REAPING THE
WHIRLWIND

REAPING THE WHIRLWIND

THE GERMAN AND JAPANESE EXPERIENCE OF WORLD WAR II

Nigel Cawthorne

David and Charles

A DAVID & CHARLES BOOK
Copyright © David & Charles Limited 2007

David & Charles is an F+W Publications Inc. company
4700 East Galbraith Road
Cincinnati, OH 45236

First published in the UK in 2007
First published in the US in 2007

Text copyright © Nigel Cawthorne 2007

Nigel Cawthorne has asserted his right to be identified as author of this work
in accordance with the Copyright, Designs and Patents Act, 1988.

The publisher has made every reasonable effort to contact the copyright holders
of images and text. If there have been any omissions, however, David and Charles
will be pleased to insert the appropriate acknowledgment at a subsequent printing.

A catalogue record for this book is available from the British Library.

ISBN-13: 978-0-7153-2282-6 hardback
ISBN-10: 0-7153-2282-6 hardback

ISBN-13: 978-0-7153-2744-9 US paperback
ISBN-10: 0-7153-2744-5 US paperback

Printed in Great Britain by Antony Rowe
for David & Charles
Brunel House, Newton Abbot, Devon

Commissioning Editor: Ruth Binney
Editor: Emily Pitcher
Assistant Editor: Demelza Hookway
Project Editors: Beverley Jollands & Nicola Hodgson
Art Editor: Marieclare Mayne
Senior Designer: Tracey Woodward
Picture Researcher: Tehmina Boman
Indexer: Tony Hirst
Production Controller: Kelly Smith

Visit our website at www.davidandcharles.co.uk

David & Charles books are available from all good bookshops; alternatively you
can contact our Orderline on 0870 9908222 or write to us at FREEPOST EX2 110,
D&C Direct, Newton Abbot, TQ12 4ZZ (no stamp required UK only); US customers
call 800-289-0963 and Canadian customers call 800-840-5220.

CONTENTS

INTRODUCTION

There is no moral relativism concerning World War II. By any standards, the German 'Führer' Adolf Hitler was a psychopathic dictator bent on building a European empire by intimidating, imprisoning, murdering and waging unprovoked war on anyone who opposed him. In the end, he was happy to see the destruction of the German nation, which he felt had let him down, and he urged others to go on sacrificing their lives, even when he had taken his own.

In the East, General Hideki Tojo and his militarist government pretended that they were liberating the yellow man in Asia by kicking the white man out. However, Japan's incursion into Manchuria and China was marked by atrocities. The Japanese Imperial Army was scarcely less brutal in the other territories it conquered – murdering, raping and enslaving. Allied prisoners of war were brutalized, maltreated and worked to death, and many more native people suffered the same fate. And, again, the Japanese began the war in the East with a series of unprovoked attacks.

Of course it is possible to criticize the excesses of the British, American, Free French and Allied forces, with the benefit of hindsight. But the Allied nations were forced into war and fought back against a ferocious onslaught with any means to hand. The price of losing was too high to bear. Even the Soviet Union under the brutal dictatorship of Joseph Stalin – though no haven of liberty – was forced into war by an unprovoked and unannounced attack. Of all the Allied nations, it sustained the greatest losses, with an estimated eighteen million dead – including seven million civilians. When Hitler sent his armies into the Soviet Union, he ordered them to use unprecedented savagery against those who lived there.

Many of the men in the front line on both sides were just ordinary blokes. They had been promised that theirs was the world's finest fighting force – only to find themselves pitted against an enemy who was equally highly motivated and often much better equipped and supplied. Some quickly realized that they had been tricked into war by a cynical leadership. But whether they were disillusioned or true believers, most of them found that they had to make the best of a bad situation. German troops, unable to criticize impossible orders, were thrown into unwinnable battles, while Japanese troops were abandoned without arms, ammunition or supplies on Pacific islands or in the jungles of Burma.

Women and children also suffered, mainly from bombing. They lost their menfolk and their homes, and millions died – whether they believed in the cause or not – though however grim their fate, it pales in comparison with the genocide carried out deliberately by both Germany and Japan. Nevertheless, one person's suffering is not mitigated by the worse torments of another.

The line 'For they sow the wind, and reap the whirlwind' appears in the Old Testament book of the minor prophet Hosea. It warns against the worship of graven images. However, the line was famously appropriated by Sir Arthur 'Bomber' Harris, commander in chief of the Royal Air Force's Bomber Command. In 1942, at the start of the bombing campaign that he was about to unleash on Germany, he said: 'The Nazis entered this war under the rather childish delusion that they were going to bomb everyone else, and nobody was going to bomb them. At Rotterdam, London, Warsaw, and half a hundred other places, they put their rather naive theory into operation. They sowed the wind, and now they are going to reap the whirlwind.'

It is true. Germany with its blitzkrieg and Japan with its attack on Pearl Harbor began the war with air attacks, while promising their citizens they would not be bombed. But Harris's biblical quotation is an apt description of the entire war from the point of view of the vanquished. The hubris of the Nazi leaders and the Japanese militarists is astounding. They told their people that their armed forces were invincible. They said that some of their enemies (the Russians, in the case of the Germans, and the Chinese for the Japanese) were racially inferior, while the others – the Western democracies – were morally weak and would never exhibit the political will they would need to withstand the German and Japanese onslaught. The wind they sowed with these sentiments caused a whirlwind that was reaped by their peoples. Their countries were devastated. Their cities destroyed. Their citizens – both soldiers and civilians alike – were killed, maimed, widowed, orphaned and rendered homeless.

Reaping the Whirlwind uses the authentic voices of German and Japanese people caught up in the conflict to relate their experiences. Their words come from diaries, letters, interrogation reports, interviews, personal memoirs and published material. These men and women were the enemies of Britain, America, France, the Soviet Union and the other Allied nations. But for them, 'the enemy' was the Allies.

Much of the material has been found in the archives of the Imperial War Museum in Duxford, Cambridgeshire, thanks to Stephen Walton; the US Army Heritage Collection in Carlisle, Pennsylvania, thanks to David Keough and the US National Archives in Maryland, thanks to the redoubtable John Taylor. A disproportionate number of the interrogation reports and captured letters and diaries preserved there come from the Battle of the Bulge – or rather the 1944 Winter Offensive, as it was known to the Germans – and the Philippines. This is because German soldiers who saw action in the Ardennes in 1944 were much more likely to have survived the war than those fighting in Russia in 1941. And Japanese soldiers in the Philippines were still holding out when Japan surrendered and, consequently, did not fight to the death like their comrades confronting the Allies in other places.

Although I was born six years after the war ended, like most British people of my generation, World War II had a profound influence on me. The attitudes formed during the tumultuous years of the 1930s and 1940s were passed on to us and coloured the rest of the century. Both my parents served in the British Army during World War II.

My father landed in Normandy. As a captain in the Royal Corps of Signals, he followed the front-line troops, setting up communications systems. He saw many of the terrible results of war – and never liked to talk about it. However, before World War II, he had been a student, studying engineering. Educated in the sciences, he was fluent in German as the text books in engineering and the sciences were mostly written in German back then. When I was a child, he took the family to Germany and certainly bore the people there no animosity.

My mother was an anti-aircraft gunner. She lied about her age to join up and won the British Empire Medal for being with the first women's ack-ack battery to shoot down a German plane. My mother is the only person I know who has killed lots of people. After the war in Europe was over, she re-enlisted to go out to the Far East, where she met my father, so both my parents had experience in both theatres of war.

Sadly, my father died many years ago, but my mother is still alive. She is eager to read this book. Even after all these years, she wants to know what those people she was fighting against thought and felt. It also has to be said that she abhors any attempt to glorify war, but the suffering and courage of those caught up in it she finds of enduring interest.

I know other people of my parents' generation who went through World War II. Few of them bear any resentment against their former enemies. Usually, they reserve this for the ingratitude of their governments and for historians who do not recognize their contribution. Others are even more forgiving. One of my parents' closest friends was a German Jew who had escaped from Italy during the war. He returned to live there, where he became wealthy. We used to holiday in his villa on Elba.

More recently, I was employed by a Jewish entrepreneur to ghost his memoirs. His wife had just died. On her deathbed she had begged him to set down his experiences for their children and grandchildren to read. He had never talked to them about what had happened, fearing it would bore them. It did not.

He had been born in Berlin, but his family realized in time what was happening and managed to escape. In England, as a young man, he was interned. But, eventually, the British authorities saw sense and allowed 'enemy aliens' to join the Pioneer Corps. Like my father, he landed in Normandy. He went on to see the liberation of the concentration camp at Bergen-Belsen. At the time, he feared that the German people could never be forgiven – although, as far as the British authorities were concerned, at the time, he was still a German national himself. But, after being part of the occupation force charged with rehabilitating the country, his opinion gradually changed. It was only after he was demobbed in 1946 that he was allowed to naturalize as a British subject. Later, as a magazine publisher in England, he frequently did business with his German counterparts and he enjoyed regular visits to the land of his birth. If he can forgive, I don't see why everyone else can't.

Nigel Cawthorne

PART 1: THE WAR IN THE WEST

European and
North African
Theatre

Legend
- – - – - – National boundaries
- |||||||||||| D-day beaches

GREENLAND

Denmark Strait

ICELAND

ATLANTIC OCEAN

DENMARK

*North
Sea*

GREAT BRITAIN

Hamburg

Berlin
Frankfurt
-an-der-Oder

GERMANY

NETHERLANDS

Leipzig Dresden

IRELAN

Gotha

Dunkirk

BELGIUM   Aachen
Malmedy
Saint-Vith
Bastogne
La Gleize

Frankfurt
Darmstadt

SUDATENLAND

Le Havre

Arromanches

Paris *The Ardennes*

Avranches

St Nazaire

AUSTRIA

SWITZERLAND

FRANCE

Milan

Venice

PORTUGAL

Genoa

Florence

Marseilles

ITALY

SPAIN

MO

NORWAY

SWEDEN

FINLAND

SOVIET UNION

•Moscow

ESTONIA

LATVIA
•Riga

Smolensk•

Stalingrad •

LITHUANIA

Minsk•

DENMARK

EAST
PRUSSIA

BELARUS
S.S.R.

Kharkov•

River Dnieper

rth
ea

NETHER-
LANDS

Berlin•

Polish Corridor

•Warsaw

POLAND

Kiev•

Lvov•

UKRAINIAN
S.S.R.

GERMANY

SUDATEN-
LAND

Odessa•

Crimea

BELGIUM

SLOVAKIA

Black Sea

•Paris

Vienna•

AUSTRIA

HUNGARY

ROMANIA

SWITZER
-LAND

Venice
•Milan•

YUGOSLAVIA

BULGARIA

TURKEY

RANCE

Genoa•

•Florence

ALBANIA

ITALY

Rome•

GREECE

•Athens

_Strait of
Messina_

Crete

Tunis•

MEDITERRANEAN SEA

TUNISIA

Tobruk•

Benghazi•

ALGERIA

•Tripoli

LIBYA

CYRENAICA

EGYPT

11

1
ACHTUNG!: THE WAR IN EUROPE BEGINS

When World War II began, Berlin resident Herbert Otto Winckelmann, like most of his neighbours – indeed, most of Europe – was asleep. He was in for an unpleasant awakening.

> Usually I awoke to the sound of soft music, but on the morning of 1 September 1939, martial music blasted into my sleeping area. Then in a few minutes Goebbels, our propaganda minister, came on the radio with a special news report announcing that our troops had crossed into Poland to liberate the oppressed German minorities there. The word 'liberate' had been used before as a pretext to invade our neighbouring countries; first, for the annexation of Austria and to split the Sudetenland from Czechoslovakia ...

Just a few hours before, German troops had rolled across the Polish border. With them was Heinz Guderian, pioneer of mechanized warfare and architect of the *blitzkrieg*:

> On 1 September at 0445 hours, the whole corps moved simultaneously over the frontier. There was a thick ground mist at first which prevented the air force from giving us any support. I accompanied the 3rd Panzer Brigade, in the first wave, as far as the area north of Zempelburg where the preliminary fighting took place. Unfortunately the heavy artillery of the 3rd Panzer Division felt itself compelled to fire into the mist, despite having received precise orders not to do so. The first shell landed fifty yards ahead of my command vehicle, the second fifty yards behind it. I reckoned that the next one was bound to be a direct hit and ordered my driver to turn about and drive off. The unaccustomed noise had made him nervous, however, and he drove straight into a ditch at full speed.

Winckelmann was initially unconcerned by events in Poland. He was over thirty so, at that time, not eligible for the draft. And he was no supporter of the Nazis, as his earlier marriage plans had been ruined by the Nuremberg Laws preventing interracial marriage when it was discovered that he had a Jewish grandparent. However, he did not feel that Germany was totally in the wrong:

> Although most Germans had not been filled with enthusiasm that war had broken out, this did not mean that they did not support Hitler's intention to free our minorities, which had been foolishly separated from Germany by the politicians under the Versailles Peace Treaty ... After three days, England and France declared war against us.

FRANCE FALLS

The 'phoney war' followed, but on 10 May 1940 Germany made its attack in the west. Leading the attack was the 7th Panzer Division, commanded by Erwin Rommel, later famed for his campaign in North Africa. On 11 May he wrote to his wife:

> Dearest Lu,
> I have come up for breath for the first time today and have a moment to write. Everything wonderful so far. Am way ahead of my neighbours. I'm completely hoarse from orders and shouting. Had a bare three hours' sleep and an occasional meal. Otherwise I'm absolutely fine. Make do with this, please, I'm too tired for more.

Overhead was *Luftwaffe* pilot Fritz Mölders, in a Messerschmitt Me109 fighter plane:

> France, 5 June 1940: ... At about 5,000m, I get my mob lined up, make a quick target allocation and then – in we go! I take the plane furthest to the right; below me lies Compiègne. After a short burst of fire, fragments of the enemy fighter are flying round my ears. I feel a hard blow on my machine – a moment of terror – but the engine is still running happily. Beside me, two Me's attack the opposition. *Leutnant* Claus shoots one of them down.
> Where has the spotter-plane got to? Must get rid of him! Down there, close to the ground, a Bloch still with him, I dive towards

the Bloch fighter, but I'm going too fast, can't shoot; suddenly I'm alongside him; I can see the pilot very clearly; he's sticking doggedly with the spotter-plane he's meant to be protecting; his cockpit is open, and I curve in on him slightly – he looks at me in horror and – whoosh – he peels off at high speed. That's what I wanted him to do. Because now I can drop straight on to the spotter-plane. But the fellow is a fantastic pilot. He flies low over a village, below the height of the church tower, and down into a river valley; I get him briefly in my sights – safety-catch off, load, we go lower, between two poplars, now I'm only 50m from him – nose up to avoid a telephone-wire – then down again, just one metre above a meadow – I've got him in my sights. Caught unawares, he flies into the ground, a thirty-metre long column of fire behind him. He won't be taking any more photos.

France fell at lightning speed, with Rommel plunging on to Normandy.

14 June 1940: On to Le Havre and inspected the town. It all went without bloodshed. We're now engaging targets out to sea with long-ranging artillery. Already we set one transport alight today.

You can imagine my feelings when twelve generals of the British and French armies reported to me and received my orders in the market place of St Valéry. The British general and his division were a particular source of joy. The whole thing was filmed and will no doubt be talked about in the newsreels.

Now we're getting a few days' rest. I can't think that there'll be any more serious fighting in France. We've even had flowers along the road in some places. The people are glad that the war is over for them ... the war seems to be gradually becoming a more or less peaceful occupation of all France. The population is peacefully disposed, and in some places very friendly.

By then much of the British Army had been plucked off the beaches of Dunkirk. On 22 June 1940 France capitulated, and the focus of the war moved elsewhere. Back in Germany, Herbert Winckelmann was still untroubled by the war. At Christmas 1940, he went skiing at Sonthofen, where he met his future wife Elinor. At Easter, they went skiing together in Kitzbuel and in July he proposed to her. However, the war now brought with it minor inconveniences:

When war had broken out, the lights all over Europe had gone out and I disliked the dark streets. Not that I had been afraid of a possible crime, for crime happened very seldom due to the severe punishment received ... It was because all the streets looked grey and the same. I suddenly recognized that I seldom looked at street signs. So far, I had found my way using the neon lights ... Nightlife in Berlin went on during the first two years as usual. In order not to bump into each other on the sidewalks, we pinned phosphor-covered buttons to the lapels of our overcoats.

NORTH AFRICA

Italy had entered the war on the German side on 10 June 1940. With colonies in North Africa, the Italians were in a perfect position to attack the British in Egypt. On 13 September, at Hitler's urging, they rolled over the Egyptian border intent on taking the Suez Canal and, possibly, the Middle Eastern oilfields beyond. But the Italians were no match for the British. By the time they surrendered, on 7 February 1941, the British had driven them back 800km (500 miles), taking over 130,000 prisoners. But on 6 February Hitler sent Rommel to Tripoli, and on 31 March Rommel attacked El Agheila. Present was Lieutenant Kurt Wolff, with the newly formed Afrika Korps:

In the yellow moonlight long convoys of trucks move along the coast road, now and again attacked by English bombers. Water, fuel, ammo, bread, food and people, everything moves through the dark night which is no different from the glowing heat of the day ... Field kitchens and ration trucks search for the tracks of the Panzers of their units. However, the important movements in the dusk are the repair groups. Men who repair the engines, clean and adjust the carburettors. Springs, track rollers and track links have to be seen to and fixed. Guns and machine-guns have to be checked. You can hear the swearing of hard-working men, the clanging of hammers in the wet and cold night. But thousands of other things come together before a battle is won. As soon as the sun rises through the morning mist, the regiment starts to roll forward. We disperse into the desert, but forward we go, 40–50km per hour we read on our tacho. But the nicest is the attack ... the German Panzer, our beautiful wide, humming Panzer. We are secretly proud that everyone needs us when the danger is high. Panzer! Panzer to the fore!

OPENING THE RUSSIAN FRONT

Soon the British were fleeing back towards the Egyptian border.

On 22 June 1941 Hitler attacked the Soviet Union. By October, the 2nd Panzer Army was advancing on Odessa, where it was briefly held up by retreating Russians who were holding positions near a bridge. Captain Georg von Konrat was ordered to clear the road with three tanks – Sea Rose 1, 2 and 3 – and two armoured cars – Sea Rose 4 and 5. He decided to use an encircling manoeuvre through a forest.

> We moved rapidly out through the trees and on to the field, immediately starting to pick up speed. At first, I could see nothing because of the smoke, but then, suddenly, we were through and into the open field, in sight of the Russian guns. Jochum, my driver, yelled: 'We're doing 55.'
>
> 'See if you can make it 65,' I roared back.
>
> Two seconds later we made our first turn, shooting out to the left in an 80° twist and heading full tilt for the Russian guns. They were blasting at us non-stop, but before we could line up again we were off to the right and heading at an angle for the river. Then we went left again and back towards the turn-off. The Russians must have thought we had gone crazy or that we were trying to cut them off from their retreating forces. We made another sharp turn back towards the river and this time I jammed the lid of the turret shut – just in case one of those grenade throwers hit bull's eye. If we had to go out, I didn't want it to be over something as measly as that.
>
> We turned left again, 55°, dodged towards the forest and then were off again on a right-hand tangent before the guns had a chance to aim. The Russians were going berserk. I had my periscope up and was watching them.

Two Russian 76mm infantry guns were set up at the end of the road where they could command the field. There were more heavy guns in the trees on the other side of the road.

Everything else was too well covered to be visible. But I had seen enough. I could have split my side watching their barrels turning frantically about. They were firing half blindly, sending out shell after shell in one continuous bombardment, but none even half-hopeful of aiming the right way.

But it was not just the Russians who were having a problem aiming:

Dita was having the same trouble and I could hear one unending stream of curses issuing from the gun turret.

Both sides were firing wildly when the Panzers closed in, so they dashed back and forth randomly so that the Russians could not work out any pattern.

Five seconds later, we were off again to the right and back towards the river. The Russians now had an old Katusha rocket launcher doing her bit, spraying the field with lollipops. The sky was a mass of exploding shells. I could see the infantry digging in ahead of the guns, so we charged them this time, machine-gunning and shelling madly. They dropped their spades with the first burst and went rushing back to the road and out of sight. I was grinning like a madman. I think we all were.

We careered off again, then right, then left, backwards, forwards, left, right, and off again. The tank heeled about wildly lurching off in another direction almost before it had regained its balance from the last zigzag. At times I thought we had been hit or lost our tracks, the way Jochum was throwing the poor tank around. My stomach felt turned inside out and I almost fainted with the sudden, violent jolts. I did not even dare to think what was going on in my lungs. Only the excitement kept me conscious ...

The other Panzers charged in. But the Russian infantry were massing again:

I ordered my driver to race back towards them. Otherwise, they could jump on my other tanks and throw grenades down the turrets. 'Right into them for 100m next turn,' I yelled. Jochum didn't answer. He didn't have time to. With a sharper spin than ever to the left, the tank seemed to keel over. But it steadied itself on the edge and righted itself again. Now the gun turret was steady and Dita was grinning. He could shoot directly into the Russian gun positions, while our machine-guns cross-fired into infantry, sending them flying.

Von Konrat ordered the tank in again. This time Jochum seemed to lose control and overrun the road itself.

If the Russians weren't laughing with glee, they were shivering in their boots. I could see men flying out and leaving their guns in all directions as our tanks roared down on them full tilt.

At the last minute, Jochum turned and the tank raced back off across the field to safety, leaving the Russian infantry positions shattered. However, the Russian guns were still firing at von Konrat's other two tanks.

Ordering Jochum to spin round completely to the south, I threw open the lid of the turret and stuck my head out so I could see more clearly. At the same time, I clung onto the sides for grim death. The Russians had no idea what was happening out on the field any more. We hadn't gone in, we hadn't retreated. We had just played cat and mouse with them like kids at a Sunday school picnic ...

He charged them again but, just as he was drawing level with Sea Rose 2, he saw the armoured car Sea Rose 4 'just one great roaring flame'.

Now we were completely surrounded by Russian guns and Dita had our gun turret turning to the left and right and firing continuously at everything. Sea Rose 2 came quickly back onto the main road and the three tanks moved down it in line, our machine-guns cross-spraying to keep the infantry off. We moved down towards the turn-off, gradually silencing every gun in the area. None of them was powerful enough to knock out a tank.

As they rolled on towards Odessa, all they saw was burning vehicles and infantrymen fleeing to the sea. But they were running out of ammunition.

It was becoming hard for me to think clearly. I felt sick – I felt lousy. All I wanted to do was to get the hell out of Russia, Odessa, and everything to do with it, and lie on a nice soft bed and sleep. Had we won the battle or not? And when the hell were the *Das*

Reich boys going to arrive? If they didn't get there soon, there just wouldn't be any of us left.

I braced my body against the side of the tank and asked Dita how many shots we had left. 'Another ten, that's all,' he told me. Sea Rose 3 had only another three salvos, so that settled it. None of us could afford to stay kicking around the highway any longer.

'Sea Rose 3,' I called. 'You and I will speed right to the turn-off. Now or never or we will have to bluff it out. I'll go in front spraying the right-hand side, and you follow about 20m behind spraying the left-hand side. Leave yourself one shot.

Meanwhile Sea Rose 2 was to head back to the forest to find out what had happened to Sea Rose 5.

While we were among them the Russians could not fire for fear of blowing each other up, so all they could do was scatter – all except for one Russian officer. We drove the tank straight at him but he did not budge. Alone on the empty road, he stood waiting unflinching for the moment when our tank would roll over him. I never felt so much for a Russian before. Just before we reached him, we turned and drove past him and down the bridge road. I did not look behind but I knew he would still be there. As soon as we turned, Dita swung his gun around and loosed off our final shell. Then we raced for the river at top speed.

By this time the infantry lines had re-formed:

They were positioned to the south-west in a half-moon arc, but there was not just one row. They were everywhere, like ants. Our low machine-gun was still intact and firing, so they shifted in a hurry. Then, to our right, we discovered an anti-tank gun facing the river. As they hadn't fired they must think we were Russians. Cursing that we had used our last shell, we blasted at the men behind the gun with machine-gun fire. 'Sea Rose 3?' I called. 'Have you still got that one shell?'

'As ordered, yes.'

'Then blast that darned gun out of existence.'

Sea Rose 2 then reported that it had found Sea Rose 5 'a red mass of fire'.

Von Konrat concluded that it must have got ahead of the tanks, or that it had been caught by a gun they had missed – but he consoled himself with the thought that his men might have survived:

> Maybe the boys had managed to get out and save themselves. But even if a quarter of the Russians in that arc of infantry had been anything like their officer who stood on the road, they would have eaten not only them, but all of us, steel and men.

When von Konrat returned to the German lines, he told his commanding officer of his high-speed attack across the field.

> 'I saw that,' said Major Horst, 'and I nearly died laughing too. Those Ruskies must have used up half the ammunition in Odessa lighting up the sky like fairyland for you – while you did exhibition dancing underneath.'

Von Konrat agreed that it had been fun.

THE RUSSIAN WINTER

The Red Army surrendered in their hundreds of thousands, but then the Germans had to face Russia's greatest soldier, 'General Winter'. On the eastern front, infantry commander General Gustav Hoehne felt that his forces were ill-prepared:

> Western Europeans will be hard put to imagine the masses of powdered snow that, during the most severe part of winter 1941–42, buried western Russia beneath a blanket averaging 1.2m in depth ... During 1941–42 even Germans accustomed to the rigours of the eastern climate faced a situation in which all lessons of the eastern winters of World War I, and all experiences gained in the bitter East Prussian winters were useless.
>
> During January 1942 the Russians had succeeded in encircling a German force of about seven divisions that had its easternmost elements on the high ground around Valdai. Thrusting south along both banks of the Lovat River (a tributary of Lake Ilmen), the Soviets had established themselves between Staraya Russa and Koholm. The solidly frozen Lovat served the Russians as a road. During the winter, frozen rivers are the best roads in Russia ... The deep snows protected the encircled German troops around

Demyansk from annihilation. Even the Russian infantry were unable to launch an attack through those snows. Russian ski troops got nowhere. The Germans were supplied by the *Luftwaffe*. This means of supply, however, proved inadequate and, starting late in February, German forces assembled west of Staraya Russa to relieve the encircled forces at Demyansk.

The movement was effected by rail. The transport I travelled on arrived at Volot, about 30km west of Staraya Russa, on a clear winter afternoon. We could feel the cold, which was intense but not too unpleasant. Yet, all of a sudden, the men noticed the symptoms of frostbite on each other's face. The mercury registered –35°C. While detraining, the sun went down; before complete darkness set in the sky turned a deep blue, like blue-black ink, and poured its colour over the virgin snow. With the disappearance of the sun a light breeze started up, hardly noticeable but incessant ... Paths for sleighs and vehicles were laboriously shovelled through the snowfields, only to have long stretches buried again within a matter of hours by the evening wind. To make matters worse, we no sooner had detrained than marching troops and supply columns caused traffic jams. All of which adds up to the following lesson: prior to detraining large troop units, a detailed map of winter roads must be procured, for even the primitive Russian road network cannot be kept altogether clear of snow ... The winter roads frequently do not follow the course of regular streets and roads.

The countryside was only sparsely settled; one must remember that the Russian peasant usually owns a single house rather than a group of farm buildings. Billets therefore became so scarce that troops had to be quartered even in houses occupied by Russian civilians. Their eviction would have meant certain death in that temperature. The German soldier did not do such things. The upshot was numerous cases of typhus, a disease transmitted by lice. Lice are found in many Russian homes.

Despite the weather, the Germans fought on. Two divisions of German riflemen, supported by twenty tanks and assault guns, were to attack across enemy-held territory in an attempt to reach the westernmost salient of the encircled German troops. Hoehne was with them:

The southern division had to traverse more than 2km of snow-blanketed plain, offering no cover whatever, in order to reach the enemy lines. That feat would have required hours, and merely the job of struggling through the powdery snow would have drained the infantrymen of all their physical strength. An attack conducted in this manner held no prospect of success, even if it were aimed at weak enemy forces. Tanks, for that matter, were likewise unable to manoeuvre in the powdery snow.

A page was therefore borrowed from the way the Russians had cut off Demyansk in their attack up the Lovat River. It was decided to launch an attack from the north, up the frozen Polizt River ...

Conditions were more favourable for the division to the north. It had to aim at reaching two points that marked the beginning of Russian winter roads ... Even in Germany the surfaces of heavily travelled roads occasionally crack, once the thaw follows a severe winter. The phenomenon is caused by the fact that heavy traffic deprives a road of the snow blanket that otherwise would protect it from the cold. The Russians close improved [paved] roads as soon as the winter freeze sets in and establish winter roads either alongside the regular right of way or simply straight through the countryside.

Snow was compressed by tanks, and water was poured on to give the road a smooth surface of ice. Snow fences also had to be built to stop the wind drifting snow across the road. There were other difficulties:

The infantry was equipped as follows: cotton-padded winter uniform (which unfortunately had not yet been available at the beginning of 1942); felt boots; and two small hand sleds per squad, loaded with blankets, two shelter halves per man, some dry wood and some boughs. In addition, each platoon had two small trench stoves ... Platoon tents were pitched; dug into the snow, they did not protrude above its surface. The floors of the tents were covered with boughs, over which the second shelter halves were spread for protection from the cold ground. A stove was set up at each end of every tent, and fires were started. The temperature in the tents was not uncomfortable ... The pack animals were simply sheltered in pits dug into the snow alongside the winter roads. So long as the animals are protected from the wind, they can withstand temperatures even below –30°C ... In the deep snow of the winter in question, any calibre smaller than 150mm was completely ineffective because the snow stopped the shell fragments. This was particularly true of mortar shells ... Contrary to expectations, the mountain howitzer of the Jäger [Rifle] divisions proved to be highly effective, even though its calibre was only 75mm. By a great stroke of luck, eight per cent of the ammunition brought up for these pieces were armed with combination fuses. Most of the field fortifications which the Russian infantry had built into the snow were not splinterproof.

After one attack in February failed, Hoehne and his men tried again:

On the clear, frosty morning of 21 March the two divisions of Group Seydlitz went over to the attack. According to plan, the right division succeeded in cleaning out the stubbornly defended southern part of Ivanovskoye and rolled up the enemy positions west and east of the Polizt.

Then things began to go wrong:

Because of the dense underbrush the snow was so deep that the forest could not be used as flank protection ... Enemy nests of resistance that had formed around battery positions could not be eliminated in the deep snow. Partly sparse and partly dense shrubbery, low in height and in most instances as thick as a man's finger, had permitted the snow to pile up so high that the infantry sank into it up to their armpits. Without very thorough and careful artillery preparation, a continuation of the attack was out of the question. Aviation could not be used because of the difficulty in recognizing the front lines, nor could tanks be committed, since the Russians had failed to build a winter road to Invanovskoye from the east ...

A winter road in the direction of the Russian battery positions was begun at once. The entire engineer battalion, a sizeable unit to start with, was reinforced by approximately one thousand men for the purposes of this project. Nevertheless, building the winter road took almost twenty-four hours ...

The left division likewise effected the penetration into the enemy position according to plan. After enemy resistance had been broken, the attack towards the east was continued at once ... The left regimental combat team thrust almost to the Staraya Russa–Ramsuhevo highway, but could not get possession of it. Here the attack stopped dead in its tracks. The right combat team pushed far beyond the enemy position ... In the forest east of Svinushovo the attack slowed down because of the deeper snow and the increased enemy resistance ... In hard fighting the combat team reached a point about halfway between Svinushovo and Bol'gorby. The woods, however, became more and more dense, so that on 23 March this attack also bogged down.

The failure of a Russian counterattack – they were little better than the Germans at manoeuvring in snow – allowed the German offensive to resume. Now it was a race to advance down the winter roads before the thaw set in.

On 4 April the mercury began to rise and the daytime registered temperatures above freezing. As a result, the infantry had much more easy going in the snow. Nevertheless, the onset of the thaw was one of the reasons for the failure of the attack. The few, largely obsolescent German tanks had become damaged and were out of action. Russian armour, on the other hand, began to move now that the snow had hardened somewhat. German anti-tank artillery could not be set up. For that, the snow was still too deep.

After a week, the attack had to be called off. The Russians counterattacked, moving through the forest where not even their tanks could be spotted by German bombers.

Winter warfare in Russia requires heavy tanks, like the German Tiger, that can move through the deepest snow. Under those conditions the tank is superior to the assault gun, because the tank's artillery piece is farther off the ground and can be rotated with the turret above the level of the snow ...

But spring was on its way, and improving weather conditions favoured the Germans. They took the village of Vazvy, but the battle was far from over.

In the depths of the forest, the enemy had established several lines of defence. The Russians are masters in the construction of shell-proof wooden field fortifications. About 3km southeast of Yazvy the attack of the division bogged down.

So the German spearhead swung to the northeast and, after bitter fighting, broke through.

Now the snow began to melt with a vengeance. The water in the woods was knee-deep ... But the weather brought one advantage: the enemy evacuated the woods south of the Yazvy–Ramushevo highway, and withdrew to the high ground of Ramushevo. On the west bank of the Lovat he held only one small bridgehead adjacent to the village. Thereby the threat to the southern flank of the attacking forces had, at least temporarily, been removed. Now the infantryman could protect himself against the water. The forest provided sufficient cover to permit the hasty construction of simple wooden shelters. In the meantime, reconnaissance was conducted for the continuation of the attack. After all, our encircled comrades were waiting to be freed. Every man knew what was at stake.

Lucky indeed was he who found a large bomb crater. Most Russian swamps are the result of an impermeable layer of clay, usually only shallow. Large bomb craters were frequently deep enough to penetrate the clay. As a rule, they did not fill up with water and, as long as they were not located within large inundated areas, their edges were often the only patches of dry ground. There infantrymen sat, there and on islands either provided by nature or man-made from tree trunks. The ground below the water was still frozen. Wide, shallow streams ran through every field and forest. The flood waters had washed out every bridge. Heavily travelled roads were covered with a 1m layer of mud.

Ramushevo on the River Lovat was now the objective, but the thaw presented another problem:

The fields of the peasants are located to the west of the town. Through them runs a stream which had, at this time, swollen to a

400m-wide river. The northern part of the river had solid, steep banks, indicating deep water at that point ... With the disappearance of the snow, the artillery had finally regained its normal effectiveness. After the most painstaking reconnaissance, the attack on the bridgehead got underway on 15 April. It succeeded with surprising ease, although the bridgehead, too, was protected by the overflowing stream. Despite the arrival of numerous enemy replacements, the Russian troops were no less exhausted than our men.

Since the distance to the northern edge of the village was only about 300m, the obvious next move would have been to attack Ramushevo from the captured enemy bridgehead. No attempt, however, was made as the banks of the stream were steep and high, and the water was bound to reach above a man's head ... At this time patrols had to wade though snow water, which was knee-deep south of the highway ...

On 20 April, German forces assembled for the attack on Ramushevo ... The enemy had not counted on a German attack through the flooded area ... The men had to wade through more than waist-deep snow water. Soon after, other German units penetrated the village from the west and, by 22 April, Ramushevo had been completely cleared of the enemy. The Lovat had been reached. From the east, a combat team of the units encircled at Demyansk launched its own attack in the direction of Ramushevo and on 22 April reached the river. The first boat crossed the Lovat and the first telephone cable was laid. Contact with the encircled units had been established. As yet, the link was only slender, in places no wider than 1km. Nevertheless, supplies soon began to roll through. Unfortunately Demyansk was not evacuated at once. Instead, our troops finally pulled out almost a year later ... The fighting in the so-called land-corridor resulted in serious German losses, because the Russians launched one major attack after the other. Almost every month, and sometimes twice a month, it appeared as though a new encirclement was unavoidable, and it is indeed a miracle that the German units fighting around Demyansk did not suffer the fate of those at Stalingrad. Had

Demyansk been evacuated in the spring of 1942, the men that would have been saved could have bolstered German forces at Stalingrad enough to avoid that catastrophe.

DUGOUT LIFE

Dr Lothar Rendulic spent nearly three years on the Russian front and later wrote a report on the hardships encountered there:

> In the later fall, when the dugouts in the front line had to be heated, the freshly felled wood produced a large volume of smoke which during daytime drew enemy fire on the dugouts. As charcoal was known to generate hardly any smoke, the troops set out to make that type of fuel for use during the day. They established behind the front lines a number of small kilns, which soon produced the required amount of charcoal. [However] the production of charcoal was taken up at a rather late date, after a good many casualties had been suffered ...
>
> In the German Army, a supply of stoves for dugouts in winter positions had not been provided for from the onset. Thus the troops resorted to fashioning stoves from bricks or stones, or to the use of empty gasoline barrels and cans. Stovepipes were always the major problem as they could not be made without sheet metal. Brick chimneys take up too much room in the cramped dugouts, and require a good many bricks. Moreover, brick chimneys cannot be used for every type of stove. Thus, whenever sheet metal could be obtained, it was used for making stovepipes. To a limited extent, we procured that material from the ruins of houses and factories in larger localities, where the roofs frequently consisted of sheet metal.

In central Russia the temperature regularly dropped to $-35\,°C$ ($-31\,°F$) and sometimes to $-46\,°C$ ($-51\,°F$). Dr Rendulic recommended the use of the 'Finnish igloo' for shelter, yet:

> I went through the first two Russian winters without having witnessed the use of snow huts, except in very rare instances, not even in 1941–42 when my division went through the entire winter campaign in the centre of events.

... It was possible to requisition some furs and felt boots from the natives for a small fraction of the troops. Winter clothing was also removed from the enemy dead. But it was not until the spring of 1942, furs, warm underwear, gloves and ear protectors arrived from home, and these too sufficed to supply only a small part of the troops ... If a man had a reserve of underwear, he wore two lots. The divisions and army issued the entire supply of underwear they had on hand. Finally, each man succeeded in providing himself with more protection for his head and ears by using pieces of cloth and waistbands. The most difficult problem, for which there was no solution, was that of footwear. Consequently, there were frozen limbs.

'The people of Russia and the east in general are greatly plagued by vermin,' Dr Rendulic wrote. Apart from countless mice that gnawed their way into the wooden food boxes, there were other problems:

Bedbugs, which can be found not so much on the human body as in houses, are unpleasant, but as carriers of diseases they are harmless. The flea which was present in large numbers during World War I seems to be dying out. It was encountered very rarely. But the louse is dangerous. It nests on the human body, in personal effects and also in dwellings ... The louse is a carrier of typhus, the most dangerous disease of the east. Persons over fifty years of age hardly ever survive it, but the death rate among the young is also high. At that time vaccines could be produced only by a very complicated and expensive process. Since November 1941 only nurses and attendants in typhus hospitals, doctors, people in important positions and those over fifty years of age could be vaccinated ... The troops used a delousing powder; it was sprinkled on the body and underwear. But the results were not too promising.

Quarters were frequently cramped to such an extent that on several occasions even I had to share the same room as four officers of my immediate staff and the orderlies ... Living in crowded quarters and positions furthered the rapid increase of lice ... our troops were constantly lice-ridden.

Drinking water had to be boiled, on pain of punishment, to prevent typhoid.

But soldiers who had suffered from respiratory diseases and rheumatism seemed to be miraculously cured.

> Cases of dysentery occurred in a few instances, although inoculation against it was begun only in the middle of 1942. The disease had spread among the troops very seriously during the Polish campaign of 1939. At that time, the cause was undoubtedly the eating of spoiled or unripe fruit. This danger did not exist in central or northern Russia.

Epidemics of jaundice and trench fever both occurred widely, but the cause had 'not been clearly determined at that time'. Then there was malaria:

> As protection against the swarms of mosquitoes, especially in the swamp regions, it is wise to provide the troops with mosquito nets and window screens for shelters, also as a protection against the numerous flies.

The horses brought for transport also suffered from numerous diseases.

> Mangy horses were isolated in special stables ... In mild cases, the troops treated the horses locally by rubbing the infected parts with a tar preparation. Before this preparation was applied, the troops substituted kerosene, available locally and normally used for lighting purposes; although effective, it strongly affected skin ... The most effective and quickest treatment consisted in placing the horse's entire body – except for the head which was left sticking out in the air – into a gas chamber and exposing it to a gas which killed the mites. But the veterinary company had only one gas chamber; that was not enough ... More than 1,000 of the 5,800 horses in my division, the 52nd Infantry Division, were mangy in the spring of 1942. This number decreased considerably during the summer, but mange could not be wiped out completely.
>
> In the summer of 1942, we found that many horses in the Shisdra area (about 100 kilometres northwest of Orel) suffered from large festering boils that were caused by the bite of certain flies. This disease had been unknown until then ... Horses withstood the severe winters well, even though for long periods they had no stables.

And the horses had insufficient fodder, Rendulic said. The severe conditions also affected the *Wehrmacht*'s weapons:

> The extreme cold of the winter of 1941–42 showed to our surprise that the mechanism of rifles and machine-guns and to some extent even the breech-blocks of the artillery became absolutely rigid. It was necessary to apply heat to them carefully in order to make them fit for firing again ... It became evident that the lubricants used (grease and oil) froze in the extreme cold and became as hard as stone ... The troops immediately made various experiments and determined that kerosene was cold-resistant and suitable as a lubricant ... The only drawback was that it had no lasting properties and had to be renewed frequently.

Motor vehicles suffered similarly:

> Completely unaware of the fact that grease and oil had frozen and hardened like stone, we tried at the beginning to make the vehicles start by towing them. The result was that the motor was badly damaged, and the differential was ripped to pieces. It was necessary to thaw out the vehicles by carefully applying heat to them before moving. It took up to two hours ...
>
> From the very beginning Chrysantine [anti-freeze] was available which was mixed with the water for the radiator, preventing freezing in temperatures not below –25°C. In extreme cold the water had to be drained from the vehicle after driving and had to be brought into the quarters.

CALLED UP

The invasion of the Soviet Union had left the German Army stretched to its limits. There were occupation forces in Norway, Denmark, the Low Countries, France, the Balkans, Greece, Czechoslovakia, Poland and now the Baltic States, vast tracts of Belarus, the Ukraine and Russia itself. The *Wehrmacht* needed fresh troops, so the draft age was raised and, in September 1941, Herbert Winckelmann, who had avoided the war so far, was conscripted.

> I had not been enthusiastic about going to war, but was determined to do my duty by defending my country. I had no ambition to become a general or a war hero.

He was sent to boot camp at Zuellish, a small town east of Berlin, and emerged as a member of the 4th Company of the 39th Infantry Regiment. After three months' hard training, he expected to be sent to the Russian front with the rest of his company. However, at the last moment, he received an order to report to Sorau for training as an officer in the reserve. There, on 24 January 1942, he married his fiancée Elinor, 'on the coldest day of that winter, with the thermometer dipping to -22°. After a further three months' training, he was made an NCO. 'Before I could receive the patent for commissioned officer, I had to prove myself on the battlefield.' So he was posted to Artemovsk in the Ukraine.

> It took almost five days by train ... I could hardly comprehend that
> we had conquered so much land in just six months. Since the
> Ukraine is only a small part of Russia, I wondered how much
> further we would have to go before the Russians would surrender.

Winckelmann had been trained to ride motorcycles and drive heavy trucks, but he was in for a shock. His new squadron leader in the Ukraine, *Rittmeister* (Captain) Ahrbecker, said: 'You will soon realize that what you learned back in Germany and the reality of the situation here are two very different things. Come, I will select a gentle horse for you and personally give you a crash course in horseback riding.'

> With the first rain I learned how valuable horses were to us here.
> When I had arrived the sun had baked the black clay to a rock-
> hard surface, but after only a few hours of rain the entire
> countryside was one big mud puddle. Motorized vehicles were
> useless in this weather, bogging down to their axles.

His company had abandoned their trucks. Instead they used horse-drawn wagons captured from the Russians.

2
THE BATTLE OF THE ATLANTIC: FIGHTING ABOVE AND BELOW THE WAVES

The German surface fleet did not discharge itself very well in World War II. On 13 December 1939, the pocket battleship *Admiral Graf Spee* was cornered in the River Plate between Argentina and Uruguay by three British cruisers. In the ensuing battle the *Graf Spee* put into Montevideo for repairs. Forced to leave port four days later, the ship was scuttled just outside the harbour. In a note to the German ambassador in Buenos Aires where many of the crew were interned, its captain Hans Langsdorff explained:

> After a long and inward struggle, I reached the grave decision to scuttle the *Panzerschiff Graf Spee* in order that she should not fall into the hands of the enemy. I am convinced that under the circumstances this decision was the only one I could make after I had taken my ship into the trap of Montevideo. With the ammunition remaining, any attempt to break out to open and deep water was bound to fail ... I decided from the beginning to bear the consequences involved in this decision.

After writing to his wife and parents, Langsdorff wrapped himself in the ensign he had taken from his ship and put a pistol to his head. The first shot grazed the back of his head. A second, through the forehead, blew his brains out.

Then on 18 May 1941, Germany's biggest battleship, the *Bismarck*, sailed, accompanied by heavy cruiser *Prinz Eugen*. They were attacked by the Royal Navy in the Denmark Strait. In the engagement HMS *Hood* went down, with the loss of 1,416 men. The *Bismarck* then escaped into the open sea. Thirty hours later, it was sighted by British aircraft in the Atlantic around 500km (300 miles) off the west coast of Ireland. A torpedo crippled its steering gear, and HMS *King George V* and HMS *Rodney* closed in for the kill. On board the stricken ship was *Matrosengefreiter* (Able Seaman) Georg Herzog:

> The destroyer attacks subsided at about 0100 hours. I surmised that the enemy had lost contact with us. First, the Chief-of-Fleet

addressed the crew between 0100–0200 hours. I did not hear his speech. My comrades told me the Chief-of-Fleet said: 'We will fire until the last shell.' I did hear the speech wherein he said: 'A telegram with the following content was sent to the Führer: "We will fight until the last man. All is for you, my Führer."'

I later heard by loudspeaker that the Führer had awarded the Knight's Cross to the 1st Artillery Officer for sinking the battle cruiser *Hood*. It was also broadcast that every available U-boat has been put on high alert, and that 80 aircraft, two ocean tugs, and one tanker were proceeding with all haste. There was great joy among the crew, but the mood had been good all along. The '*Bismarck*' hymn and other seamen's ballads were sung.

I slept in the deckhouse until approximately 0500 hours ... Shortly afterwards, the alarm sounded. I saw that the ship had ceased to make headway as I emerged from my battle station. The ship was abeam to the sea and breakers crashed over the portside. The ship showed considerably more list.

All the 38cm turrets swung to port while I was still on deck. Then, I went to take cover. Enemy shells splashed 100m ahead of the ship. Then, our guns opened fire. I felt shocks in the ship that must have resulted from hits. I left the deckhouse with my comrades. I observed white smoke ascending from the funnel. The antennae were shot to pieces and I saw hits on the ship's forward section. Splinters and ship parts were flying about. Several comrades tossed life rafts from the deckhouse to the upper deck. I assisted them with this. I then went to the upper deck, where the majority of the flak crew was. We sought protection behind turret 'C'. Other comrades were standing in the gangway descending to the battery deck. There were already chunks of the superstructure lying on the poop. The funnel was torn open on the starboard side. The *Oberbootsmann* and two *Obergefreiter* were readying the rescue rafts and laid them on the upper deck. Comrades tossed inflatable boats over the side and jumped in after them. Along with several comrades, I tried to toss an inflatable boat overboard. But we did not succeed because a hit struck in our vicinity and splinters made the inflatable boat useless. I received a flesh wound in the calf of the left leg. We then sought shelter behind turret 'D'. There was an inflatable boat behind turret 'D'. We tossed the boat over the starboard side and jumped after it. I had luck on my side in immediately grabbing hold of the raft. Other comrades tried to swim to the raft. Only comrades *Matrosengefreiten* Manthey and Höntzsch made it to the raft. All our efforts to fish out even more comrades were unsuccessful ...

After this, we drifted off very rapidly ... After we had drifted for some time, we saw a second raft with approximately seven men, but we quickly lost track of this raft. We could see *Bismarck* only when our raft was atop the crest of a mountainous wave. Firing continued. It became silent after an hour. An English cruiser with three funnels passed within approximately 200m after we went overboard. The cruiser was on course for *Bismarck* ... During the day we only saw a single Kondor plane. In the twilight, we were seen by U-boat (U-74) and taken on board.

Another survivor was *Maschinenobergefreiter* (Leading Stoker) Bruno Rzonca.

When the skipper gave the order to abandon the ship and leave the doors open, we looked for an exit. I was looking around and saw men sitting on a bench and I asked: 'Don't you want to save yourselves?' They said: 'There is no ship coming, the water is too cold, the waves too high, we are going down with the ship.' A little bit further there was a wounded guy, he lost his heels; I said: 'Come on, I am going to help you out first and then find me an exit.' He replied: 'Leave me alone and don't step on my feet, I am going down with the ship.' I couldn't believe that. A little later we found a stairway. When I came out I couldn't believe it. The British were still shooting, and we looked for cover behind one of the six-inch turrets. Bodies were piled around the turrets, they were all dead. The whole deck was full of blood and body parts. There were a couple of guys sitting there and said: 'Help me to get in the water, we can't walk any more.' So we help them out into the water. Now the ship started turning over more and more to the port side and I stayed on the starboard side. I took off my heavy leather suit and jumped into the water. I thought this would be the end. I was 23 years old, only starting living. I was engaged, and there was no chance to save myself. You just have to jump into the water and swim as long as you can. That's what I did. It was at least 50 or more feet to jump into the water. I was 100 feet away when the ship started to turn over to the port side all the way, and then a couple of guys that didn't get over on time, jumped and slid down the starboard side of the hull until they hit the stabilizer and never came up again. They drowned. Then, we had to swim for almost an hour, the water was 15°C and the waves 30 feet high ...

First I was swimming and I could see nothing, then a guy came by me and held on to my neck and I said: 'I can't help you.' I was looking and I saw a mast coming up. I couldn't distinguish the ship, and then a while later I saw the flag on it. It was a British flag. I told the guy who was swimming beside me: 'There is a British ship coming there.' He said: 'I don't want to do anything with the British; they want to shoot us.' I didn't see him any more.

Bruno Rzonca was rescued by HMS *Dorsetshire*.

They took my clothing off, dried me up, and gave me a blanket. They brought us downstairs, offered us whiskey. I had swallowed some of the oil in the water and the whiskey was better.

Matrosengefreiter (Able Seaman) Otto Maus also survived.

Towards 1100 hours, large numbers of comrades were being washed overboard every time the ship heeled to port; I was among these ... After a short time I reached a raft which was already occupied, while being respectively grabbed onto by 40–60 comrades. I grabbed on too. A lot of oil floated on the water. I met the ordnance mate from our turret there. We talked. We could still see the ship which was still firing. But after about an hour we could no longer see the ship ... Many comrades became unconscious as a result of swallowing oily water and let go of the raft. Among them was my turret's ordnance mate. I drifted with five men for about two more hours. The air and the water appeared warm to us. At about 1700 hours the raft capsized.

Maschinengefreiter (Stoker) Walter Lorenzen was in the same raft.

Five of us got into the raft. But the raft repeatedly capsized, whereby two more comrades drowned – one a staff officer and one of the mechanics ... There were two soldered-shut tin cans and two signal flags in the rubber bag in the raft. One of the cans contained a flare pistol and ammunition, the other a bottle of Schnapps, one bottle of seltzer water, cookies, chocolate, cigarettes and matches. Our joy was great when we opened the tins. But we were to be disappointed. The charged water bottle had burst and the entire contents were wet. We decided to deal very frugally with the Schnapps. After a short time we discovered that the contents of the Schnapps container had leaked out because the seal was defective ... We three drifted along during the night. Sometime during the middle of the night as I was woken from drowsing by a breaker, I noticed that the comrade from the prize command's head was lying face up in the water. He had drowned. We took the dead sailor's life vest off and cast out the corpse. Now I was alone on the raft with my comrade, Seaman Second Class Maus. In the morning, we again saw, at a distance of 200m, a raft occupied by two men – evidently, it was the same raft we had been alongside the previous evening. But the raft soon disappeared once again from view. My comrade woke me up with the scream: 'A steamer!' We fired flares. The steamer instantly veered toward us and took us aboard. It was the German steamer *Sachsenwald* [a German weather ship]. I found out the following day that we had been picked up about 2300 hours.

INTO THE U-BOATS

After the sinking of the *Bismarck*, there were no more surface actions involving the German Navy. The *Bismarck*'s sister ship, the *Tirpitz*, remained hidden in a Norwegian fjord until it was damaged by bombing in September 1944. Meanwhile, the Battle of the Atlantic had been waged by German U-boats. These submarines were metal tubes just 67m (220ft) long, into which were crammed four officers, three or four senior non-commissioned officers, 14 petty officers and 26–28 enlisted men. Around half the crew lived in the bow compartment, where they ate, slept, serviced torpedoes and whiled away their free time. According to *Oberfähnrich* (Midshipman) Volkmar König:

> They shared their bunk with a comrade who did the same job aboard. While one man was on watch for four hours, another would have time to rest. When the watch changed, the other man would take over this bunk, still warm.

And with a full load of torpedoes there was nowhere to sit or stand. Submariner Gerhard Schwartz recalled:

> It was awful, one bunk above another. And next to it a small locker. Sometimes there was butter stored in it. And all the food stuff hanging around. It was hard to get used to.

Not all those who volunteered for the U-boats were hardline Nazis. Radio operator Georg Högel recalled listening to jazz. Some U-boats even tuned into enemy radio stations to hear forbidden 'swing' music. Gerhard Schwarz remembered his crew being collectively punished with a reading from *Mein Kampf*, after a portion of *Kujambel* – a type of fruit soup – was eaten despite orders that it was to be kept until the end of the next shift. This did not foster a sense of solidarity. Usually people stuck together in small groups, and submariner Herbert Arnecke recalled:

> You did not run to and fro. If you lived in the aft compartment [on board a Type IXC U-boat] you did not know what was going on in the bow compartment unless you talked about it on watch.

In all weather conditions, the cook managed to produce four meals a day in a tiny galley with a three-ring range, two small ovens and a 40-litre (9-gallon) pot. But this had dire consequences, according to *Leutnant* Hans Zeitz:

> We were encouraged to eat, because we were living under such unhealthy conditions, without daylight and in poor ventilation. The result was constipation. There was no exercise but plenty of nutritious food. Sometimes we disregarded the bread and spread the butter straight onto the cheese. The consumption of castor oil was considerable.

On the other hand, going to the lavatory was a hazardous business. Known humorously as 'Tube 7', the early toilets could not be flushed at a depth greater than 25–30m (80–100ft), due to the water pressure, and porcelain cracks easily when subjected to shocks from depth charges. Later in the war, lavatories that could be flushed at a greater depth were provided, but special training was needed to operate them, leading to the bogus *WC Schein* ('water closet certificate'). But it was no laughing matter. Failure to operate the lavatory properly led to the loss of U-1206 off Scotland on Friday, 13 April 1945. An ill-executed flush allowed waste and sea water to flood the forward compartment, and the water-logged batteries gave off chlorine gas, forcing the submarine to surface. It was then bombed and strafed. Three men were killed. The rest of the crew abandoned ship and rowed ashore in what must have been the most embarrassing U-boat loss of the war.

Generally, hygiene went by the board, as fresh water was conserved for drinking and cooking. U-boat veteran Otto Giesse recalled:

> During operations in the Atlantic or Arctic one simply could not escape becoming encrusted with dirt. At first, I thought a man could get scabies or some other skin disease if he didn't wash down at least once a day. To my surprise, I soon learned that we could make do by just rinsing off our hands a couple of times a week with salt water. Afterwards, we splashed 'Cologne 4711' onto our faces and distributed any remaining dirt with ointment, vigorously rubbing it into the skin. Our hair and beards were soon filthy and clotted from the salt water breaking over the ship, and even the best comb broke when we tried to disentangle the hairy mess. So it was left as it was and sprinkled with birch water to neutralize the odour, which seemed to differ with each man.

Then there was the battle with the elements, recalled by Robert Klaus:

> When on lookout duty, one got terribly wet. The heavy sea crashed over one's head. We had to get fastened to the conning tower not to be washed overboard.

After his watch, he would dry his clothes near the engine, but once he found that his dry clothes had been stolen and other wet ones put in their place.

In the North Atlantic there was also the cold to contend with. Heading into Canadian waters, Erich Topp, commander of U-552, wrote:

We entered these icy waters and a number of the crew ended up
with frozen feet, limbs; we weren't dressed warmly enough. People
were standing on the bridge with icicles hanging off their caps;
everything was under ice. The water that came on deck froze
immediately; the temperature was minus ten degrees and we had
to dive to melt away the ice. That was a bad time.

In the tropics, though, the temperature inside a U-boat could reach 60°C
(140°F), with a relative humidity of over 90 per cent.

Food was also a problem, particularly when missions went on longer than
originally planned. The diet on U-340 became monotonous when its supply
boat, U-459, was sunk. One crewman complained:

We had nothing but macaroni all the way from Freetown back to
St. Nazaire. Macaroni with noodles and noodles with macaroni.
Macaroni with dried fruit and dried fruit with macaroni. And then
macaroni with ham and ham with macaroni.

However, birthdays and other special occasions were celebrated with tinned
strawberries or a cake. In 1942, U-boatman Gerhard Schwartz remembers
celebrating Christmas 30m under the Caribbean with a Christmas cake,
carols and a paper Christmas tree made for the occasion.

Then there was the excitement of an attack. *Oberfunkmaat* (Radio Chief
Petty Officer) Wolfgang Hirschfeld recorded in his diary on board U-109:

Then it is time. The men stand or crouch in tension at their posts.
'*Rohr zwei fertig!*' ['Tube two ready!'] It is absolutely silent on
board. Then I hear the muffled but decisive words, '*Rohr eins los!
Rohr zwei los!*' ['Tube one fire! Tube two fire!'] The *Aale* ['eels' was
the submariners' slang for torpedoes] leave with a hissing noise ...
The stop-watch ticks. After three minutes there is the first
explosion, immediately followed by the second ... Suddenly fierce
shock waves hit us like a hammer ...

The captain looked through the periscope to see that the ship had been
ripped apart by the explosions. Then came what Werner Kronenberg, the
engineering officer on another U-boat, called 'the death-struggle of a ship'.

Those squeaks, the bursting of the bulkhead, this noise when she goes down – a noise that gets into your bones. That is not a pleasant sound.

As sailors, the U-boatmen thought about ships rather than the loss of their fellow seamen. After sinking the Danish-registered tanker *Danmark* in Inganess Bay off Kirkwall in the Orkneys on 11 January 1940, U-23's first watch officer, Hans-Jochen von Knebel Doeberitz, said:

> We were very proud and happy. The English didn't believe we could be so close by in the anchorage, and when the torpedo exploded they searched the air with lights because they thought we were the *Luftwaffe*. They were even firing into the air. Of course, for me on this first voyage, it was quite an experience. Then we turned back and again we sailed very close to the lookouts, but got out of there in one piece.

Others grew more aware of what they were doing. Herbert Arnecke recalled:

> The war was ugly ... I personally only realized that when I heard people crying in the water, because they were drowning. Until then I really focused upon the tonnage rather than the people.

Of course, once men were in the water the attitude to the enemy changed. *Korvettenkapitän* (Lieutenant Commander) Peter 'Ali' Cremer said:

> For us U-boat commanders, the humane treatment of shipwrecked seamen of the enemy powers was a matter of course. They were not enemies any more, but simply shipwrecked and had to be helped as far as possible.

DEPTH-CHARGED

After an attack, there was always the danger of retaliation and the horror of being depth-charged. Hans Börner recorded:

> After each depth-charge we were so relieved, when it was over, that nothing had happened for now. And you knew that the next would come. Often you heard the splash of it falling into the sea above us. We could hear that. But where was it? In front, aft, to port?

Depth-charging took a terrible toll. A submariner from U-37 wrote home from captivity in the Tower of London:

This is what happened. After an attack, we were simultaneously pummelled for three hours with terrible little depth charges by seven destroyers. The charge goes off with a most uncomfortable bang. Near the boat, they change the nature of material which breaks up into the form of atoms. We came to the surface, damaged and we were all saved by the British destroyers ... Our treatment is good, and there is no need to worry. This is in itself astonishing, given the anti-German agitations stirred up in the English people by their newspapers.

Men endured depth-charging for two or three days. *Kapitänleutnant* (Lieutenant Commander) Hartwig Looks, commander of U-264, which was sunk on 19 February 1944, described the loss of his vessel:

We got around two hundred depth charges and they exploded beneath the U-boat. We were accustomed to depth charges exploding above us, but the full wave of the explosion came from below. I tried to shake them off by taking evasive action, but that didn't work. Equipment broke away from the pressure hull, and there were various leaks. The water reached above our ankles and a fire was reported in the electric motor room, and when you are submerged and there's a fire on board that's the end. I thought, 'There's nothing for it – we have to surface.' We shot out of the water like a champagne cork and found ourselves inside a circle made by Captain Walker's submarine chasers. The crew jumped in the sea. I was on the tower holding on to the antenna to stop my legs being pulled into the tower hatch, where a whirlpool was forming. Then the U-boat sank below me.

Looks was rescued by a British rating:

I was hanging on the scramble net limp as a lettuce leaf. Then a British sailor jumped over the rail, climbed down the net, got hold of my collar and said, 'Come on, sailor!' and hauled me up on deck.

The entire crew of U-264 was saved, but of nearly 800 U-boats sunk during the Atlantic campaign, most went down with all hands.

3
HOLDING THE LINE: ATTRITION ON TWO FRONTS

During 1942, the Germans suffered further reverses in North Africa. In the summer, Hitler ordered an advance on Cairo. But Rommel found his supply lines overstretched and complained that 'support only arrives when things are almost hopeless'. On the night of 1 November 1942, the British, under General Bernard Montgomery, stopped the German advance with a counterattack at El Alamein. Two days later, Rommel wrote to his wife:

> Dearest Lu,
> The battle is going very heavily against us. We're simply being crushed by the enemy weight. I've made an attempt to salvage part of the army. I wonder if it will succeed. At night I lie open-eyed racking my brains for a way out of this plight for my poor troops. We are facing very difficult days, perhaps the most difficult a man can undergo. The dead are lucky, it's all over for them. I think of you constantly with heartfelt love and gratitude. Perhaps all will yet be well and we shall see each other again.

Unhelpfully, Hitler sent a signal saying:

> The situation demands that the positions at El Alamein be held to the last man. A retreat is out of the question. Victory or death!
> Heil Hitler!

It made no difference; the German army was soon fleeing back towards Tripoli, then on to Tunis. During the battle at El Alamein, Leutnant Heinz Schmidt's Special Group 288 was left out of the fighting:

> We listened to the heavy battle going on a dozen miles to the east of us, while our weapons lay idle and there was nothing for us to do except swim or lounge in the sun.

But they became Rommel's rearguard. Schmidt described the conditions they then faced:

We went without sleep, without food, without washing, and without conversation beyond the clipped talk of wireless procedures and orders. In permanent need of everything civilized, we snatched greedily at anything we could find, getting neither enjoyment or nourishment ... The daily routine was nearly always the same – up at any time between midnight and 0400; move out of the *lager* [camp] before first light; a biscuit and a spoonful of jam or a slice of wurst, if you were lucky; a long day of movement and vigil and encounter, death and fear of death until darkness put a limit to vision and purpose on both sides; the pulling in of sub-units which had been sent out on far-flung missions; the final endurance of the black, close-linked march to the *lager* area; maintenance and replenishment and more orders – which took until midnight; and then the beginning of another 24 hours.

On 8 November 1942 the Americans, who had now joined the war, landed in Morocco and Algeria and began closing in on Rommel from the west. Then, in early December, the British First Army under Lieutenant General Anderson led an attack on Tunis, the last Axis stronghold in North Africa. It was repulsed, but as the British, Americans and French were preparing to have another go, Colonel Rudolf Lang was moving 10 Panzer Division from Marseilles to Naples, ready to be shipped across the Mediterranean.

As soon as the last transport train had been expedited on 4 December from Marseilles, which – contrary to the rural population – was not altogether friendly towards us, last but not least because of the occupation of Toulon, I proceeded through Nice, Genova, Florence and Rome to Naples, driving by automobile to save time. It rained almost all the time so that we could not enjoy the beauty of the countryside. Many anti-tank obstacles had already been erected along the roads which we travelled; everywhere lighted signs, posters and large inscriptions on houses and walls expressed the determination to attain a joint victory. Many places in the part of Italy we crossed were literally swarming with Italian soldiers, who appeared to be friendly, happy and ready to burst into song.

But Colonel Lang did not want to wait around in Naples while the tanks were loaded on to ships.

I wanted to take charge of my Panzergrenadier Regiment 69, known to have reached a high degree of perfection and training during the last months as part of an excellently equipped division ... I started across on 14 December on a Ju 52, flying in an enormous fleet of aircraft of all kinds, including one giant aeroplane. We had a wonderful trip, flew at low altitude, encountered no enemy interference and reached the airfield of Tunis safe and sound ...

I was terribly eager to see the place where the division had recently earned its laurels. Everywhere there were the marks left from the fighting, giving evidence of a hard German blow. Major General Fischer, who had led the combat near Tebourba and had thereupon been awarded an oak-leaf cluster to the Knight's Cross and had been promoted Lieutenant General, met me on the combat field. The General showed pleasure in greeting me, briefed me on the situation and told me that I might expect to go into action soon.

While the hurried trip of the last few days had taken in localities and places of world-wide fame, such as Nice, Monte Carlo, San Remo, Florence, Rome, Pompeii and the top of Mount Vesuvius, while during my flight across the Mediterranean, Sicily had floated by below me, during the few days before my employment I had the opportunity and time calmly to enjoy Carthage's rich collections from ancient times, and to become somewhat acquainted with the country and the people.

On 17 December, Lang was given a command to the southeast of Tunis.

A command post of the *Kampfgruppe* [combat group] was a well-taken-care-of farm, owned by a courteous Frenchman, who as an officer during World War I had been seriously wounded, and who, afterwards, like many others used the financial support granted by the French government to settle in Tunisia. In his home he had a small but choice collection of antique objects found or excavated, paintings including some very good ones and a well assorted library, indicating his artistic understanding and wealth. Even though it was cold because the windows were broken, one could be very comfortable there and do good work. Since the owner, staying with relatives nearby, was exposed to hostile actions by the Arabs, which at times took rather serious proportions, I granted his request to let him keep his hunting gun, together with some ammunition to defend himself in case of emergency; I also promised him protection.

Lang sized up the situation:

The enemy could not fail to notice that because of the considerable enlargement of the bridgehead as a consequence of the Tebourba battle, the German lines had been seriously thinned out there, as a matter of fact, had to be left entirely unoccupied for stretches kilometres in length ... Later on barely enough forces were available. In the Lanserine mountain range in the west, there was not one single German soldier in an area of about 20km in length ... Furthermore, the enemy had to be aware of the fact that the number of German units to be moved up from Italy was limited, and that transports carrying troops and all kinds of material were sunk by torpedoes, bombs and shells ... Reconnaissance groups were sent, by day and by night, deep into no-man's land and even into the enemy lines ... Although Arabs, throughout favourably disposed towards us, had been promised tobacco, blankets and clothing, they, at first, brought in only little unusable results from their spying expeditions. However, they confirmed observations made by our own forces. Statements by prisoners who were brought in – French and British – were contradictory and of little use.

However, it became clear that an attack was coming soon – particularly when Allied air reconnaissance was stepped up on 21 December.

Following a brief expenditure of ammunition reminding us of the First World War, the attack started on 22 December. In that coverless, hilly terrain, which produces only some miserable and thorny bushes and afforded no chance whatsoever for digging in, the brave German soldier was mercilessly exposed to the hail of shells and rock fragments. The fireworks claimed their victims ... After hours of enemy fire, the enemy infantry rose to an assault on the decimated defenders, but was unable to reach its immediate objectives. All day long and during the night, the battle fluctuated back and forth ... General von Arnim, as commander of the Axis forces in Tunisia, took the opportunity to express Field Marshal Kesselring's approval and, disregarding the proximity of the enemy, he decorated some of our valiant fighters in the most advanced line ...

Again the fighting flared up. Fighting went on all night long. The enemy finally succeeded in gaining possession of the summit of the mountain and some hills towards the west. The situation had grown to be very serious ... To get us out of this difficult situation I assembled a counterattack for Holy Night. The commander who knows his men is entitled to make a demand of this kind on them, even though they had suffered severe casualties, were tired from extensive fighting during wet and cold days and nights, and were, furthermore, in an extremely unfavourable situation ... The enemy forces, fighting stubbornly and obstinately, were caught in the frontal fire as well as in that from the Panzers to their west flank and were forced to give up. The group making the main effort reached the enemy's east flank unnoticed. The enemy was completely wiped out or taken prisoner in close combat. The Panzers continued their thrust, cut off all of the important enemy elements from the chance of escaping, and proceeded up to a point where a mine field made a stop imperative ... This troop had not only inflicted considerable losses to a British regiment and to an elite regiment from London, but it had also proved its ability to make a stand in defensive action.

The troops received congratulations by radio from the high command at 0955 hours on Christmas day. Even the enemy grudgingly acknowledged defeat.

The British newspapers did by no means conceal the failure of this action at Christmas time to the public, but they attributed its cause to the stormy, cold and rainy weather conditions, and to the commanding position of the Germans. It was during the close combat fighting there that the British earned the respect of the German soldier.

Although the Axis forces in North Africa were on the back foot, there were other small victories to be recorded. The March issue of the Army newspaper *Die Wehrmacht* crowed:

> Through the streets of Tunis rolls an American Sherman tank – bouncing along on its mobile tracks, its engine rumbling, with captured ammunition in its gun barrels, and on board, its crew – the German scout patrol that captured it in the hills of Sbeitla on the foggy morning of 22 February. Down it travels from the hills through the sea of olive groves, headed towards the seaport of Sfax. It's a journey of some 210 miles, lasting four-and-a-half days, which testifies well to the overall march capacity of this steel colossus. The thing weighs about 31 metric tons. It was loaded onto a ship in the harbour while German fighter planes wheeled overhead in the clear sky of Africa, and not one enemy bomber dared intrude on this deadly zone. Now, after many intermediate stops, this star of American armament has arrived at its destination, a proving ground near Berlin, in the hands of German arms experts who are testing its combat efficiency and durability. Preliminary investigation in Tunisia had already revealed that this rolling steel mine is not a bad product. It was captured by a German Panzer regiment.

But defeat was inevitable. On 7 March 1943, Rommel was recalled to Europe to prepare the Atlantic defences against the Allied landings the Germans knew would come, and on 6 May the remaining Axis forces in North Africa were overrun.

AFTER STALINGRAD

Things were little better on the Russian front. In June 1942 Herbert Winckelmann had been with General Friedrich Paulus's 6th Army as it prepared to advance, fatefully, on Stalingrad, but he had fallen ill with trench fever and had been sent back to hospital in Germany. On 30 January 1943, Paulus surrendered at Stalingrad, so Winckelmann was not sent to rejoin his unit. What remained of the 6th Army mustered at Savenay in the Loire Valley and celebrated their survival with 'good red wine'. While his regiment was being reconstituted, Winckelmann was offered a command and a commission, but refused.

To become a commissioned officer one had to swear allegiance to Hitler, which I was not inclined to do. I have never regretted this.

Rebuilding the regiment took five months.

> We filled our leisure time with sight-seeing. One of the more relaxing trips was one taken to LeBaule ... Now all this was boarded up and the seawall was spotted with bunkers and other obstacles to hinder the possible landing of the Allies. At any rate, the miles of beaches, although now deserted, were beautiful and it was peaceful to lie in the sand and forget the ugliness of war ... I had longed to visit Paris before the war but had to postpone it several times because it was too expensive. However, now with the devalued franc I could patronize the most luxurious hotels and restaurants with their exquisite cuisines.

The first thing Winckelmann did in Paris was catch up with his old school friend Goetz Bannay, whom he had not seen for four years. Bannay was now a staff officer in Field Marshal Kesselring's headquarters there. He had lost a brother on the Russian front, who had written in his last postcard, 'Just today I saw through my binoculars the towers of the Kremlin.'

> The following days were filled with sight-seeing. Although we were on our feet from morning till night, we were only able to see the highlights of Paris. We strolled along the wide avenue of the Champs-Élysées from the Arc de Triomphe to the Place de la Concorde. Here and there we stopped for some window-shopping. It was too bad that we did not have more money on us as these stores offered goods that were already scarce in Germany. When our feet were tired we rested them in one of the many sidewalk cafés and watched passers-by while enjoying a *café au lait* with some delicious *petits fours*. Paris was still bustling as though the war did not exist. It was regrettable that the Louvre was closed ... There was a special order in effect that groups could not split up at night. Being an opera fan, I would have loved to have seen a performance there, but I was overruled by my comrades and instead we visited the nightclub Folies Bergère. Although they were practically naked, the performance was artistic and not vulgar. A woman's body does

not exist for man's lust alone ... On the last morning in Paris we went to Montmartre where the artists lived, viewed some of their exhibits, had lunch at one of the bohemian restaurants ... It was like a vacation except that our spouses could not be with us.

Back on the coast in LeBaule, there was serious business afoot:

We occasionally had to hunt down spies who worked amongst us like moles, mostly at night, except for one who made a daring daytime appearance and almost succeeded ... One day while my friend Achim Peglau was on duty, an officer unknown to him but in a very snappy staff-officer's uniform demanded, in a very commanding tone, to know the location of certain of our units. Achim who was only a private was intimidated by his forceful manner and went on to show the locations on a map. While opening his overcoat to put a copy of the locations in his jacket pocket, Achim noticed that he wore the Iron Cross on his right-hand side. Before Achim could apprehend him, he reached his motorcycle and sped off. Achim called headquarters who put up road blocks and intercepted the spy.

TYPHUS, BEDBUGS AND RATS

Without the 6th Army the Germans in the east were in disarray. In February 1943, General Walter von Unruh took over as commandant of Roslavl, a city in the oblast of Smolensk.

The town held 20,000 civilians, 20,000 rear-echelon troops and 10,000 Soviet PWs. Among the latter a typhus epidemic had broken out ... All billets were overcrowded, including the unheated church. Field hospitals were crowded to capacity and could not receive additional patients. Evacuation of the wounded had come to an almost complete standstill. The hospital basements were full of corpses that could not be buried because the ground was frozen solid. Almost all the town's people lived off our soldiers, who were billeted in their houses. In the beginning of February, Christmas packages for the soldiers at the front lay solidly frozen in front of the post office because there was no room inside. It was a sad and disagreeable situation. I added to the worries of the officers by telling them that a ground and air attack on Roslavl could not be ruled out ... I lived in modest quarters, where I was well acquainted with bedbugs and rats ... Since the few guards and sentries were always posted in the same place, the partisans who passed at night called them by names. This was proof of how well informed the partisans were, and I had the feeling that they were playing cat-and-mouse with us.

SECRET ORDERS

By July 1943 Herbert Winckelmann's division was ready for active service and soon to be transferred.

The first ones to know this were the 'market wives of Savenay'. I had gone into town on Wednesday with the intention of buying some fruit and vegetables to supplement our monotonous food. Thankfully I heeded the market wife's advice – 'buy today, next week you will be on your way to Russia'. I proceeded to buy some lingerie and also some hand-knitted items that France was famous for and a cute outfit for our soon-to-be-born baby.

Soon after, 'secret orders' came telling the division to ship out for an unknown destination: not Russia, however, but Acqui, a spa town in the hills above Genoa. Winckelmann enjoyed the trip.

We reached the sea just east of Toulon in about two days. To enjoy the beautiful Côte d'Azure in this gorgeous weather I transferred from my passenger compartment to the more open freight car. We rode passed Cannes and Nice and even stopped for an engine change in Monte Carlo. To kill some time, I walked up to the famous casino, but being in uniform, was denied entrance.

Soon there were unpleasant duties to attend to. On 10 July 1943, the Allies landed on Sicily and on 25 July Mussolini fell from power and was arrested. The Allies crossed the Strait of Messina on 3 September and, on 8 September, the Italians capitulated, announcing their intention to change sides.

When the Italian government surrendered to the Allies, we were in a very unpleasant situation. Yesterday the Italians had been our allies, but today we were ordered to disarm them. Fortunately most of their units were war-weary, surrendered peacefully, and went home.

But, for Winckelmann, there were compensations.

> The three months in Acqui, up to this disaster, has been even better than my stay in Savenay. My mornings were filled with paper work, but the afternoons were spent enjoying the spa's beautiful swimming pool or the nearby vineyards where the grape harvest was in full swing. How delicious these sweet red Italian grapes were and their many varieties of wine. Unfortunately sightseeing was out of the question as Milan, Florence, Venice, etc were outside our divisional sector.

On 30 September 1943 a telegram arrived at Acqui telling Herbert Winckelmann that he had become the father of a baby daughter, named Ulricke. He celebrated with a bottle of red wine. The birth did not entitle him to leave, but furlough was granted when his home in Berlin was bombed, and he set off to inspect the damage.

> I found the house in better condition than I had anticipated. The house across the street had been destroyed and the vacuum from the exploding bomb had left the front wall of our house bulging. The remaining walls, though cracked, were still standing. To my surprise, the electricity as well as the plumbing were still working and most of the furniture was unharmed. I therefore decided to spend the night in my house. I was extremely tired from my long trip and fell into a deep sleep. So much so that I did not even hear the air-raid sirens and did not wake until a window shattered about two o'clock in the morning. I jumped from my bed to witness the horror of an air raid over Berlin ... It was clear to me that our furniture had to be moved out of Berlin for safekeeping. This was easier said than done, especially to convince the bureaucratic channels to give the necessary permissions, not only to move the furniture but to move it out of Berlin. This was a logical move, but the bigoted Nazis still maintained that Berlin was a safe town.
> Having anticipated some difficulties and the need to grease

some gears, I armed myself with some Italian and French cigarettes. They were black looking and awful tasting, but we soldiers at the front had them in abundance, while cigarettes at home were scarce. With great luck I found a moving company that was eager to get one of its trucks out of Berlin and with the cigarettes I was soon provided with the necessary papers to get my furniture on its way. Within a week the furniture was in Dresden ... I had presumed Dresden to be safe as it had been declared a hospital town ... I spent the remaining days of my furlough with Elinor and our newborn princess in Kaufeuren.

That November Winckelmann was back on the Ukrainian front.

The Russian winter, which we feared more than the enemy itself, has already initiated a standstill on the battle front. This was due to the continuous rain that had fallen for weeks and had bogged down both sides in soaked black clay. I had not forgotten my first experience with this awful mud ... As we disembarked from the train, the rain was still pouring down and the strong east wind had resulted in a chill factor of below freezing.

The car designated to take him to his quarters got stuck in the mud and he was stranded for the night.

We were miserable in our rain- and mud-soaked boots and uniforms, and when the gas tanks ran empty we shivered to our bones.

Horses were called in to extricate them, and Winckelmann found himself in a 'cosy' hut under thick snow. With motor vehicles next to useless in those conditions, *Rittmeister* Ahrbecker helped out again, bringing Winckelmann a small Cossack horse:

Next to the captain's tall mare stood this tiny, shaggy animal which looked more like a colt than a full-grown horse. It looked so uncared for, his hair covered his sad eyes and I wondered if he could see. His coat was covered with mud and his tail almost touched the ground. Ahrbecker, noticing my disappointment, put his hand on my shoulder and explained: 'Herbert, he might not look like much but he has a good body and good legs.' ... At least twice he proved to be my guardian angel.

Winckelmann was constantly teased about his little horse and challenged the scoffers to a race.

They never won. Their heavier horses, even with their longer legs, were no match, especially on the loose snow.

He was also wary of his 'comrades'.

In my many years of service, I would name only two people to have been my comrade in the true sense of the word. These were Achim Peglau, from my regimental staff, and Rudi Peterson, from the PoW camp in Russia. With Achim I had many things in common. I could discuss things that made life valuable; we were both anti-Nazis, etc.

To the troops on the eastern front the situation was hopeless, though they could not say so. After the debacle of Stalingrad, half of the Ukraine had been lost and the Germans had withdrawn to the River Dnieper, more than 800km (500 miles) behind the German high-water mark. But the Führer was not downhearted and was planning a new spring offensive.

At this time, Hitler's propaganda was still strong, telling us 'just one more push and the Russians will collapse forever'.

TRUE BELIEVERS

There were still some true believers. On 1 September 1943, when the war was already going badly wrong for Germany, Hans Niedermejer gave a speech at a prisoner-of-war camp in Huntsville, Texas:

Comrades: A great event, which took place four years ago, induces me to call you here together today. You all know that four years ago on this day the greatest of all wars broke out. When we remember that time when our armies following the orders of the Führer crossed the German borders, when we remember the day we took leave of our mother and father, when we gave the farewell kiss to our wife, child or bride, when we remember the day we left brothers and sisters who had to fight in other countries and on other fronts or who had to take care of wounded soldiers, when we remember how men and women, in many cases without any aid, are working to give weapons and food to the fighting front, then now as prisoners of war having much time for such thoughts, we understand completely, how resolutely and compactly our fatherland, that is the whole German nation, stood for the Führer and will stand for him in the future too.

Since that day four years have passed and we have been fighting on many fronts, in Norway, in France, Yugoslavia, in Greece, in Crete, in Russia, in Libya and in Tunisia and on all the oceans. Many of our comrades died on the battlefield and there they bear witness to German heroism, German union and strength. Their blood obliges us to go on fighting and winning.

Now I ask you my comrade, who you are far from your family and from your fatherland? Do you remember still that this blood of your comrade does oblige you, also now in the prisoner of war camp, to stand for Germany as he did? I ask you, do you remember the day when you left your mother, father, wife, child or bride, brother and sister, when they were saying to you 'goodbye'? Do you think that they are trembling and praying for you and that they are longing for you? Do you remember that it is German blood running in your veins? Do you remember that day when you stood in formation and raised your hand to heaven to swear by God loyalty to the Führer and to the German people for life?

It was our fate that we were taken prisoner and confined behind barbed wire. Disarmed and powerless we have to await the end of this war. But in spite of this we remain soldiers of our Führer, soldiers of that great army which is the best in the world. I see that looking at you, my splendid young German men, standing here upright with closed ranks. When you are marching and singing German songs, I see that. Those are German military soldiers – that is, disciplined men – I thank you with all my heart for your proud and German attitude, and I ask you to remain so in the future.

If one of us should sleep,
Another guards instead of him
If one of us should doubt,
Another faithfully will smile,
If one of us should fall,
Another stands for two,
For every fighter gets from God
His comrades true.

So as your attitude has been until now, you are worthy to be named German soldiers, you are also worthy of your dead comrades. On this day, on which four years ago the war broke out, we renew our vow to stay always with our Führer and our German people with firm loyalty. We will not finish this day without having thought of our dead heroes, who died also for us and for the greatness of our fatherland. One minute of silent memory.

We do think of our fighters on all fronts and we call to you, our dears at home, we shall come back, as we have left you, strong and German. To our Führer and chief commander of the *Wehrmacht* and to our German people a three-fold *Sieg Heil*.

This speech was transcribed and translated into English. The translator helpfully added: 'There followed the national hymns (*Deutschland-Lied* and *Horst Wessel-Lied*).'

4
REAPING THE WHIRLWIND: FORTRESS EUROPE UNDER ATTACK

At home, the German populace began to notice the discrepancy between Nazi propaganda and their own experience. At the beginning of the war they had been told that they would never be bombed. When raids became a fact, the authorities sought to play down their effects, but noted that this drew murmurs of discontent. In September 1943, a report from Dortmund said:

> The official Army bulletin was long and critically discussed when, after the daylight raid on Bochum, it was stated that 'enemy air units flew under cloud cover'. There was much comment, for the enemy raiders were widely visible. Very few clouds were noticed.

After an attack on Augsberg on 20 March 1944, a report was sent to Berlin of out-and-out disloyalty:

> The increase of air raids leads to expressions like the following: 'Now we finally get the reprisals (a reference to the much-touted V weapons) but unfortunately they come from the other side ...' One can hardly talk of reprisal without eliciting a pitying smile ... They say, 'If we didn't have this government we would have had peace long ago. With the tenacity of our leadership an end of the war can only be hoped for after Germany's complete annihilation.' Members of the intelligentsia state that 'it was a matter of course to be a German, but not quite understandable that one could still be a National Socialist'.

The same report emphasizes that the air war 'proves as hitherto the crux in the moulding of morale' and ends:

> Comment on the often quoted poet's word: 'Germany must live even if we have to die.' The question is often raised: who in this case will represent the surviving Germany? Will it be the people in the bomb-proof shelters? ...

In other words, Hitler and his cronies. Chain letters and leaflets expressing criticism appeared, particularly in the industrial areas of the Ruhr and Rhine Valley. A poster pasted under the mail box in the post office in Krefeld read:

People awake! Down with Hitler, Goebbels, Ley, Rosenberg, Himmler, etc. These swine who have plunged us into misery; every night these raids. Do we need to stand for that?

In April 1943, leaflets found in Krefeld were sent to the Gestapo Regional Headquarters in Düsseldorf. Typically they read:

No more of these raids, unite, arise. Down with the Hitler murderers. No more of these raids! The people arise. Down with the murders, down with Hitler.

Jokes also circulated. One went:

A man took his radio to confession in Cologne Cathedral because it had been lying so much lately.

Another described Hitler and Goering flying over Bochum to survey the bomb damage from the air:

Goering points out the ruins to Hitler and comments: 'Wouldn't they be pleased, Adolph, if we dropped them a sackful of meat and fat coupons?' The pilot, a native of Bochum, on hearing this, turns around and says: 'You have no idea how happy the Bochumers would be if I dropped you too.'

In 1943, a Rhineland wit posed the riddle:

What is it? It is naked, stands on a meadow and carries a bank savings book under the arm? Answer: The German of 1946.

The Nazis were well aware that they were being ridiculed. A Party morale report dated June 1943 read:

The most vulgar jokes are circulated that assign to the leader, in the most indecent manner, sole responsibility for the war.

These jokes were circulated easily, as people were huddled together in air-raid shelters. However, not everyone was disillusioned. On 21 June 1945, a 21-year-old woman who worked in the Focke-Wulf Munitions factory in

Bremen was interviewed by the occupying forces about the effects of carpet bombing. Although she claimed not to be a Nazi, she was unrepentant.

> I had absolute confidence in Hitler and the whole political leadership. Only with regard to the military leadership did I have misgivings.

Why did she have such confidence?

> For the simple reason that they were men from the ranks of the common people.

Naively, she said:

> I thought that I would not be affected by the war, for at that time there were not yet any air raids; all of the stores were open. I and the rest of us expected things to remain like that.

But the air raids did come – 'all other hardships revolved around them', she said – and she soon found that the provisions the authorities had made were inadequate:

> In the early part of the war, alarms came well ahead of attacks; one had an hour or more to get to the shelter. But later on the alarms came at the same time as the fliers themselves or only a couple of minutes sooner. The air-raid shelters were too few and too small. The one which we used where I live was intended for eight hundred people and was actually used by three or four thousand. In there we were so crowded and hot that one after another vomited and the air became worse on that account. We just took off our clothes without shame because of the unbearable heat.

THANK OUR FUHRER

On 27 July 1945, a 25-year-old housewife from Duisburg was interviewed about the effects of bombing, which had begun there in May 1940 but reached a new ferocity on 14 October 1944.

> On the fourteenth we had an early alarm about 6am, but no planes came. I stayed up and did my housework. At 9am, a preliminary alarm came and then a full alarm almost immediately thereafter.

My baby, who was only a few weeks old, was in his carriage.
I snatched him out and rushed to the cellar. The other people in
the house were also in the cellar and there was much crying and
praying because almost immediately large bombs began to fall
directly on our section of the city. The house shook so that men
had to hold the timbers that propped up the walls and floor above
to keep them from falling. We opened holes in the walls into the
next cellars and called out to see if the people in there were alive.
People were crying and praying. They said that we had to thank
our Führer for this. The Party leaders had their safe bunkers and
most of them were in Berlin ...

After the attack was over, we came out. The doors and windows
in our house were broken. There was much destruction around
us, particularly in the Thyssen Works just opposite us. A great
many large bombs had dropped. That night we took turns keeping
watch, listening for the alarms across the Rhine. The alarm came
about 2am, but it was too late to go to the bunker. We went to
the cellar, where again there was a fearful scene of crying and
praying. After about fifteen or twenty minutes of bombing there
was a pause. My sister and I put our babies into their carriage and
with my father ran to the bunker. Many phosphorous bombs were
dropped, and everywhere houses were in flames. All the while my
father was shouting at us to hurry. Finally, I took my baby out
of the carriage and ran with him in my arms. By the time were
reached the bunker bombs were falling on all sides.

I was completely exhausted and said I could never go through
this again. We stayed all night in the bunkers. After we went home
there were still continual alarms. We did not have time to wash
our children or eat. All that day we were running from the house
to the bunker and from the bunker to the house. The night that
followed we stayed all night in the bunker and the babies got some
sleep. Father remained at home and he brought us something to
eat. About 4am we went home. Our house was damaged and there
was no water running, but we brought some from a pump and
washed ourselves and the children. Then we got some soap from
the NSV and for eight days thereafter we got food in this way.

Our flat was badly damaged but we could live there.

Did the bombing affect her morale? This was her answer:

> I always thought I would surely be killed. I lost the desire to live.
> The smut and dirt covered everything and it was impossible to
> keep anything clean. There was so much work to do. Life was no
> longer beautiful.

Did she blame the Allies for the bombing?

> Really no, I heard the English radio and knew that we had bombed
> cities. Goebbels made a great speech in which he challenged the
> Allies, saying that the German people were strong and could take
> the bombings. [But] the leaders were sitting safe in Berlin, but we
> had no flak and poor bunkers ... If the Allies had not bombed the
> cities, the war might have lasted longer and more men would have
> been killed at the front.

So who did she blame?

> Those who let the war go on. Our Party leaders. They should
> have brought the war to a close. The Party leaders looked out
> for themselves first of all ... [The newspapers and radio] said that
> the people were not affected, as if we lived in Berlin, which
> wasn't attacked much at first. The people couldn't say much
> about how they felt, but in the bunkers they cried out against
> the Party leaders.

And why had the war started?

> I haven't thought much about the fundamental cause of the war.
> I suppose the big people such as Hitler wanted more power.

THE ENGLISH DESTROY OUR HOMES

The bombing of German cities was also having an effect on morale at the
front. As early as mid-1942, a German soldier wrote home to his mother:

> I have talked with comrades who returned from leave in Cologne.
> They told me that one-third of the city is a pile of rubble and that
> there is much anguish and misery ... it is no use for us to destroy

the Russians, while the English destroy our homes.

In an attempt to correlate the weight of bombs dropped with the effect on the civilian population, the Allies analysed captured mail. In one letter, a woman from Bingerbruck complained:

> We have alerts day and night and the fighters are coming always. It really is a misery on this earth. If the war does not come to an end either our nerves will be shattered or else we shall be dead. It's becoming nearly impossible to work or even to prepare lunch at noon time. On Sundays we can't go to the cemetery. We scarcely receive any milk deliveries at all. If we go to town for milk there is a constant alert on. People here are about to lose courage. In Mainz and Boon they possess less courage yet. There they are in the process of moving and going away.

A woman from Stolberg described the general mood:

> All you hear all day long are the sirens, the anti-aircraft guns, the sound of the motors and the dropping of bombs; despite all that, they won't get us down. It's out of the question.

From Petch, a woman who was not made of such sterling stuff, wrote:

> I am a nervous wreck from all the excitement. It was terrible again today; the enemy planes do not stop coming. We had luck, but I am completely exhausted.

A German prisoner of war had noted the effect when taking leave from the front in an attempt to visit his family.

> I left by train on 2 December 1944 ... difficult journey, experienced air attacks ... found out that my mother and sister left Saarbrücken three days before, after having lived in a cellar for some time after their house had been bombed ... My dear wife had taken refuge with her brother in Neustadt ... I went by bicycle to Niederhausen (near Darmstadt) to see my sister and find out where my dear mother was ... No one in Saarbrücken, neither city nor Party official, had been able to tell me ... I had to go to Darmstadt to apply to the local commander for an extension to my furlough ...

was granted two additional days ... was about to leave Darmstadt when the air-raid alarm sounded ... the raid lasted forty-five minutes ... When it was over, the city was a sea of flames and smoke ...

By this time, it was clear that Germany was in difficulties and Herbert Winckelmann's unit was ordered to pull back 24km (15 miles) to a village that the map showed had a distinctive church with two steeples.

A church? So far I had not seen a church in all Ukraine, so I asked how old the map was. Later I found out that the church had been demolished during the Russian revolution – this map was probably from the time of the Czar.

Winckelmann was offered the use of a car to scout the unit's new quarters, but he already knew how useless wheeled vehicles were in the Ukraine. Instead, he took his Cossack horse. This was a good decision, as soon there was a shower that would have rendered the roads impassable to motor vehicles.

Things got worse when the shower turned to sleet in the howling east wind. My coat got stiffer and stiffer while visibility diminished to zero. My little horse was no better off but kept going faithfully, his head drooping lower and lower. The icicles on his mane rang out like little bells when he occasionally shook his head ... Suddenly the little horse stopped in front of a small hut and gave out a loud whinny. It wasn't long before the door was opened by an elderly Russian peasant. We were both petrified for the first few seconds, neither knowing what to do next ... He eased the situation by making a friendly gesture for me to come inside ... I accepted his invitation. But first I had to get off my horse – because of the ice covering me, I was unable to move. I had literally become an ice statue unable to move either my arms or legs and my shoes had been frozen to the stirrups. Realizing my predicament, the old man opened his arms and I slid into them. My prayers had been answered, I could not have found a better or more hospitable place. As I went into the hut, the old man took my Cossack into the stable next door to bed him down for the night.
The cottage was the usual one-room adobe house, with a stable

attached, under a thatch roof. The room was sparsely finished ... The white walls were bare except for an icon hanging in the corner ... Across from the entrance was a huge clay stove with a platform over the top covered with straw which served as a bed during the winter.

As I entered, I saw the peasant's wife sitting next to the fireplace. With a friendly gesture she invited me to sit next to her. When she noticed my wet uniform, although I resisted at first, she insisted that I undress and in a motherly manner hung a blanket around me. Her husband smiled kindly at my costume when he joined us by the fire.

Our conversation, mostly in sign language, progressed slowly. Of course, they were curious to know who I was. But how to explain this was sometimes difficult even when using words. So I pulled from my tunic photographs of my family and they showed me some of their family. Suddenly we were not strangers any more.

My anticipated one-night stay became two-and-a-half days, since our regimental staff had been delayed by the snow storm. I was aware that I was a burden to this old couple, for they had not much for themselves and I was another mouth to feed. I reciprocated by giving a chicken I had caught earlier that was still hanging on my saddle to the old woman who served us a delicious borscht.

To kill some time while the weather played havoc outside, the old man challenged me to a game of chess. I did not even win one game ... This was a very special couple, both in their upper sixties. They put aside the war that was going on and that I was one of the soldiers who occupied their land, and treated me like a fellow human being who was in need due to the horrible weather conditions.

ON LEAVE

In May 1944, the Germans retreated across the River Dniester into Romania, then still a German ally. Winckelmann was due some leave and managed to hitch a ride on a plane back to Berlin. It was the first time he had flown. Flying without a radio, the plane barely missed a mountain when landing at Krakow in cloud. At Berlin it touched down during an air raid. He spent a week at Kaufbeuren in Bavaria with his mother, wife and newborn daughter, then he travelled back to the front by train via Vienna.

> It was no longer the city I had loved before the war. There were no more *sacher torte* or Grinzing wine. The opera and the Burgtheater had also been closed ... At the front all was quiet ... It was so relaxing to see the beautiful countryside, still so peaceful while we were preparing to destroy it with everything our factories could supply in just a short period of time and the human race would kill each other again in senseless war.

By 1944, the Germans were expecting an invasion in the west, and in preparation Hitler had ordered the construction of an impregnable 'Atlantic Wall'. One of those defending it was Gotthard Leibich. He and his comrades knew the Allied landing was coming:

> It was talked about quite a bit and we felt 'well, we are ready for it', so to speak, because Rommel came in February if I remember. [It was March.] I was right on the beach in a place called Vierville. It's one end of what was, later on, Omaha. He came there and he organized that the fortifications should be much more improved, you see, and they worked on it like the clappers, but they didn't finish it because, you know, it was too late.

And Leibich's impression of Rommel?

> Big-wigs like that, they just walk around a little bit and then they shoot off again. But he did inspect the coastal defences. Rommel was a very good man and he was a decent man and everybody liked him. Even the British in Africa spoke highly of him. But Rommel had problems. As you know, he later had to take his life. It was very sad. My feeling is that he didn't really want to know about this rotten chap Hitler. But he said: 'Well, if you need me, I am there.'

Generally Leibich respected his officers, who were especially scrupulous about their behaviour towards the French.

> We had to treat the French with kid gloves. We weren't allowed to do anything that you do to hurt them. I was just seventeen years old and I went with my friend Walter Holland – he was higher up and a bit older than me – to have a meal or a drink in a French pub

one evening and he started talking to a Frenchman. He spoke a bit of French I think, and he got in a real heated argument with him and told him off and I said: 'God, what are you doing?' I was so – Why did he have this violent argument? He nearly came to blows with the Frenchman.

Alfred Mertens was also manning the defences in Normandy on 6 June 1944 – known, by the Allies, as D-Day.

Around 14 days before 6 June our company had received 24 new machine-guns ... Four wouldn't shoot at all and a number of them could only produce single shot fire ... All at once 12 English fighter-bombers flew over ... I ran to the anti-aircraft gun and was able to aim and fire, but it was a great disappointment ... we'd only got off 42 rounds.

Then came the big day itself.

Around midnight on 5–6 June we received a telephone call raising security to level two. The deafening noise of aircraft engines confirmed that the invasion had begun. As our company assembled early that morning our area was carpet bombed. I was on my way to a meeting and found myself on the edge of the attack. Five soldiers of our company were buried in their foxholes and killed ...

Mertens retired to the system of trenches built to defend the beach there.

It wasn't long before we met machine-gun fire in front of us. We carried on in the trench that ran along there. Going over to the left side of the trench I could see to the enemy on the other side of the field. All at once I got a blow on the right side of my head. I dived to the left of the bank and ducked down under cover. I shouted: 'Sniper, to the right!' I took off my helmet and saw on its edge a deep indentation which caused a massive swelling right up to my right temple. My captain, who was near me, sent me straight away with a colleague who was slightly wounded in the neck, along with an English straggler, to the main first-aid post.

We ran like hares – fighter bombers above us and a ship's battery bombarded our path. The shells would fall first on one side, then the other, then there would be a new salvo. We finally reached the first-aid post, but, because we were only slightly wounded, were transferred to the next unit engaging the enemy.

But the Germans were forced back and Mertens and his comrade became detached from their unit. On 7 June they were taken prisoner.

The Allies quickly established a significant beachhead. But heavy rain in July bogged down the advance, and the Germans managed to confine them to northeast Normandy. The US VII Corps would eventually break out southwards along the Avranches corridor, where medical sergeant Walter Klein was stationed:

On the morning of 24 July 1944, I just came back from the dressing station to the position when we were attacked by artillery. Our anti-aircraft platoon had two dead, three severely wounded. My own company, the heavy company of *Kampfgruppe* Heintz, lost only one man. With the help of two stretcher-bearers and the medical unit of the neighbouring company, we went back to the dressing station, to bring the wounded there. We arrived there at about 0900 hours. At 0915 hours there was such strong air activity over the combat line that we had to take the St-Lô–Vire road to get back from the dressing station to the position. We had the prescribed insignia, and knew that the American aviators would not fire on us.

Over the sector held by my company were approximately 18 to 25 Lightnings, which were firing systematically on every hedge. Our position was situated in a wooded sector. We left the road to reach the position and took a sunken road. It was 1100 hours. According to orders I had to report back to the company command post, but on the sunken road I found five wounded parachute gunners of the 5th Para Division, injured by a splinter bomb ...

What happened during the following hours was terrific. By our calculation, 1,000 to 1,200 bombers took part in the attack ... The effect was devastating; all our anti-aircraft guns and artillery were destroyed. Tanks that tried to get away were destroyed by pursuit planes. When a wave of planes had passed, one could hear the crying of the wounded and shouting for help of medical personnel. I had just the time to carry one of my comrades, who had been wounded badly in the thigh, into the dugout when a second wave started bombing. It was impossible to give help as long as the air raid lasted. Several companies of the 5th Para Division who tried to withdraw to the north in the direction of Marigny were entirely destroyed by Lightnings, pursuit planes and bombers. On that day my company lost one officer, and 34 non-commissioned officers and enlisted men. The attack lasted approximately three hours ...

At 1930 I brought the last wounded to the dressing station. The unit had moved to another position. The general opinion of my comrades and even the officers was that, if the enemy made another attack, it would be our end. Only one heavy weapon was left and it only had six rounds of ammunition. Of our heavy trench mortars only two were left. The St-Lô front had suffered very much from this attack. Worse than the loss of weapons was the effect that the attack had made on our morale.

On 25 July, the Americans started to make the breakthrough. At daybreak, as on the day before, innumerable pursuit planes and artillery-spotting planes were over the battlefield. Almost every rifle pit was shelled. At 1400 hours, when I accompanied some wounded to the dressing station, I found that American tanks were already driving along the St-Lô–Vire road. Canisy was taken at 1500 hours by assault detachments of the infantry, but could not be held because the enemy pressure was too strong. An observation post on a tree reported a big concentration of tanks north of Canisy. When our assault detachments withdrew, they were fired on by tanks moving up behind them. At 1900 hours the enemy had advanced on the right and on the left side past Canisy. Parachute units that were situated on our left were captured by the enemy, and we were in great danger if we did not try to withdraw. But not until 26 July at 2115 hours, a lieutenant of the 302 Infantry Regiment brought the order to withdraw in the direction of Vire. We managed to withdraw at the beginning of the night, harassed by enemy trench mortars. However, we had to leave the dressing station with 75 severely wounded in the hands of the

Americans. Two stretcher-bearers who were slightly wounded, one medical officer, one surgeon and half of the medical equipment of the troop were left with the wounded. I was ordered to follow the rest of the combat group with 14 wounded who were able to walk.

On the morning of 27 July we occupied a new position northwest of Vire ... The morale of the wounded comrades who were recovered from the combat sector was, when they were not too badly wounded, good. Most of them gave vent to their feelings, declaring the whole resistance, the whole war is a 'cramp'. A corporal, who was decorated with the Deutsche Kraus in gold for having destroyed five tanks with anti-tank mines on the eastern front, said to me: 'I tell you one thing, medic, this is no longer a war here in Normandy. The enemy is superior in men and material. We are simply sent to our deaths with insufficient arms. Our Highest Command doesn't do anything to help us. No aeroplanes, insufficient ammunition for our artillery.' And he concluded: 'Well, for me the war is over.'

An infantryman of my company, who was severely wounded in his shoulder, said: 'This piece of iron that hit me should have hit the Führer's head on 20 July, and the war would be over already.'

On 20 July 1944, Count Claus Schenk von Stauffenberg, a Panzer officer, and others had attempted to assassinate Hitler by planting a bomb in his headquarters, the Wolf's Lair, in Rastenburg, East Prussia. A heavy table had shielded Hitler, and Stauffenberg and many of his co-conspirators suffered a painful death.

MORE PLOTS

The July Plot was not the first attempt on Hitler's life. Lieutenant Colonel Rudolf von Gersdorff claimed that he had been involved in several other attempts. From April 1941 to September 1943, he had been an intelligence officer with Army Group Centre in Russia. It was there that he met Colonel Henning von Tresckow, who was with the general staff and later recruited von Stauffenberg for his bomb plot. Witnessing the 'cruel methods used in Russia' that had been advocated by Hitler, von Gersdorff said, it became 'clear to all that this man deserved death a thousand times'.

We – the circle around Tresckow – had already made up our minds in 1942 to kill Hitler and if possible to remove Goering and Himmler. At other places different plans were being considered, as, for example, the proposal to kidnap Hitler and then to force a change in the top military leadership. However, it was always clear to Tresckow that such a half-way measure would only lead to civil war, and that only the shock of the death of the 'mystic Führer' to the entire German people would make it possible for a coup d'état to proceed according to plan ... It was clear from the beginning that the attempt had to be made in such a manner as to assure absolute certainty of success. And it was axiomatic that the attempt must be carried out as soon as possible ...

An assassination by pistol was ruled out because it was generally believed that Hitler always wore a bullet-proof vest. Tresckow finally decided on a bombing attempt. Requesting me to prepare the explosive and fuses, he set up the following requirements:

1. An explosive about the size of a book or bundle of documents with sufficient force to destroy a small house and its occupants.
2. A time fuse which would function with absolute certainty but without any audible ticking.

I decided on English plastic explosive, an English magnetic mine, and an English chemical fuse. These devices had been dropped by enemy aircraft over Germany for use in sabotage by agents and foreign workers, and had been systematically collected by us. None of the available German devices were suitable, being either too large or too conspicuous.

Tresckow made many tests with these devices. The power of the explosive seemed quite satisfactory, although naturally it was impossible to make tests with living beings. The fuse was especially suitable because of its rod form and its simple operation – the crushing of a foil cap. There were fuses with a time delay of 10, 30, 120 and 360 minutes. Experiments showed that the surrounding air temperature affected the time delay: at less than room temperature the time delay could be increased by as much as 100 per cent ...

The first assassination attempt was carried out by Tresckow on the occasion of Hitler's visit to the Army Group headquarters in Smolensk. Tresckow was to personally bring Hitler from the airfield and had planned to place a bomb in the side pocket of the automobile, next to the place Hitler was to occupy. But it was not possible to plant the bomb in advance since, although Hitler himself travelled by train, he always had his personal car and driver sent on ahead. He never sat in anyone else's automobile. Even though, to avoid attention, Hitler had only a few SS men present, the attempt failed because of their ceaseless vigilance. It proved impossible for Tresckow to approach the car unwatched. Several subsequent attempts were undertaken but most were disrupted in their early stages ...

Then came von Gersdorff's chance.

Army Group Centre had prepared in the Armoury in Berlin an exhibition of captured Russian arms and equipment, war pictures, models, etc. A few days before 15 March 1943, General Schmundt [Hitler's adjutant] gave out information that Hitler would personally open the exhibition on the occasion of Heroes' Memorial Day. Since Goering and Himmler, as commanders of their respective organizations, were always present at this celebration, this was an opportunity that might never repeat itself. Upon Tresckow's request, I declared myself ready to make the assassination attempt.

Before flying to Berlin, I had asked Tresckow to tell me whether the coup d'état could be successfully carried out once Hitler had been assassinated. Since I did not expect to survive, I wanted to know if my act would be justified in the eyes of history. At that time Tresckow told me that the organization already existed and would go into action immediately; that arrangements had already been made with the Western Powers; and that the enterprise was the only chance to save Germany from complete destruction. Other than this, I knew only that Tresckow was in close contact with various branch chiefs in the Army High Command ...

Together with Field Marshal Model, I was flown to Berlin where I learned from General Schmundt that, after Hitler's address in the glass-roofed court of the arsenal, he would spend about half an hour going around the exhibition, accompanied by Goering, Himmler, Dönitz and several aides, and would then carry out the traditional review of the honour guard ...

After investigating the layout of the arsenal, I concluded that the actual attempt could only be made during the time that Hitler's party was going through the exhibition ... That the tour through the exhibition would last at least 20 minutes was a fact of decisive importance, since in the unheated rooms of the arsenal the temperature was only a few degrees above zero and I was therefore forced to calculate on the basis of a fuse time of 15 to 20 minutes ...

Tresckow had asked me to use any favourable opportunity which promised absolute success. Since everyone involved in the conspiracy was to be forewarned ... I told him that I intended to set off a bomb in each of my coat pockets during the time that Hitler passed through the exhibition.

But there was a last-minute change of plan.

As Hitler, together with Goering, Himmler, Dönitz, von Bock and three or four aides, entered the room, General Schmundt came up and told me that there were no more than eight minutes available for the tour of the exhibition. The possibility of assassination had gone, since even at normal room temperature the fuse would have required ten minutes to set off the bomb. This last-minute change of schedule, indicative of the extreme precautions that Hitler took, was responsible for saving his life once again ... Meanwhile Lieutenant Colonel Count von Stauffenberg had joined the conspiracy.

USELESS SACRIFICE

Medical sergeant Walter Klein, out in Normandy in 1944, had to cope with the consequences of their failure.

Another comrade who helped me to carry the infantryman said: 'I don't care for anything. Two of my brothers were sacrificed at Stalingrad and it was quite useless, and here we have the same movie.'

Few were sorry to have been seriously wounded.

Men who were slightly wounded were sent back to their units after five days. Men who had lost a finger or were shot through their legs without breaking the bone were sent back. Men wounded by a grazing shot were only sent to the troop dressing station. Therefore the young thought it better to be seriously wounded in order to be sent to a field hospital, or home, which would be best ...

It was plain to Klein that the Panzers that had given the Germans such advantages early on in the war were now ill suited to their task.

The German tanks were too large to be used in Normandy. When they were driving along the sunken roads, they could not see, nor could they operate between the hedges. In contrast, the Sherman tanks, with their high and narrow construction, had all the advantages. The hedges, however, permitted our tank destroyer troops to approach the enemy tanks without being seen.

Klein also compared the two sides' tactics.

If the American infantry did not approach our lines, it was not from cowardice, but because they were ordered to withdraw as soon as they met strong resistance and to wait until the air force and the heavy weapons had exhausted the enemy. Our infantrymen, who could not count upon any such help and who had seen the Russian infantry in action, could not have had a better opinion of the American infantry.

Nevertheless the Germans counterattacked.

During the night of 26–27 July we received orders by radio to join a part of the Panzer Division 'Goetz V. Berlichingen' northwest of Vire ... in order to make it possible for the rest of Hitler Jugend Division, of 'Goetz V. Berlichingen', of 'Das Reich' and of the 5th Para Division, to escape.

At 1200 hours we started the attack. We were promised an artillery detachment and a pioneer company with heavy weapons as reinforcements. The whole reinforcement, however, consisted of 16 dismounted gunners and 15 men of the pioneer company without flame throwers under the command of a lieutenant.

Covered as much as possible against enemy observation, we
tried to approach their lines. The American infantry, however,
having observed our approach withdrew in the direction of
Marigny, and we were heavily attacked by artillery. A direct hit
killed all our officers ... During the attack I saw no Tigers of the
tank detachment of the SS Division 'Goetz V. Berlichingen', and
only one tank of the medical service. The enemy received more
reinforcements from the direction of Granville, and two hours
later, at 1400 hours, he took the offensive. The proportion of
strength was approximately 20 to one without mentioning the fact
that our only heavy weapons consisted of two 8cm trench mortars.
50 to 60 enemy tanks were pitted against 36 men when the attack
started ...

We assembled in the valley of the Vire. Approximately 10 per cent
of our combat strength was left. Of my company 11 men were left.
Once more the Army was sacrificed in order to save the SS units
from being taken prisoner. Again we had to leave behind our 178
wounded. We spent the night in a brushwood that borders Vire.

On the morning of 28 July marching along the hedges, we tried
to find a gap in the encirclement. Our suggestion to surrender
because of lack of ammunition and our hopeless situation was
refused by our officers. We avoided villages. In the evening, we were
fired on from a farm by some terrorists who escaped when our men
were approaching. For five days we had nothing to eat but unripe
fruit and the iron rations we took from our dead comrades. We
spent the night and the day of 29 July in an oak wood.

That night a French farmer had told us of a gap in the
encirclement near Vire. He showed us the exact location of the
point on a map. On the morning of 30 July, when we passed
through a wood, approximately 150 men joined us. They were
dispersed from different units. When we arrived at 0600 hours at
the point that the French farmer had described, we received terrific
fire from a brushwood which was occupied by Americans. I made
field dressings for the wounded, while nobody fired at me. I want
to reiterate the fact that the American infantry, tanks and aviators
fought in a fair way. Already during the fighting for St-Lô, we had

the experience that all men who were wearing the Red Cross could help their wounded without being fired on. The losses in our medical personnel were caused by artillery or bomb attacks.

I was taken prisoner at 0700 hours. The American captain, who was commander of the position, allowed us to recover our wounded, assisted by a surgeon and three medical officers of the American Army. I also helped to bring in the American wounded. Eighteen hours later this work was finished and I was transferred to a collecting station for PWs.

Out on the Dniester, Herbert Winckelmann heard news of both the D-Day landings and von Stauffenberg's assassination attempt on Hitler.

Although neither of these events had a direct effect on our situation on the Romanian front, we were inclined to discuss them. That, however, was impossible since any opinion that deviated from the official explanation could have far-reaching consequences, even life-threatening ones. Goebbels' official but absurd explanation of D-Day was: 'The invasion is nothing more than an ingenious, strategic coup by Hitler. The Allies have been lured into France so they are no longer out of reach as they were when they were in England. Now that we have them within reach, our troops will destroy them with our V-2 bombs and other secret weapons to follow.' That explanation was accepted by men who wanted to believe it, but I and many others were shocked to hear that the Atlantic Wall, which had been so highly praised by Nazi propaganda, had failed to withstand the assault by the Allies.

No less absurd was the announcement after Hitler's assassination attempt: 'The unsuccessful attempt on Hitler's life was only an act by a handful of infamous men. His life was saved because Providence has chosen him to lead Germany to victory.'

The inevitable attack came in Romania on the morning of 20 August 1944, when 8,000 Red Army artillery pieces opened up. The Romanian units crumbled and fled, forcing the Germans to retreat in confusion. On 23 August, Romania switched sides, opening the skies to Allied bombers. Winckelmann had a narrow escape:

I jumped on my Cossack and he, perceiving the imminent danger, ran as fast as he could, straight for a row of hedges. We had never jumped together before. So I let him have his head, hoping he would know better than I what to do. We survived both our first jump together and the nearby exploding bomb.

Comrades who had witnessed the explosion concluded that Winckelmann had perished, and he was posted 'killed in action'. But 12 days later, he caught up with them in the Carpathian Mountains, staying with a community of ethnic Germans who wore traditional German folk dress. Realizing they were in great danger from the invading Red Army, the people packed up their belongings for the trek westwards.

It was a heartbreaking sight when our host family loaded their horse-drawn wagon to capacity with their furniture and other belongings. I wondered how far these horses would be able to pull such a heavy load, since their destination was so far away in either Austria or Germany. When the time came to say farewell, the old woman of the house came to me with tears running down her cheek and said, 'Comrade, take good care of my house and don't forget to feed the pets ...' I assured her that I would. As they pulled out of sight, I entered the house and found it spotless. She must have even swept the floors before leaving. I wondered what must have been going through her mind to make her think that she would be returning to her home so soon. The eventual reality, that I am sure she had to face, must have been very painful.

CIVILIAN MORALE

By September the Americans had reached the Western Wall, the fortified line along Germany's western frontier also known as the Siegfried Line. On the 15th the US Army breached it near Aachen. Now fighting on home soil, the Germans were expected to put up fierce resistance. However, civilian morale was not high. 'You will not stop the Americans,' the villagers of Langerwehe called out as the 2nd Battalion of the 89th Grenadier Regiment marched through. With them was Alfred Braun. Things, he reported, began well enough:

When the machine-guns opened up, we penetrated Schevenhütte in the darkness. The US forces were caught by surprise asleep.

Vehicles, rucksacks and blankets were found on the sidewalk.

Nevertheless the Americans resisted. In the morning, the Germans had to pull back into the forest, and 7 Company set up a command post in the village of Buschhausen. Then a patrol was wiped out except for a single man – and he was wounded.

> Afterwards the Americans started mortar fire and shelled the village using phosphorus grenades. Even the brick buildings were set on fire.

Braun was in the thick of the action.

> I had a narrow escape. A dud mortar shell passed between my legs and landed in my foxhole. I jumped out and raced away.

After two days, 7 Company moved into the forest and the headquarter's staff were called to a battalion meeting in the forester's house.

> The signal people had forced open a door leading into the cellar which was filled with a good supply of wine – we used the lot. After we returned to the forest making our way through an orchard. We heard mortars fire and shells landed in our way, forcing us to take full cover. Captain von Ahn, who was CO of 2 Battalion, was wounded by shrapnel in the thigh. First Lieutenant Lück was hit worse; his head and one eye caught several fragments, which were removed by means of an electro-magnet in Eschweiler. He got an eye patch and returned to 7 Company.

Next, 2 Battalion were moved to Stolberg.

> Its command post was set up in buildings at the edge of town near the limestone factory. The men had wrapped their boots with patches to avoid any noise when crossing the street. There, too, we had many casualties from the phosphorus ammunition ... The distribution of food was at night-time only to avoid casualties ... In screening the area we discovered two women and their adult daughters in one of the buildings. They were evacuated the same evening.

They had to fight off attacks by US tanks and fighter-bombers. While they often gave as good as they got, German casualties mounted.

On 22 September, First Lieutenant Hans Zeplier, company commander to the 14th Company of 89th Grenadier Regiment (Tank Destroyers), was made local commander of the villages of Hastenrath and Scherpenseel.

This involved arrangements such as clearing the roads of rubble, compiling a guard and defence plan, and, above all, the evacuation of civilians still living in the place. The inhabitants of the village – elderly people, but women and children too – were requested by me in person-to-person talks to leave Hastenrath and Scherpenseel. As cattle could not be taken along, I purchased the animals and submitted a retrospective report to the regimental staff for the purpose of further action by the butchering company of 12th Volksgrenadier Division. The prices were fixed by the cattle owners and I had their quotations checked by one of my messengers, a farmer by profession, and there was not a single case where a quotation gave rise to complaint. There was no trouble either concerning the evacuation of the civilians. People were allowed plenty of time to make their arrangements and no deadline was fixed; the ever-increasing artillery fire spoke a clear language ...

Mid-October I received instructions to collect all sewing machines, radio sets and the like from heavily damaged buildings. Equipment of that kind was badly needed in the rear areas, but commercially hardly available. The idea was to save these items from the rainwater that came in through shell-holes in roofs, walls and ceilings, which even penetrated to cellars, and take them to the rear. Along with my messengers, I collected the sewing machines and radios, and compiled a list showing the names and addresses of the owners, equipment trademarks and the number of items found in each flat. The outcome of this action in the 46 flats in Hastenrath were 32 sewing machines, 32 radio sets and six loudspeakers which, after registration, were taken to rear areas, as instructed.

Shelling by the Americans continued to increase. Then there were the fighter-bombers.

Their bombs very rarely came down on the villages, but rather exclusively on identified artillery and trench gun positions. I observed an incident where American planes laid a volley of bombs on a single horse-drawn supply vehicle. A soldier led the horse by the bridle, walking beside the vehicle. Four or five American planes approached from the direction of Düren. When they were over the vehicle, they released a volley of bombs. I heard the bombs screaming, the impacts were to left and right of the vehicle. All I saw were flames and dust, and I thought: 'Poor sod – he's had it.' After the fighter-bombers had disappeared and the dust had settled I saw the horse – upright and dust-covered – just standing there on the road, its head dangling a little. Nothing could be seen of the driver. Eventually he crawled out of a ditch, took the bridle and off they went. When they passed a trench-gun position, the driver told the soldiers there in his Mecklenburg dialect: 'We just got bombed.' This stoicism is very typical of the Mecklenburg people.

Many American tanks were knocked out by bazookas fired from covered positions the Germans had prepared.

In their attempt to avoid rocket fire, the American tank crews used to put any suspicious shrub or the like under machine-gun fire until they could be flattened with their caterpillar tracks. Of course, that could not be done with all shrubs in the area, particularly extended hedges. So the bazooka-ists had the possibility of raising their 'stove pipes' unseen from their covered holes and to fire at the attackers. This naturally required great courage in the face of the superior fire power of tanks on their approach with their loud roaring engines.

The 'stovepipe' bazooka – Raketen-Panzerbüchse (RPzB) 54 – was extremely effective, according to Lieutenant Zeplier. But, otherwise, the Germans were ill equipped.

Neither motorcycles nor bikes were provided to the messengers carrying orders. Rather they had to cover long distances on foot. As a result, the company commander was unable to coordinate the action of his platoons in the course of anti-tank combat. Not only that: the platoon-leaders' influence on their platoons and bazooka squads involved in action was very nearly nil.

Even a successful attack could bring trouble in its wake, as when the lead tank of an American column was knocked out.

> A soldier came running towards us and shouted: 'I've got him, I've got him.' He was a member of the 12th Tank Destroyer Battalion and as the company's battlefield observer he had been watching from a shell-hole a little beyond that road. Those tanks had arrived there on their way from somewhere near Werth, but had obviously not yet advanced into the firing range of one our 7.5cm anti-tank guns waiting to kill them from the flank. After that one tank had been silenced, the others had turned and slowly moved back to Werth. Dusk was coming on when, armed with two *Panzerfausts*, we rushed after the tanks. Through a messenger I ordered a bazooka team of the tank destroyer group to the spot. Passing the knocked-out tank, we saw the exhaust flames of the retreating tanks in front of us as the darkness increased ... It was dark when we approached the outskirts of Werth and an American sentry challenged us with the words: 'Hey, Charlie!' He might have mistaken us for crew members from the killed tank. He soon saw that, by our number, we could not possibly be the expected tank crew but rather a German tank destroyer party and we soon received fire from a submachine gun, or perhaps a machine gun, which we immediately returned with our burp guns. We were now fired at with anti-tank guns and machine guns, but they were firing too high. A little later American artillery and tank gun fire set in. Tier after tier came down and hit the area of the crossroads behind us. We stopped our advance and took cover on both sides of the street. The shells got us anyway and out of the five men who had advanced with me, Sergeant Tonagel, two messengers and one man of the bazooka crew were wounded.

However, Zeplier's tank destroyers proved themselves very effective. Returning to the battlefield in September 1946, after the war was over, he found the remains of 14 Shermans. But American fire power eventually proved too much for them and nothing could stop the Allies advancing into Germany. The villages of Volkerath, Hastenrath, Scherpenseel and Werth were all completely destroyed.

5
THE LAST OFFENSIVE: COUNTERATTACK IN THE ARDENNES

Hitler had one last trick up his sleeve, an operation he called *Wacht am Rhein* ('Watch on the Rhine') and later *Herbsnebel* ('Autumn Fog'). One of those involved was H. Rammes. He had trained as an aircraft wireless operator, but the *Luftwaffe* had few planes left and he was retrained as a forward artillery observer for the forthcoming German winter offensive in the Ardennes. Launched on 16 December 1944, it would be known to the Allies as the Battle of the Bulge. Rammes recalled:

> I cannot say that we were excellently equipped. The radio equipment was intact, and the Volkswagens were in working order, but the heavy Büssing lorries were obviously completely unfit for cross-country rides, and their camouflage was good for desert warfare in Africa rather than for a winter battle. On 14 December we were in a forest near a road leading to Prüm ... At this place we saw for the first time a V-1 passing overheard. Was this the famous wonder weapon? With a feeling of utter dislike I noticed the strange and disgusting screeching of this remote-controlled device.

Neither were V-1s the invincible, war-winning weapons German propaganda had promised, as Alfons Strüter recalled:

> En route we experienced for the first time a V-1 being shot down. Some of these 'things' did not go very far and crashed soon after they started. The V-1s that flew on were fired at by the Yanks with all barrels.

Emil Bauer also visited Prüm on the way to the front.

> I have been here before, but I do not recognize this place. It is totally destroyed. Undestroyed a few weeks ago and now only ruins. The situation here must have been very severe. American prisoners are standing in a courtyard ... They looked like a bunch

of tramps ... The company are confident; we are moving forward again. 'The Americans clear out in their underwear,' people are calling to us.

Bauer did not share their optimism.

Civilians talk a lot about magic weapons, new assault divisions – 'Soon you will be at the Channel!' I tell them: 'Listen, it's impossible, we cannot win any more. I've been in Stolberg, Aachen, Venio, Roermond, Arnheim and so on. I know the Americans and I am aware of what they have and what we have not. In 14 days we will run past you again in a long-distance race.'

The night before the attack there was something of a celebration, as Klaus Ritter of the 12th Volksgrenadier Division recalled:

Dinner was comparatively opulent that evening. Additionally, every two men received a bottle of wine and 20 cigarettes were allocated per head. We younger people were soon getting euphoric. Four weeks to get to Paris, the Champs-Élysées, pretty girls, the Eiffel Tower. And hundreds of German combat planes of the latest design would support us in this assault of decisive importance for the whole German nation. Finally, after so many weeks, we shall send our greetings to the Yanks ... The older men were silent. Many of them had seen the invasion. They seemed to feel what was ahead of us.

While Klaus Ritter was partying, forward observer Rammes was moved into position with the *Nebelwerfers* – German rocket launchers.

Suddenly our foxhole was as light as day. The recoil fire of the rockets cast a ghostly light over the country ... In the light of the recoil fire we could see infantry companies, part on bicycles, on their way to the front. Our gunners worked until the last rocket was fired ... The onset was a bad surprise to the Americans. The front units immediately involved in the fire strike ran for their lives.

Rammes said that, for him, the attack on 16 December did not hold 'any further excitement or events of particular significance'. However:

In the late afternoon the first ambulances came back from the front line, heading for the dressing stations. My first thoughts: Are they badly wounded? Have they died in transit?

Even so Rammes shared none of Bauer's pessimism.

In the late evening a trailer stopped at the entrance of our pillbox heavily laden with foodstuff. Rumours went round that large quantities of American petrol had fallen into our hands, that progress was fast, and that Liège would be taken very soon. General Eisenhower was said to have his HQ there, and once he had been taken prisoner, the war would be over pretty soon. We were also told that new German jet planes were about to intervene in the battle, identifiable by yellow waving lines on their body sides. On no account should we fire at them. Rumours, opinions, latrine talk spread fast ...

The following day, the 12th SS Panzer Division 'Hitlerjugend' were ordered to take the Meuse. They were promised the upper hand:

New types of aircraft are available to cover you and to support your operations with efficiency. V-weapons will cause embarrassment in the rear areas and eliminate the supply centres ...

The general purpose of the attack was 'to force the Americans out of France'. The unit history recorded:

That was it! We now knew what was ahead of us. That order of the day reminded us of glorious times. Anyway, we felt this all looked so definite as if this would be the last possibility of getting this war to turn in our favour.

Gunther Holz was more cynical.

We could not believe in a winning blow of this kind. During the recent months we had gained only too clear an idea of the inexhaustible material supremacy of the enemy ... We were even told that the Luftwaffe was available at full efficiency.

That day the troop movements towards the front line seemed incessant. But Rammes had more personal concerns.

Who might be thinking about me? Do my parents know anything about our onset? ... But they do not know that I am here. Better perhaps. I smoke my first American cigarettes and can even select the brand – Camel or Chesterfield. Strong stuff on the lungs ...

By evening I am in the pillbox, along with Hermann Brambrink, Gregor Kehrer and some other comrades. First Lieutenant Freitag enters, sad and depressed, and says: 'There's Second Lieutenant Deparade lying in a Volkswsagen outside – hit by an explosive bullet during a low-level raid' – our first dead ... Is that war? Who will be next? Why just he? He was 20.

Moving up to Grosslangenfeld, they found some buildings on fire.

We move on, our pistols drawn for the sake of safety. You never know. At the other end of the village we find three armoured patrol cars and a jeep outside an old house. We search the fully packed vehicles. In one of the patrol cars we find a heap of sleeping bags, food – all tinned – and cigarettes – bars and loose packs. I walk over to the entrance of the building, hear some noise and go inside, finding some pigs in a pigsty – but no Americans ... The company commander is more than happy with the sleeping bags – enough for the whole battery.

BEHIND THE LINES

Willy Volberg was in charge of a unit of paratroopers landed behind the lines in the Ardennes, but high winds had dispersed them and caused some injuries.

During the dawn of the following day some of us were resting in a ditch beside the road when suddenly a column of US trucks approached. It was too late to hide. We unlocked the automatic rifles, ready to fire. But nothing happens. Passing our position, the GIs sleepily wave their hand comrade-like and we quickly respond in the same way. They must have been deceived by the shape of our paratrooper helmets which look like US steel helmets.

But they soon found themselves perilously low on ammunition.

What will become of us? The whole stock of ammunition available will only allow us to fight for five seconds. So there is no need to mount a guard. We are all going to sleep. If our hiding place is discovered by the Americans, nothing can be done but surrender ... What a windfall. Next morning, when one of us penetrates the wooden terrain to relieve nature he discovers a parachute container full of ammunition ... The magazines of the rifles and machine gun are filled, and everybody gets a belt with 300 rounds to be carried around the neck. Hand grenades are put into the big pockets of the parasuits. We cannot take all the ammunition with us ... One of the men who is a specialist in preparing booby-traps proposes making such a device by using a hand grenade, the ammunition container and the rest of the ammunition we cannot carry with us. Due to the possibility that the trap could be found and opened by civilians, I forbid him. They would have paid with their life, and there already had been enough harm done to the population.

Soon, as Klaus Ritter recalled, the advance of the 12th Volksgrenadier Division was halted:

On the top of the bridge crossing the Alfbach, short of the village, the column stops. American mortar fire lies on the entrance to the village. Some of the vehicles are already on fire. The ammunition on their platforms explodes and spreads a shower of steel into our own files. Cries, curses and groans are mixed with the sound of impacts. I flop to the ground and try to find shelter between the wheels of our gun. Four weeks to get to Paris? The hell with Paris! I want to get out of this inferno alive ...

In the late afternoon we are back at Brandscheid, dog-tired ... And there – the first groups of captured Americans ... Well-fed men in warm winter clothing, their boots in rubber overshoes. I hardly dare to make the comparison with our equipment. Near the church another larger group of prisoners, embarrassed, frightened, and surrounded by very young German soldiers ... Greedily we make for the chocolate, the ration packs and the numerous tins with cheese, ham and eggs and other dainties. And heaps of cigarettes. Soon all pockets are stuffed with Camel, Chesterfield and Lucky Strike.

On a Dodge troop carrier I search the kit bags for warm underwear. In no time my worn and damp underwear is off, and I put on Bill's or John's comfortably warming things, if I only had not to pull back on my damp and dirty uniform. And then my sore feet slip into a pair of brand-new shoes with rubber soles and fist-high leather spats – how comfortable. I hurl my old and worn-out *Wehrmacht* slippers on the street. Like a newborn child, I feel in that army outfit 'Made in the USA'.

FIELD GREY AND KHAKI

In Schönberg, Klaus Ritter noticed traces of fighting on the walls and abandoned enemy vehicles in the side streets.

Here and there I see killed soldiers – in field grey and khaki. Frightened civilians are standing at the front doors of their homes. The street had provisionally been cleared of battle equipment. Dead horses have been pushed aside. They formed an obstacle to the war machine. And now the tracks of our RSO grind over human bodies rolled flat, a pulp of flesh and bones, mixed with uniform rags and what has been left of their equipment. I feel like vomiting.

Ritter was then mortared with phosphorous shells.

The rain of fire can still be seen as glowing dots of light after minutes. The impacts are very close to one another. The first curtain gets steadily nearer. The impacts are now hitting the road as I flop into the hard-frozen ditch. Others take shelter beside or on top of me. A whizzing and the night is as light as day. Paul Richter, lying on top of me, yells: 'My eyes! My eyes!' My face feels like burning, like a thousand red-hot pins sticking into my face. The smell of burning flesh! Those nearby jump up and leave the ditch with loud screams. I jump to my feet, frightened to death, and dash into the darkness, tearing the blanket off my shoulders and pulling off my heavy overcoat. 'I'm burning! I'm burning!' I yell, and try to find a building with a Red Cross flag. There are more human torches in the yard, rolling to and fro on the ground, when I arrive.

Funnily enough, the feeling of fright eases down, although my face aches ... Funnier even are my thoughts: this injury will certainly get me that black badge, perhaps even a bronze one. Medical orderlies take care of me. And then I faint. Hours later

I wake up in a dimly lit hospital room ... My fingers are so cold that they hardly can feel the thick bandages around my face. Mouth, nose and eyes are uncovered, the pain is negligible. With some effort I lift my head, look to the right and left. Wounded lie everywhere, groaning here, screaming there.

'Oh man, was I lucky! Shot through the arm – should be just sufficient to get out of this shit. And you?'

'Phosphorus burns,' I reply.

Again loud groaning and rattling comes from a corner of the large room.

'All belly shots,' my neighbour remarks. 'Safe tickets for a better world.'

The early morning sends its light into our room. I have sat up and now I see all the misery which a war can bring. Wounded Americans are sitting and lying about among the field grey.

Aircraft approach. I crouch against the wall. Several wounded Americans have leapt to their feet, trying to find shelter, their eyes horror-stricken.

'Don't be afraid. They are your own fighters,' I shout at them with some sarcasm. But I am just as frightened as they are.

Medics instruct us to move into the basements. Field-grey clusters of buddies, bandages around their heads, their arms, jostle to the exit – a stumbling, jerking and swearing mass of human beings. The air in the basement is cold and stuffy. I find a place near some thick heating pipes. The muffled noise of explosions and a screaming comes close and a deafening crump. The walls shake. Dust and dirt. The air now becomes insufferable. Breathing becomes hard. Someone tears the door open. A mud-covered human queue jostles outside, yearning for fresh air. Outside clouds of dust are hanging over the major portion of the hospital, covering the ruins. Along with the others I hasten into the street, away from the hospital area. Who knows when another formation of these damned Americans may come again to unload their deadly burden.

A few hours after the bomb raid, the wounded are instructed to assemble. From all corners they arrive, panting and limping.

A doctor, his overall still covered with dust, announces: 'The major part of the field hospital attached to the general hospital of Saint-Vith will be dissolved. Assembly areas for the disabled are Bleialf and Gerolstein. Those who think they could manage to get to the Andernach main hospital [on the Rhine] should try.'

Apathetically I move into the next street. Undamaged in the middle of the crossing is a group of sign-posts – German and American. One catches my eye. It reads; 'Prüm 33km.' This entirely clarified what I should do – go home to Meinsheim, 5km from Prüm. It is Christmas 1944. On 3 March 1945, American soldiers overrun the place, but I escape captivity.

PERFECT TANK GRAVE

On 18 December, the 12th Panzer Regiment made a disastrous attack on Rocherath-Krinkelt. Willi Fischer, a tank commander, said that they stumbled into the 'perfect tank grave'.

> The tanks of A Company moved ahead, followed by our company with Brödel as the company commander. I was driving behind Beutelhauser, my platoon leader. When he arrived at a place near the church we were offered a cruel sight. Beutelhauser was shot down ahead of me, just when both tanks had passed the second crossroads. When Beutelhauser was knocked out, I could make out the probable location of the enemy anti-tank gun. Beutelhauser managed to get out and escape to safety. The gun loader was killed by rifle fire when he tried to escape. Under the cover of a building I moved my tank into position ... Beside me I noticed Brödel's tank burning slightly. Brödel could be seen sitting in the turret – lifeless. Ahead of me on the road all the tanks were shot out of action. Some of them still ablaze.

They had been hit by a damaged Sherman tank which, though unable to manoeuvre, was otherwise in fighting condition. Fischer managed to withdraw, though a shell destroyed one of his tank's tracks and the radio equipment. Even so, he covered the escape of the surviving tank crewmen and captured 20 Americans. However, he was threatened with a court-martial for retreating and spent Christmas taking shelter in a farm building 'as the cold inside the tanks was much in excess of what a man could stand'.

At 3pm on 18 December 1944, gunner Horst Helmus watched as American Mustangs came under attack by Me109s.

It comes to a wild fight. We watch it with scissor telescopes and binoculars. Every knockout arouses applause, like at a sports game. One American after the other buzzes off. Later we learn six losses have been inflicted on the enemy to one on our own ... Five hundred metres ahead of us an American two-motor plane has been forced down. Unfortunately it has burned out completely. The landing ground is totally wrecked, the meadow torn up, fences broken down and torn to pieces. The crew is charred beyond recognition and the bodies have shrunk. They can only be identified as such by the helmet.

But the victory was short-lived.

The sky gets dark, plane by plane, close together, not even a span's space between. Each plane has transport glider in tow. We get frightened. What would happen if these fellows came down in our line? A real nasty feeling. No soldier is running around any more. Everybody is staying inside their holes, looking upwards.

Next to me is an eighteen-year-old infantryman I had been on guard with last night at the window. Suddenly there is an aircraft attack. I jump into the entrance hall and rush into the last room to lie down flat in front of a wardrobe ... But my fellow infantry soldier got it. A splinter went right in the carotid and he bled to death.

On the afternoon of 19 December, Rammes and a party of four left for a reconnaissance mission in the Bleialf area.

Moving through brushwood, we find a German infantryman lying on the right-hand verge of the road – shot through the throat. On the left of the road, we discover the remnants of an American camp, slices of white bread lying around, empty tins, tents partly dismantled.

Crossing a railway line, they found a village.

Things look ugly here, the buildings around are more or less damaged. We look to the left and see the church – or what has been left of it. And wherever you look – German tanks and soldiers. A depressing sight.

On 21 December, Rammes went to an area near Schönberg where 9,000 Americans had been captured. The following day, after a hearty breakfast of American rations, he and his men were ordered up to Saint-Vith in Belgium. On the way they commandeered an American half-track.

It is cold and the countryside is covered with a thin layer of snow, the bright sunshine goes into even the remotest corners. It is noon and our 'tractor' is parked in the yard of a mill. A quick-fire gun is mounted on top of the driver's cabin. A belt of ammunition is inserted. We wonder whether the thing is ready to fire. Suddenly a fighter-bomber dives towards the mill, out of the sun. Second Lieutenant Bauer jumps onto the bonnet and grabs for the gun. I and a few comrades escape to safety, taking cover in the barn. The plane's guns fire. Bauer fires back – a terrible noise all around. No bombs – we are having some luck. I see the impacts of explosive shells around the vehicle. Again Bauer pulls the trigger. The plane crosses overhead and takes a curve over the valley for a repeat attack. Our second lieutenant opens fire at once, but unfortunately fails to hit the aircraft. Luckily the plane turns away ...

The miller and our first lieutenant appear at the entrance of the building, both gesticulating. The miller feels that there is no sense in shooting, since the fighter-bomber has the advantage and our presence would put his mill at risk. Everyone looks at matters with his own eyes.

Reaching Saint-Vith, they found it under shell fire.

In the fields to the left we notice many tanks of the 'Tiger' and 'Panther' types. Second Lieutenant Bauer talks to one of the infantry officers, an old acquaintance of ours. He advises us to turn around at once to get out of there as fast as we can ... On 22 December, at 1400 hours, Saint-Vith had finally been taken by German troops ... [But] the planned surprise assault of the German Army, aimed at the early capture of Saint-Vith and Malmedy in the north, and Bastogne in the south, had failed.

This was what had actually decided the outcome of the Battle of the Bulge. But for us the fight had to go on.

That night they decided to stay in Saint-Vith.

I notice a few nice houses – their inhabitants seem to have been evacuated. There is a garage attached to one of the houses where we put our car. Some soldiers have already been billeted in the building. After a look about we decide to take a room on the east side, opposite the front line. The soldiers have already lit a stove. There is wood and coal in the basement, and someone even finds a big bag of noodles.

Gregor and I go to the basement for water, as the taps in the house do not seem to be working. But there is no water in the basement either – the system seems to have been damaged. Instead we find shelves of preserved foods, such as beans, cranberries and even a large jar of preserved eggs. Should we take them or wait until everything gets smashed? Our buddies in the warm room are happy: today is cooking day – how eventful a soldier's life can be.

But how to get water? Someone claims to know that there is water in the school building near the open place near the main street. We take a tub from the basement ...

They made their way down the street in complete darkness, then noticed other people heading for the building.

Inside a large cellar some water is dripping from a stopcock connected to a main pipe, the pressure being only a little above zero, and we place our tub underneath. Some light from the side illuminates the basement. It takes a long time until the tub is half full and we can walk back to our billet. Again we have to cross that open place and turn right into the main street. All of a sudden there is some howling – rather short – and there is the impact. We flop down with our tub. We survive, but there is only a little water left in the tub. Never mind, that must do ...

Everyone is happy when they see us entering the 'living room'. Now we can cook. The dish is simple: noodles, cooked with ten eggs and cranberries. Delicious – particularly the cigarette afterwards. We get some mattresses from the bedroom and place them on the floor of our room in the back of the house. Soon we are asleep.

FIGHTER-BOMBER WEATHER

The next morning Rammes and the others headed for Rodt, but 'this will be a clear day with a blue sky; fighter-bomber weather'.

> Halfway, the engine suddenly stops. I open the bonnet: the driving pulley between the engine and the dynamo is broken. One half lies on the bottom of the engine casing: the pulley is made of wood! We push the car to the wall of a farm building for cover against aeroplanes. My three comrades start walking, and I remain with the car. The farmer's wife is inside and we have a chat. She does not believe that the Americans will come back very soon ...
>
> In the afternoon my comrades come back from the direction of Rodt with an American track-type vehicle ... It is too early now to drive back. To avoid the risk of air attack we wait until dusk.

Soon after they set off, they ran out of petrol. Then they discovered that the vehicle had two tanks, one 'on either side, the left one empty, but the other one filled to the top'. The lieutenant sent one of the men to a nearby house to get a hose to siphon the petrol from one tank to the other. Meanwhile the others searched the vehicle:

> After all, there must be some cock to change over the petrol infeed from one tank to the other ... During my search I get hold of a few bars of cigarettes and fresh potatoes. Second Lieutenant Bauer and Gregor continue their search in the driver's cabin. Then Caspar is back, a hose around his neck and both hands packed with big sandwiches ... Soon the engine is humming again. Caspar has told me that there are nice young people living in the second house ... We want to stay overnight ... so we persuade the lieutenant ... Everything is settled, so we park our vehicles outside the house as we want to be off early in the morning.

Rammes and his comrades made a good choice to stay indoors overnight. 'It was a grim winter night,' recalled Fritz Langanke, who was with the 2nd SS tank division *Das Reich* near Odeigne.

Deep winter snow crunches under one's feet. The frost is biting even through the winter clothes, and we feel as if we were in Russia.

Even so, his Panzer unit went on the attack.

The approach route leads through marshy shrub and woodland. We get stuck several times and it costs us lots of time. American artillery is spreading harassing fire over the area and target markers in the air to guide the enemy night bombers ... It is much brighter than our plan allows, but unfortunately it cannot be altered.

They suffered for it, coming under concerted attack from anti-tank guns.

We have been hit more than twenty times and, as we cannot see the anti-tank guns, we decide to back up. Past our own tanks – one of which is still ablaze – we slowly roll back until we reach the point on the road where we had set out. In the end, our radio operator cracks up completely. He jumps out of the tank and must be taken to a field hospital ... The shells have left deep marks on the bow plate. Amazingly it held out. Fortunately, the shells hit at angles which could not do too much damage ... I also learn who was killed in knocked-out tanks. Among the dead are some close friends of mine with whom I spent a long stretch in the service. We all are in low spirits. Over our head, floods of bombers are flying towards the Reich. With a heavy heart and helpless in my rage I can only stare after them, full of despair ... That was our last Christmas in that war. It was pitiless and it demanded the utmost of us. It suppressed any shimmer of hope because we came to realize more and more that the end and our defeat were already inevitable.

While Langanke's tank was being battered by shells, Rammes and his comrades were settling in with their hosts.

They have two little children who have now to go to bed. And everything is as in peacetime, an oasis of tidiness amidst the battlefield. Soon dinner and drinks are served. The housewife opens jars of preserved black-pudding – unique! ... We soon realize that our hosts are definitely pro-German ... An unforgettable evening indeed!

Lieutenant Bauer gets his own bed. We three want to sleep on the kitchen floor on mattresses, which is arranged too. In fact, we are looked after as if we were their own children. Haven't slept so well for a long time. In the morning we help clear the kitchen. Then we are given breakfast before we say good-bye. We make as little noise as possible in order not to wake up the neighbours.

Christmas Eve, when Germans have their Christmas dinner, found them near the front line.

Most members of the battery have joined in the celebration ... The room is packed, but the atmosphere is good. A small Christmas tree with candles lights the room. Erich Beckeer of Völklingen, a baker by profession, has baked a large crumb cake – quite a change. There are many comrades whom I have never met before. Everyone is talking.

I am thinking of my parents. How are they getting along? I have not heard from them for quite a long time, and was unable so far to write to them, so they do not know my post number. In a way this is all rather depressing. How can a short hour of peace match with the reality of a cruel war!

On both days of Christmas, Saint-Vith is destroyed by American bombers. Malmedy was heavily bombed on 23 and 24 December, although that town had never been in German possession. Three raids carried out in error turn the place into a heap of rubble.

Elsewhere in the Ardennes, German soldiers spent 'a rather sad Christmas Eve in their positions, only slightly animated by gifts from captured stocks of alcoholics'. Others, particularly staff officers, were better off, as General Heinrich von Luettwitz recalled:

Our Christmas was made happy by the number of K rations which were dropped over Bastogne, because a large amount of them fell into the area of my chateau. On Christmas day, I was able to issue two K rations to every member of my staff and to each of the Belgian children.

Lower down the chain of command, Emil Bauer also had a jolly time:

I have found a can of coffee and I make coffee for the company. The commander is happy. At night, the canteen bring some roast pork – Christmas dinner. Together with the four people of my crew I am sitting on the floor in a room of a farmhouse with a 'Hindenburg' light burning. We are singing Christmas carols and soldiers' songs. I tell about the concentration camp. We talk about home. The soldiers' hearts melt. The commander and the top sergeant come and wish us a merry Christmas and that it may be the last one of the war.

On Christmas Eve, C Company of the 12th SS Panzer Regiment assembled in a small woodcutter's shack in the wood near Loseheimergraben in Belgium. 'In view of the particular character of the evening, and also because of the cold, we have lit a fire which, taking into account the possibility of airborne observation, has to be very small, thus involving the development of much smoke,' said *Untersturmführer* (Junior Storm Leader) Engel.

We remember our dead comrades and send our thoughts to our dear folks back home. But my thoughts also wander along to the woods beyond Büllingen and Bütgenbach and to the ridges around Elsenborn. Perhaps the boys from New York or Kentucky, from California and the Colorado River are having their Christmas services right now. Perhaps the commander of an American tank is cursing the war and the blasted krauts who have spoiled his quiet Christmas celebration in one of the snowed-up Ardennes villages. Others, a No. 1 behind an anti-tank gun or an infantryman on his outpost, may curse the cold or hum a carol or a boogie. Above all, they should be thinking of home – just as we do.

Despite the hardships, the *Führerbegleitbrigade* (Leader's Escort Brigade) was feeling festive too. One of their number, named Meins, recalled:

Our infantry was actually smashed up – to say the least. Poor sods – I knew most of them from our time at Cottbus. Very few of them were older than eighteen. But on that day the fighter-bombers were obviously not keen on bothering us. Even the artillery spotter plane which, day by day, was hanging around overhead like a kite did not show up. This was a bright winter day and we were on the verge of dreaming of peace on earth. There was only one thing that detracted from this. From behind the corner of a building there protruded the long barrel of a 7.5 anti-tank gun controlling a road that led to Eschdorf.

Christmas brought with it a certain complacency.

We listened to the morning air and our first impression was that a group of Mickey Mouses was approaching ... The jabbering became louder and turned out to be American. On the road a steel helmet of a shape we disliked became visible. More and more followed. An assault party of ten with their Tommy guns hooked up approached along the middle of the road. We waited motionless and Second Lieutenant Ovenbeck whispered: 'Never saw anything more stupid during my whole time with the army.' ... Nearer and nearer the Yanks came, in Indian file, one after the other – it's a wonder they did not sing. But they were loud enough anyway, obviously thinking erroneously that we had gone home to celebrate Christmas. But no such instructions had been issued to us – much to our regret.

In the meantime, the Yanks had advanced to a point close to our positions and a sharp 'Hands up!' terminated their stroll. Nine of them laid down their arms and lifted their hands, as requested. Only the leader of the group had a different view. Bringing his Tommy gun into firing position, he pulled the trigger and shots rang out from both sides. The second lieutenant of the anti-tank platoon was shot in the thigh. And now the two opponents had to be taken to hospital as fellow sufferers, while the remaining nine, accompanied by comrades from the anti-tank unit, march on into captivity.

This was the calm before the storm. It seems that American observers had watched their men being taken prisoner and 'waited until their comrades were out of their firing range'.

The surprise fire came in all of a sudden and we thought this was the end of the world. During the previous days we had got some idea of the squandermania shown by the American artillery, but these season's greetings definitely left behind everything we had experienced so far ... The earth thrown up by the impacts formed something like a curtain – a horrid sight – steadily moving towards us ... Obviously the Americans had not yet found out that ammunition can be handled in a more economic matter.

The Americans quickly overran their positions and Meins was captured.

The Yank told us to move to the road. At the moment we were going to move, I heard someone call my name, and I made the American understand that I had to look after a comrade. In front of the foxholes I found a comrade from our platoon who asked me to take him along. He was in an awful condition. A splinter had torn open his abdomen, one of his arms was smashed and one of his thighs was slashed. I tried to help him up, but he yelled in pain.

The American pushed me aside. Two shots into the head of the tortured comrade put an end to his pain. I was stiff with horror, and I could have strangled that brute with my bare hands! But things got even worse. We had to pass the other foxholes, but this time I simply could not look at the places holding the bloody remains of what had been human life.

When we arrived at the road, everything, including cigarettes and handkerchiefs, was taken from our pockets and stamped in the mud. They were not only Americans, but Poles with them too. After everything had been taken from us, we were ordered to move in the direction of Eschdorf. I had to march ahead, my comrade behind me, and we were followed by a gang of utter killers in American uniforms.

We had not even moved 50 yards when I heard a rifle firing at me. The bullet went through my clothes to the left. A second shot, and my comrade yelled with pain and collapsed. I stopped and slowly turned around; the chap lay at my feet. What now happened before my own eyes was simply unbelievable to me – the work of merciless criminals. Right in front of my eyes, Tommy guns were emptied into my comrade, and still today I see the blood-red bullet marks on his snow-jacket. Turn around, move on! At that time I did not give a dime for my life and waited for the bullet with my number on it. I have never been a coward, as anybody who knows me can tell. But

December 1944: during the German Winter Offensive in the Ardennes called Herbsnebel – 'Autumn Fog' – or the Battle of the Bulge to the Allies, German soldiers take cover in a ditch beside a disabled American tank. Despite early advances, they quickly realized that the war was lost.

In Luxembourg Province, Belgian-captured German film shows German troops advancing. They are going towards Malmedy, where the SS massacred 100 American prisoners of war.

The Berlin Armoury, where an early attempt on Hitler's life was planned. Lieutenant Colonel Rudolf von Gersdorff later revealed how he plotted to kill the Führer and other high Nazi officials as early as 1942.

By the time the Red Army turned up in Berlin in May 1945, the population was starving. Although they were grateful for food, inhabitants later revealed the rapes and other attacks and privations they had suffered.

To the Allies, Erwin Rommel and his Afrika Korps seemed invincible in the North African desert. But his men enjoyed few comforts at the end of long supply lines. Enclosed in their Panzers, they suffered from the intense heat and were pummelled by overwhelming numbers of British anti-tank guns.

German motorcycle teams scouted the desert in North Africa. But by 1942 they faced Allied troops with superior equipment and air cover and they were hampered by a commander in chief who constantly told them to fight to the last man.

Heinz Guderian was the architect of blitzkrieg warfare. He spearheaded the attacks on Poland, France and the Soviet Union. But he later saw the failure of his Panzers and, towards the end of the war, constantly fell out with Hitler.

German soldiers enjoyed visiting Paris, where the shops still sold luxuries unobtainable in Germany. Although many French people were sympathetic to the Nazi cause, German visitors were not allowed out alone at night.

Captain Hans Langsdorff, commander of the Graf Spee, explained his decision to scuttle her off Montevideo in December 1939 in a letter to the German ambassador in Buenos Aires. Shortly afterwards he committed suicide.

German troops rode into Paris with Swastikas on their vehicles, then paraded down the Champs-Élysées on 14 June 1940. However, Rommel noted that the French had even left 'flowers along the road in some places' and, in 1940 that, 'the people are glad that the war is over for them'.

The ruins of Nuremberg after an Allied bombing raid towards the end of World War II. It was women who bore the brunt of the air raids. They told their stories in letters and debriefs to Allied interrogators who wanted to discover how effective the carpet bombing of civilians was.

German soldiers reported that many of the French were very friendly. Most were grateful that, following the swift German invasion, the war seemed to be over. For the occupation forces, Paris was mercifully free of bombing.

'We strolled along the wide avenue of the Champs-Élysées from the Arc de Triomphe to the Place de la Concorde... When our feet were tired we rested them in one of the many sidewalk cafés and watched passers-by while enjoying a café au lait with some delicious petits fours. Paris was still bustling as though the war did not exist.'
– Herbert Otto Winckelmann.

Erwin Rommel, hero of the invasions of France, North Africa and Normandy, wrote home to his wife Lu, sometimes several times a day, leaving a personal account of the war rarely found from generals. Held in great esteem by the Allies, Rommel was also a committed acolyte of Hitler.

The German Reich overran borders at will. It redrew the map of Europe, so that Poland did not exist. Here German troops tear up any evidence that there had ever been a border between Germany and Poland to the west, while the Soviet Union did the same to the east.

'Western Europeans will be hard put to imagine the masses of powdered snow that, during the most severe part of winter 1941–42, buried western Russia beneath a blanket averaging 1.2m in depth. Not every Russian winter is marked by that much snow, nor does the snow always remain so powdery...' – Gustav Hoehne.

with those killers behind me I soon learned what fear means.

Meins feared that his captors would throw him into a burning building or run him over with a tank. However, he escaped with his life and was loaded on to a truck and taken into captivity.

> On the way, we passed one of our assault guns, or rather, what was left of it. It looked like a skeleton. Then we saw the American gun position in an open field, uncovered, gun by gun, arranged in a staggered pattern. Unbelievable, these masses of material! And what did we have against all this? The courage of despair? ...
>
> At Bastogne we, about 15 men, were put into a chicken pen. Obviously the building itself accommodated some staff. There was a Christmas tree behind one of the windows, reminding us that it was Christmas Eve ... When the Americans dropped the remains of their meals into the dustbins, I was suddenly aware that we had not eaten anything all day long. I remembered the parcel sent by my mother which I had seen the day before in the company office.

But the company sergeant would not give it to him on the grounds that it was not yet Christmas.

LA GLEIZE

Karl Wortmann, commander of an anti-aircraft tank, had witnessed even more American ruthlessness during a counterattack against the small Belgian hill village of La Gleize the night before. His tank was hidden in a hollow, and he watched as the Americans brought up a large artillery piece.

> Shell after shell follow at short intervals, and after the fourth shot the spire of the church subsides and crashes to the ground. This sends shivers down our spines. The church, school and all the cellars are full up with our own as well as American wounded. The civilian population have also sought shelter in the cellars of their houses. Right in the centre of the village ... 164 American prisoners are also accommodated in two cellars.

According to the group's commander, Waffen SS Colonel Joachim Peiper, the church was 'conspicuously marked with the red cross because some rooms served as a clearing station'. Wortmann looked on helplessly.

Considering our short range and the good position we are in, it should not have been difficult for us to destroy the enemy gun. But without a single shell left, the best of positions and the closest of ranges are no good. Uninterruptedly, the Americans keep on firing deadly incendiary shells into the village. On this afternoon in December we witnessed La Gleize being completely razed to the ground ... When it gets dark I try once again to reach the command post but smoke and rubble make any advance impossible. I am confronted with a dreadful sight. Comrades to whom I try speaking are hardly able to utter a single word. On the way back to my tank I remember my crew jokingly shouting after me, when I set out, to bring back something really good to eat. Thank God they have not yet lost their gallows humour ...

The night that is closing in is going to be colder and some snow is falling. Freezing and starving we lie there in our foxholes. Of course, we must not fall asleep. Every now and then I doze off. Each night we have to spend out here seems longer and more unbearable than the one before. Then suddenly I do not know whether I am dreaming or really making out someone calling from a distance ... I run towards the caller, saying 'Merry Christmas, Merry Christmas.' I hear them repeating twice, 'What's going on? Christmas is tomorrow.' I give the reply, 'No, it's right now.'

This was the password. The man approaching was a messenger who brought the order: 'Immediate – blow up tanks and follow.'

I wake up my crew. It does not take them long to realize what is up. Erich Miechen, that loyal tank-driver of mine, jokes: 'All you need is sound sleep and pleasant dreams and you are bound to attract another alarm.' The blasting compositions are fixed within a few minutes. There is no time left to take anything with us except for the clothes which we have already been wearing for the past weeks, day and night. With pistols already fixed to our belts we quickly fill our pockets with some oval hand-grenades, grab our machine pistols and run across country towards La Gleize. We have hardly made 100m when we hear two detonations – our tanks have blown up.

One of Wortmann's crew found some footprints in the snow and they caught up with the column:

> Everyone is standing stock-still, so we would not hear them. Some
> have taken off their boots and shoes and are walking in their socks
> to avoid making any noise on the hard-frozen ground. Bringing up
> the rear is not an easy thing to do in this situation. Each of us
> thinks the enemy is hard on his heels ... Passing by the last house
> we see the outline of a tall and massive viaduct and close to it a
> small wooden footbridge which is still undamaged. It leads across
> the River Ambleve.

Wortmann learnt from whispers passed down the column that they had with them an American, Major Harold McCown. Their commander, Colonel Peiper, had made a deal with him. They had left behind the other Americans and the German wounded, along with medical officer *Obersturmführer* Dittman, who would be exchanged for McCown if the breakout was successful. McCown was then to advocate the return of the German wounded.

> The steep and narrow forest path demands of everyone the very
> last ounce of strength. You hear panting and groaning. Small
> wonder all of us are weakened by more than a week without food.
> Our knees dodder; each of us is near collapse and ready to drop ...
> After a fairly long time we have reached a height which allows us
> to pause for breath. We are standing in a clearing and the eyes of
> 800 men turn back to where La Gleize lies. What we can see is like
> a burning graveyard.

Peiper walked down the column to assess morale and offer encouragement.

> Overcome by exhaustion most of our men have sat down on the
> cold and frozen ground or have laid themselves down under the
> big trees ... Gradually it has become day – it is dawn of 24
> December, Christmas Eve. Everyone is exhausted to the limit and
> nobody knows the end. Our single goal is to escape captivity.
> Surrendering to the Americans would have meant this hour to be
> kept alive and decently fed ... Even in the heart of Russia I never
> experienced Christmas in such a way. The only thing we are
> offered as some sort of Christmas atmosphere is the charm of

wintry mountain scenery ... Meanwhile it has become late afternoon. Nearly all the comrades have laid themselves down under the big conifers. The wide branches, heavy with snow, are sagging almost down to the ground and make good cover. There is a long silence; everyone is too worn out to talk. Then, from everywhere, a low tune can be heard: 'Silent Night, Holy Night.' One of the 800 has subconsciously begun to hum the tune. Others have joined in. In no time the melody has sparked over from man to man. It is like a large choir singing in a cathedral. The emotion the song evokes touches our hearts. At this moment each of us knows that it really is Christmas. My thoughts wander back home to my relatives, and I feel sure it is the same with all the others.

We are still half dreaming when there is a loud booming from the sky ...The noise grows louder and louder and we have already realized that it is three formations of heavy American bombers on their way east. There are more than 40. They paint long condensation trails in the sky. Our hearts bleed watching them fly past in parade order towards Germany.

ARE THE AMERICANS CELEBRATING CHRISTMAS?

Wortmann was sent ahead with a scouting party – 'with my machine-pistol in firing position'. He reached a deserted asphalt road at the edge of the forest and wondered: 'Are the Americans celebrating Christmas at this moment?' Returning with the main column, he got his answer.

Having reached the edge of the forest again, we meet with an unexpected and unpleasant surprise: Americans come out of the forest, jump at us and try to pull us into the thicket. The comrades who are immediately behind us become aware of the attack and the Americans are frightened and let go of us. There is a wild shoot-out. The better part of the column has not noticed what is going on ahead. The sudden shooting gives them a fright. Some of the guys panic and part of the column run towards the slope and scatter. There are wounded and shouts for medics. Major McCown takes good advantage of the situation ... Our confusion, combined with the terrain and the darkness, give him a chance, and he makes a dash for freedom.

Somehow Wortmann and the bulk of the column managed to disengage.

> About half an hour later, after the exchange of fires, we make a
> jump across the road as one body. We land in a very deep ditch
> with a lot of tree-roots in it and a small streamlet at the bottom ...
> The comrade next to me has been shot through his right shoulder.
> Another had his thigh grazed by a bullet. He is groaning in pain.
> Hardly recovered from the shock, we hear a vehicle coming nearer.
> 'It never rains but it pours,' someone whispers to me. The vehicle
> comes near. We slip even deeper into the mud. There is dead
> silence. An American armoured scout car is passing by us at low
> speed ... Small wonder the Americans are searching for us after our
> escape from their encirclement. More than 800 men simply cannot
> vanish into thin air.

After waiting a few minutes to see if any more American vehicles were
coming, they continued their march.

> The comrades take turns linking arms with or carrying the
> wounded. The Americans' assault has noticeably stirred us up. No
> wonder we have almost forgotten hunger and cold. Now somehow
> we must cross the Salm River ... All the bridges are watched closely
> by the enemy. On either side stands an enemy tank. We continue
> on our way – again steeply uphill. The silence of the 'Holy Night' is
> every now and then broken by the barking of dogs. From the near
> distance we can hear American machine-gun fire. We hear the yells
> for help from comrades who have been shot ...
>   Ahead the path leads steeply downhill. The ground is frozen and
> slippery. We sit down on our behinds and slide from tree to tree
> downhill. Down at the bottom we talked in a whisper. In front of
> us the River Salm runs along the valley and we can clearly make
> out the rushing water of the mountain river.

On the river bank, they started chucking rocks in, in an attempt to create a
ford across the torrent, then the swimmers began to form a human chain.

> The water is cold as ice and with all our remaining strength we
> lean against the strong current. Though I stand 1.93m high the
> water reaches my chest. We balance on the big rocks that lie on the

river bed. The 30 to 35m width of the river seems endless. The chain gets broken frequently by the strong current. Some comrades are carried off and drowned.

On the opposite bank, the forest lay close to the river's edge and they took refuge among the trees.

By the time the last comrades cross the river, it has become day. All the time an American tank has been along the road beyond every 20 minutes. This time will be sufficient.

They crossed the road and went up a steep path on the other side.

When the American tank returns we have already reached a considerable height. The wags we are wave good-bye to 'the comrades below with the enemy Field Mail Number'. Some hours before we would rather have said a silent prayer. It is about 10am on Christmas Day 1944. We are in no-man's land and feel safe. The path leads over an open plain. A biting wind blows the snow in our faces and we are soon frozen in our wet rags.

Wortmann and his men then suffered a heavy bombardment of artillery fire and watched the landscape being 'ploughed and sown with the blood' of his comrades. They managed to contact advanced German units at Wenne. With six comrades – the survivors of two tank crews – he was billeted in a farmhouse that boasted 'a stove, a table and chairs, and even two beds'.

Baggage of our own we do not have. All things that were part of our personal outfit we had to leave behind at the hurried escape from La Gleize. Only things that we had on us were left. Not even a shirt for changing, no pants, no socks, no razor, not even a bar of soap were left in our possession – absolutely nothing!

But they knew where they could get supplies.

On a nice clear afternoon between Christmas and New Year's Eve we start out to search for the American trenches. Some days ago the Americans had dropped everything and rushed out of them ... The fresh fall of snow over the last few days has almost covered them and hidden them completely. Suddenly we find a large area,

covered deep communication trenches, storage silos, covered
with thick stems and made weatherproof.

We crawl into the storage silos. Our hearts leap with joy at
what we find there. It seems as if we have come to paradise all of
a sudden – unimaginable. If we did not know that the Americans
have fled from here we would assume that the troops have gone to
the leave centre or the front-line theatre for a few hours.

The wealth presented gives us difficulty in choosing. In the
ghostly darkness of the silos, we ransack the sea-bags that we
find in large quantity. We dash out the contents to fill the bags
again with things that we need and that our hearts desire. We
have enough to choose from: unused clothes, food, toilet articles,
chocolate, cigarettes in whole packets, best alcoholic drinks and
many more things.

We have put on some American furred uniform parts. On the
whole, we are totally Americanized, only the language is not right.
In our joy we act crazy, talk double-Dutch to each other, partly
American, Russian, French – and German, some of everything. The
things we are saying have no sense or meaning. We are suddenly so
jolly and cheerful like little children who have been surprised by a
belated Christmas present.

Carrying two bags each, Wortmann and his comrades walked back to Nieder-
Emmels in rapture, enjoying the clear winter afternoon and a glorious sunset.
Then they noticed 'a wall of clouds that seems to be getting larger and larger'.
It was smoke, with 'the bitter and acid smell of something burning'.

When we are to enter the house we meet inhabitants and we ask
them for the cause of those mysterious thick dark clouds. We learn
about the disaster that had come upon Saint-Vith a few days ago.
We find it hard to believe and understand what is covered by the
impenetrable wall of cloud that we had seen in front of us. Still
there is smoke rising from the burning and smouldering ruins and
the remains of the houses, under which a lot of people are buried.

On the first day of Christmas, in the afternoon, a sentence of
death was carried out upon the small German-speaking town of
Saint-Vith. Countless American bombs had turned a small town

completely into rubble and ashes on the day we talk of peace on earth – an event of which no sense can be discerned even in the cruellest war.

A GOOD CHUCKLE

Other German soldiers managed to secure their Christmas goodies from their own side, by subterfuge. Traugott Schmidt and his prisoner-escort detail were sent to a rest area in Luxembourg, about 15km (9 miles) behind the lines. They had no food and there were no civilians in the village, only soldiers. 'What was to be done now?' asked Schmidt.

> Sergeant Geiger, a man from Swabia, had an idea. We started digging holes in the hard-frozen ground – as if we were going to defend the village. A captain approached and enquired what we were doing. Geiger explained that we were the rearguard – the Americans had broken through. He unfolded a map and showed the captain a 'gap' of about 5km which they could escape through. His unit, he said, was going to defend the place to the last man ... Ten minutes later a combat-ready company on bicycles, young fellows, rushed out of the place with their commander in an attempt to escape through the 'gap'. Everywhere inside the buildings they had left behind meals they had prepared. So we had plenty of food and a good chuckle too. Furthermore they left four Type 42 machine-guns and several *Panzerfausts* that we could use.

Emil Bauer's crew were denied the spoils of war when they were billeted in a civilian's house.

> When I came back to the kitchen I can see that my crew have made themselves comfortable. They have unbelted and are now lying on beds which they have organized. My row about it makes them jump up. 'Gentlemen, we are at the front now. Now there is no more unbelting. Everyone stays with his belongings. Put your steel-helmets on.'
> Suddenly a shell hit somewhere near the house. We stumble into the basement. It is deep and crowded with civilians. They look at us with anger. 'C'est la guerre,' I say apologizing. But I cannot stand to stay down there very long. I go back upstairs. There I find

soldiers plundering. I chase them off and tell the civilians to take their belongings down into the basement. They do as I say and thank me kindly.

Even when the soldiers tried to treat civilians kindly, accidents still happened, as engineer Alfons Strüter recalled:

The house was full of soldiers. The inhabitants, however, had a room in an upper storey. A soldier sat with his gun in front of him. While falling asleep, his finger touched the trigger and the gun fired. The bullet went through the ceiling and through the leg of a woman upstairs who had lain down in bed.

After the shelling Bauer was ordered on a mission to attack three tanks that had been menacing the German guns.

To me this is a death-command, and I start thinking of how I could escape from this danger. I will certainly 'not find' the tanks and my crew will never betray me if I do not carry out the order ... the whole show will end in total failure for sure. It can only take a few days before the enemy has enough reinforcements to beat us to hell. Our dash has come to an end. We have spent ourselves completely. For replacements we have a lot of airmen who can hardly handle a machine-gun. The first sergeants with the German Cross and a war-fighter badge cannot even be appointed section leaders, because the old soldiers will not follow them.

We have only a few tanks and we have no more assault guns. So we depend on our infantry weapons only since Guderian took the heavy trench mortars and heavy machine-guns away. In Russia, the Panzer Grenadier Company still had 32 light machine guns, four heavy machine guns and four heavy trench mortars. That was a force that represented something. But now it means nothing any more ... It is getting towards the end.

Soon after Christmas the Americans struck back in the region of Bastogne. According to *Wehrmacht* Major Loos:

The advance made by the *Führerbelgeitbrigade* [Leader's Escort Brigade] was met by a concentrated American tank assault which penetrated and again encountered the left flank of the blocking unit with full force. Needless to say they pushed though the time switch-lines, causing heavy casualties. Three companies were rolled up and only a few soldiers were able to escape to safety. From my battalion command post I could watch the assault rolling on, and helplessly I saw the American tearing a wide gap into our front line. With breakneck speed on a motorbike and sidecar, my adjutant and I advanced behind the gap in the front line in an attempt to close it. This was the first time I encountered panic among German soldiers. In a stampede, with no one to lead them, and in utter confusion they ran about and made the situation a complete mess. Only here and there a few determined people clustered around leaders who had not yet lost their nerves. I saw officers and NCOs literally steam-rolling their soldiers under cover. This all happened in a matter of a few minutes.

Some were captured, including Leonhardt Maniura, who volunteered for the *Luftwaffe* in July 1944 but at the age of 18 found himself in an infantry unit in the Ardennes.

We had been encircled by US troops. There was no escape after the ammunition ran out. At about 0900 hours we showed the 'white flag' and the Americans stop firing. In the barn we put down our weapons and belts. I tried to hide my pistol somewhere with the intention of picking it up in the near future. Then we left the barn ... The GIs were close to the door already. We never thought they were so close to us. One of them tore the helmet off my head. At once my fellow soldiers took off their helmets ... We unhinged the doors and carried our wounded on them. I still remember that, when we were marching to the rear, the last American to the rear was hit by a German shell and disappeared completely. We were all white from terror. Continuing the march we noticed a V-1 which tumbled down the rear side of 'Haussart' hill. We were only 200m from the place of impact. Fortunately the rocket did not explode. All of us, including the GIs, were paralysed with fear ... German guns and mortars continuously exploded near the column. Could it be that we were the target of our own troops because of our 'capitulation'? We were very angry. Then we thought that could not be the reason, for they would not have been able to identify us from such a distance. But there was a rumour that German soldiers who had been taken prisoner without being wounded would be called to account at some later date ...

We arrived at a road crossing. There we were shown shot US soldiers, half-covered by snow. We had to pass to and fro in front of the killed, still with our hands raised, and a one-star general addressed us about this being done by the SS. There were war reporters present too, and we were filmed and photographed marching up and down the scene with our hands raised ... I felt something like being shot could happen to us. In my confusion I took the star on the general's helmet to be that of a Bolshevist commissar. However, nothing happened to us. We wondered about being so many reporters and staff officers so close behind the front line. I had never seen a thing like this on the German side. Then we had to continue the march towards Malmedy, our hands about our heads all the time. They had taken our gloves and so we had to suffer from cold ... I found myself a prisoner of war instead of having a furlough at home. However, a vacation at home at that time would not have turned out a pleasant one in so far as my home town Beuthen in Upper Silesia had been occupied by Soviet forces on 22 January 1945.

LETTERS HOME

On 17 December 1944, nearly 100 American prisoners of war were machine-gunned by the SS at the village of Malmedy in Belgium. Lieutenant Arno Krause wrote to his fiancée in Leipzig from Eupen, just 24km (15 miles) north of Malmedy:

> Dear Ruth,
> I have just been informed that, together with six other comrades, we have been condemned to death by the American military court. We will be shot in a few hours. My love (excuse this expression), I want to thank you for the wonderful hours we spent together. I am deeply in love with you and had only the one desire, to make you my wife. Unfortunately, that will not happen. Keep the golden ring as a

souvenir and keep me in good remembrance. I am not a criminal. Ruth, you know it, I had to obey my oath and therefore became the victim of a development for which I, personally am not guilty.

The only souvenir I have of you is a little picture, the first I received. This picture will accompany me on my last walk. I am only sorry for my parents and worry about my mother. If you can, please go and visit them. At least write to her ...

I am not afraid of death and will take it upstandingly and with courage, because I want you to think of me with pride. I believe in life after death, I don't know in what form. I want to wish you only the best and a very happy life. I hope you will find somebody who loves you as much as I do and that you will be very happy with him because you are young and your life is still ahead of you. Don't forget the monument that we built together at Cobeln. Those were my happiest hours, to be together with you.

Finally, let me thank you again for the happiness which you gave me in those hours we spent together, I am terribly in love with you.

Forever your Arno.

My last thoughts will be for my parents and you. I was captured 23 December at Malmedy. Now I am close to Eupen.

In their last letters, other SS men also protested that they were not criminals. Indeed, Hitler had issued an order that no prisoners were to be taken during *Herbsnebel*, though most German soldiers ignored it. Gunther Saltz told his father in Den Haag, Holland, that he 'will die as a German soldier without crying and without complaint, because I have been an honest man who only wanted the best for his fellow man'. Nevertheless, his father should tell his mother that he 'was killed in action'. However, Corporal Robert Pollack told both his girlfriend and his parents:

Just on the day of your birthday I was captured under such circumstances that the enemy must shoot my comrades and me.

'Pappa' Gorlich was also more realistic. He told his wife that, while he was 'not a criminal',

I broke the laws of the Geneva convention while carrying out orders and we will be shot according to the law ... With this letter I say goodbye to you and to our dear parents. The shots that will extinguish the flame of my life will destroy a happy marriage. But we don't want to be angry with fate and neither leave room for hate. The men who are performing my execution are fighting without hate for a better, happier Europe. Therefore, I ask you, may you also be without hate, try to understand. I have understood. My verdict may be very hard, but it is correct according to the laws of Geneva.

This was an SS man talking!

Despite Hitler's order, other American PoWs were treated well, according to Matthias Druyen of the 26th Volksgrenadier Division.

About twenty prisoners were brought to us. Some of them spoke German very well. Upon request, they told us that Goebbels had demanded that all American prisoners were shot. Of course, we ignored that and confirmed that they would be well treated. In the officers' absence we could talk with them. They said that our wireless set was primitive. When they were taken away, they secretly waved to us. A nice gesture. The subject of our talk was clear of course: as we hadn't wanted the war, they hadn't wanted it either.

HAPPY NEW YEAR

On 31 December, the 12th SS Panzer Regiment received some good news from the maintenance company:

Eleven tanks, a PIV and PV [Panther] mix, are combat-ready. During the night the Armada is seen moving towards Bourcy. A short distance off Houffalize, the time is 0000 hours. The turn of 1944–45, with moonlight and sparkling stars – just like a fairy tale. We stop. The crews are standing on the turrets of their tanks. Holding up bottles of booze, crew to crew signal 'A HAPPY NEW YEAR!'

By that time Rammes and his artillery observers had moved up to Pont.

New Year's Day is a day off. I tend the fire in our dugout and listen to the enemy gunfire ... For the time being, the US artillery seems to be in a rather friendly mood, discharging only some nuisance fire. But then follows a fantastic 'New Year's welcome shooting'. I can even adjust my old wristwatch – the comrades opposite are punctual – and saucy, too. One of the shells must have come down and hit the trees just above my dugout. Mud is dropping from the ceiling and, trying to get outside a little later, I find the entrance barricaded with big branches. The Yanks can afford this kind of shooting. We have to keep our limited stocks of ammunition for absolute cases of emergency.

At the beginning of January, the weather turned dangerously cold. But for Rammes and his artillerymen this brought advantages:

Heavy snowfall and, during the first days of January, a sharp frost brings bright wintry weather. We are well camouflaged in our small wood, so well that now not even the fighter-bomber and artillery-spotting planes find us ... But on one occasion the position was under fire. Some men were wounded. Fritz Sondermann, our first-aid man, sees us regularly and provides us with vitamin tablets, and on one occasion he even gave me two tiny apples. I had told him that my front teeth were getting loose.

Hugo Farné, our field cook, has, at all times, provided us with excellent all-in meals. We had plenty of meat, but we missed out on vitaminized food ... Here and there American shells are passing overhead. How nice life can be, so comfortable.

Klaus Ritter and his comrades got so comfy they even named their dugout:

The name of our dugout? The first letters of the names of the girls deepest in our hearts of each of us formed the somewhat exotic name of 'Luliekas' – we called it 'Luliekas Tabernacle'. Days passed in monotony. Sleeping, eating, being on guard, sleeping again ...

But the war was never far away, especially for Rammes and his men:

From some distance I hear the well-known howling of a V-1. Our positions are right on their lanes. The thundering noise becomes louder and louder, and suddenly there is silence, and we hear the impact a few seconds later. That was it: the V-1 – the 'Eifel Terror'!

Many of the V-1s were falling short, soon after being launched in the Eifel region of Germany.

I have seen them on bright days, very fast and fascinating. But there was many a village in the Eifel, in the Ardennes and in Belgium too, having their own experience with these monsters. These radio-controlled missiles were supposed to hit Antwerp, but controlling errors and, in many cases, sabotage must be held responsible for quite a number coming down too early.

In fact, V-1s were not radio-controlled but navigated using a crude gyroscope. Gunther Holz also saw them and was unimpressed:

Occasionally V-1 rocket bombs, fired from near-by positions, could be seen on their way overhead, noisy and with a trail of smoke by day and a fire trail by night. We felt a bit uneasy about this new invention, particularly because, from time to time, a rocket lost its direction, came back and exploded. Not so the V-2 whose launch we could watch at some distance. They rose up high into the sky and went on their way high up.

For Rammes and his comrades, the *Vergeltungswaffen*, or 'Vengeance Weapons', became a topic of conversation in the foxholes, but soon they were lucky enough to be moved up to the Siegfried Line.

Accommodated in pillboxes of acceptable standard and hardly molested by the enemy we stayed there until 12 January 1945. On that day I was told by Second Lieutenant Abelmann that the Russians had started an offensive on the Eastern Front ... I also met Second Lieutenant Bauer on my way to the farmhouse down the slope; we had not seen one another for several days. I have visited that farm a few times. Its inhabitants had not been evacuated and I often went there for a good cup of hot coffee ...

But the Americans were coming.

The commander wants me to see him in his foxhole. I report to him, standing in water up to my ankles. A thaw has set in – all our troubles were coming at the same time. My instructions are to move to the farm building and from there up the road to have the drivers get their vehicles ready to move. On leaving the foxhole shells come down only a few metres distant ... Wham! A shell hits the gable overhead. Fragments whirl around our ears, but we are lucky again.

INCIDENT AT KAISERBARACKE

Rammes and his men withdrew to Kaiserbaracke, whose historic inn had been home to Austrian troops from 1701 to 1713 during the War of the Spanish Succession:

> Beside the building and arranged in a horseshoe shape is a store shed and a wooden-roofed structure to accommodate horses. It must be wonderful in peacetime. But now, a shell comes down near the railway line, 200 metres from us: a smoke shell. A large mushroom of smoke slowly rises. More impacts nearby. Those mushrooms look harmless, but we know the Americans are registering – we must get moving ... The enemy uses phosphorous shells as well, and before long the whole area, buildings and the wood, are on fire.

As the American advance developed, Rammes and his comrades found shelter in a farmhouse.

> The cattle are accommodated in the basement. In a separate room to the rear, we find the inhabitants. The room is heated by means of a small iron stove; light is provided by a candle to a moderate extent. It is here we set up our radio equipment. Second Lieutenant Bauer wants to make contact with the infantry units and tells us to wait here. Shortly after he left us, we are covered by an artillery salvo that shakes the whole building. Gregor is hurled into the separate room, and shell splinters are whizzing through the basement. The hits must have been right near the entrance. Now we are sitting in the dark and Gregor relights the candle. And there we are! The radio equipment is buried under the ruins of a wall, so we have the pleasant job of digging it out. Gregor's overcoat is dotted with blood stains and little fragments of flesh. We walked towards the entrance. What a terrible sight: the cows and horses are stuck to the wall. It looks as if they have been fastened there with nails ... But what about our second lieutenant? Things seem to become mysterious, and Gregor and myself unlock

our pistols to be on the safe side. But at last, here he is. 'Get the hell out of here,' he says. 'The infantry is withdrawing. Their captain has been killed. What happened here? It seems a wonder that you guys are still alive.'

Second Lieutenant Bauer was determined to get back to Kaiserbaracke to assess the situation.

We find a motorized unit in the forest. Our second lieutenant is a bit nervous about our supply of petrol, but we are given a few litres in a jerry can. We move, soon reaching a bridge across a railway line. There, someone moves towards us, a captain: 'Where are you going?'

'To the Kaiserbaracke,' Bauer replies. 'What's the situation there?'

'Turn back at once,' said the captain, 'and take me with you. The Allies have occupied everything up to the railway line and, as far as I know, our defence system has disintegrated.'

So there is nothing to do but go back home! We turn our car on the spot, one man per mudguard ... Then suddenly there is a German tank in front of us – in the middle of the road. Its commander looks out of the turret and asks us how to get to Saint-Vith. We tell him straight ahead.

Suddenly there is the noise of shell explosion to the right and left of the road – those damned red-yellow patches! Stoyer drives on. We decide to move on as fast as possible. Bauer is sitting beside the driver. Gregor and I on the back seats. The road crossing is not too far away, but there again shells are raining down on either side: 'Get on, Stoyer!' There must be no stopping, otherwise we might have to put up with a direct hit. I am looking straight ahead, expecting a shell to hit that road and imagining us driving into the crater ...

At last we reach the crossroads. Now a right turn, then another 300 yards to get home. Stoyer takes the turn, and we are passing the buildings fringing the road on either side. Suddenly I feel a hard blow in the nape of my neck. Powder smoke fills my nose. I cannot hear anything. Instinctively I grab for the door and drop out of the car. I crawl through the snow until I reach a wall.

> I manage to get behind it, and then I faint ... but only for a short while. Then I shout: 'Medic, medic!' Are they still firing? Where is my first-aid pack? I feel the pronged splinter in my nape, and again I faint ... Then I hear Second Lieutenant Bauer shouting something. I am feeling terribly sick, but I notice that they lay me down on the back seats of the car. Does the car still go? I am fainting again ...

In fact, everyone in the car except Gregor had been hit. Bauer had a splinter in his right leg just below the knee, while Stoyer had been hit in the right arm near the joint. Rammes' blow to the neck caused concussion, resulting in blackouts. He was sent back to Germany, survived the war and returned with his wife to the scene of his injury in 1972.

Erich Heller also survived, thanks to the enemy. He was leading an anti-tank party, which took out an entrenched American tank with a *Panzerfaust* and pinned down its crew with machine-gun fire.

> Just when we were leaving the building one by one, some explosives hit our house. Obviously we had been discovered. Part of the ceiling came down and hit me, being the last of the group, and I fainted. But my unconsciousness must have lasted just a few seconds. Coming to, I found myself pressed down by a ceiling beam, so that I could not get free on my own. The building was now in flames and it was a problem removing the burning fragments that had dropped on my body. I called for my people, but there was no answer. Obviously they had managed to escape, if they had not been killed. Sooner or later the building would collapse and this would have been my end as well. Then three Americans suddenly turning the corner must have been as startled as I was. Later I heard that they were a reconnaissance party sent to find out to what extent we had evacuated the village. They helped me to get out, some of them suffering slight burns themselves, and carried me towards the rear area.

This action of compassion came as a surprise to Heller, who was an enthusiastic follower of Hitler. At the age of 10 he had joined the Hitler Youth and, at 17, the Waffen-SS. After fighting in Normandy it had become clear to him and his fellow officers that the war was lost due to the superiority of Allied materiel, but it had not crossed their minds not to do their duty. Klaus Ritter also witnessed the kindness of the enemy. He had been sent, under covering fire, to check whether there were any Americans in a farm and its outhouses.

I pushed my assault gun up against the open door of the shack and cried: 'Hands up!' No reaction. I looked into the shack and recognized American luggage and equipment. At the side, there was a bench with a box full of roasted cutlets on it. It was noon and I was hungry. With a cutlet in hand, I went round the corner with the intention of giving a sign to come to my comrades. At that moment, an American came out of the door, just two metres away. I shot from the hip – but I remember seeing the Yank pulled his gun as well ... It was dark when I recovered consciousness. My hands and feet were cold. I slowly remembered what had happened and felt around. Next to me, lay someone else. I touched his face. It was as cold as ice. The American lay next to me and was dead. I thought: 'You must go to the barn. There are straw and covers.' I dragged myself along ... I found something smooth – coverlets. I covered myself and sank again into unconsciousness. When my coverlets were torn away, I awoke. Three Americans stood in front of me, their guns aimed at me. It was day. When the Yanks recognized that I was heavily wounded, they dropped their guns and emptied my pockets. I noticed that my wallet and paybook were already missing. Later I came to the conclusion that my comrades had decided I was dead and took my things. The Americans had a chat, then they carried me to the kitchen, covered me with a coverlet, took a chair and put chocolates and biscuits on it. Then they disappeared. I tried to eat a piece of chocolate, but found I could not bite it. I touched my face, felt encrusted blood and pappy meat. Only now did I really understand that I had got a serious shot to my head. I got a fever and had fantastic visions. It became dark, then it was dawn again. In my visions, I thought I had been lying there for eight days. If no one found me I would die of hunger and thirst. I started to pray and cried for my mother. But suddenly I awoke. Outside there was the bark of a machine-gun and I heard German combat cries. I got up and rushed outside.

The dead American was still there. I fell down, crawled along and cried: 'Medic! Medic!' ... They took me to an evacuation hospital at Bitburg. We lay there in emergency beds in the corridor, Germans and Americans side by side ... One day there was a bomb attack. Window glass broke. The plaster burst from the walls and ceiling. We were seized with panic. A leg amputee slid downstairs and cried ... Later I learned that my company had been annihilated.

On 5 January 1944, Lieutenant Zeplier, who been with the 89th Grenadier Regiment (Tank Destroyers) outside Aachen, was also injured.

I heard another round of American shells approaching. Instinctively I threw myself down, and so did my messenger. There was the noise of explosions in the tree tops overhead, and I felt a hard blow against my upper left arm. Fumbling about, I felt a hole in the sleeve of my camouflage jacket above the elbow. We got up to have a closer look and I felt blood running down my arm under the jacket and along my hand. I told the sergeant of C Company who had made me familiar with the situation that I had been wounded and that he would have to lead the company temporarily. I and my wounded messenger would walk to the battalion's dressing station ... We were immediately taken care of by the battalion's doctor, and I went to Major Ripcke to advise him of the situation at C Company and of our injuries.

When the morning came, I asked the battalion's doctor to arrange for the transportable wounded to be transferred back to the regimental aid post as soon as possible ... Those able to walk or limp went on foot, while the rest were carried on stretchers. As I had lost plenty of blood, the doctor had given instructions to move me on a stretcher ... Then we approached the place where the artillery fire had been heavier the night before ... I ordered the transport to stop and explained to all the soldiers that it was now essential to cross this section as fast as possible after the next burst of fire ... I ran, holding the side of the stretcher for support ... I immediately went to the regiment's command post to inform Colonel Lemcke of my injury. He gave instructions to get his car ready to have me and my wounded messenger taken to the central dressing station ... I asked the corporal of the regimental staff to get my American kitbag from the company HQ where I kept my 'treasures' – such as my American quilt, coffee rations, US food rations, cigarettes and the like, all things from US supplies.

On the way to the central dressing station of 12th Volksgrenadier Division, we had again to pass the street crossing under American fire. This little game had become routine work to the driver. When we entered the central dressing station of the 12th VGD, we heard that it was being transferred to another place and that wounded could only be taken in the following day ... We moved on to the rear and, some time later, passed the central dressing station of the Waffen-SS. My upper arm was bandaged and the medical orderly had said that medical treatment was a matter of extreme necessity ... A doctor took care of us immediately. After he had taken off the bandage and examined the wound, he said that it looked rather bad and that an X-ray examination and an operation were needed. I was so thoroughly down that I took only a weak interest in this. Before I was undressed I asked that all my belongings be put in my American kitbag after wounded soldiers had told me things were stolen at dressing stations and military hospitals ... Some time later I was given an injection which carried me into the land of dreams. When I woke up, I found myself back on a stretcher in the corridor. Jackboots passed in front of my eyes. I dozed off a few times, before I realized where I was. My first reaction was to grab for my left arm to find out what had been done for my injury. Horrified I found that there was a dressing, but no arm. It came like a blow that I realized that due to the shell splinter I had lost my left arm. In a way, I refused to believe that this was so, because up to then I had still been able to move the fingers of my left hand ... I feel certain that, had I only been treated at the division's dressing station, my arm would not have been amputated.

After I had mentally overcome the fact of this arm amputation, my life spirit woke up again. I remembered my wristwatch which I had on my left arm, so I asked a medical orderly to have a look at the severed limbs to find my watch. He returned some time later to tell me that the watch was in the left breast pocket of my tunic, the doctor had told him. I asked him to open the kitbag beside me and to find the watch. He found the watch, closed the kitbag and with a feeling of relief I fell into sleep again ...

I and some other wounded were placed on a lorry which was cushioned with straw bags, and we were taken to the rear area. The journey seemed endless, the roads became worse and worse, and the bumping of the lorry became more violent and more frequent. The wounded beside me groaned more often, and later started yelling with pain. I called for the medical orderly who was sitting beside the driver, but he showed no reaction. Only after I threatened to fire my pistol into the driver's cabin, the lorry stopped. The orderly told me that the driver was lost. I told him to stop at the next dressing station and to have the heavily wounded taken care of.

After a few kilometres we arrived at an SS dressing station close to the front line ... Artillery fire could be heard and we used an empty food tin to urinate. Beside me was an American second lieutenant lying on a stretcher. He received the same treatment as us and was looked after by the nurse. My dressing was renewed ... Although the nurse did her job with extreme care – almost with tenderness – I was beginning to see stars. When the doctor noticed this, he gave me a glass of brandy which helped. As soon as a fresh supply of petrol arrived, we were taken to a military hospital on the Rhine. From there a hospital train carried me to a general hospital at Oberfrohna near Dresden.

SABOTAGE

Overwhelmed by the Allies' munitions, the Germans also had equipment problems of their own making. On 10 January 1945, *Obergrenadier* (Private First Class) Alfred Freund was with the 12th Volksgrenadier Division, when his company received two new infantry guns, straight from the factory.

'Thank God,' exclaimed the gunners. 'This is an end to the constant bumming around.' ... During the inspection, the soldiers find that the spirit bubbles are missing from both guns. 'These idiots,' yells *Stabsgefreiter* Ide, 'that is sabotage.' Without the spirit bubbles the guns cannot be regulated vertically or horizontally. It is a great pity for all the money spent on the guns. The missing spirit bubbles that cost only a few marks make the guns useless. This makes front-line soldiers lose their courage to see things through. Another reason for cursing the whole war. But what is the use of that for ordinary soldiers. They have to continue holding out their neck for the fatherland.

Gunther Holz bemoaned the lack of ammunition.

While our batteries had to cadge for a couple of shells, the enemy supply units drove to their vast supply depots and woe betide the depot commander if he failed to make the required quantities available at once. Where our gunners fired 100 shells, 2,000 shells were fired back from the other side and what we called co-ordinated fire was normal harassing fire in the eyes of our opponents ... From morning till evening American fighter-bombers dominate the sky, firing at anything that moved, no matter whether a vehicle or a single man. Only full cover and not the slightest movement ensured survival. In addition bomb carpets are dropped by small units of 20 to 30 four-engined aircraft on recognized troop concentrations.

By mid-January, the Germans were faced with a full-scale counteroffensive, as *Obergrenadier* Freund recalled:

During the night before 13 January 1945, the Americans shot as much as they can. The shells fell within the German lines. There was a hell of a noise. The soldiers were lying underneath the tanks or have found shelter elsewhere. The Americans want to fire a lane into the German front in order to get east faster. Someone screams: 'Enemy tanks.' Everyone shoots as much as they can ... The night is as light as day because of the exploding shells. Everybody is nervous. A German tank drives over a poor soldier. Some soldiers lie in the trench and lower their heads. Though all the rattling and cracking, Paul suddenly hears a scream. He turns around and sees one of our own tanks standing in front of him. It had driven right over the legs of some poor fellow. Half an hour later the uproar is over. It gets quiet again. Carefully, everybody who is still alive crawls out of the foxholes. The wounded are bandaged and carried off. The other soldiers inspect the whole area. Behind a hedge eight killed Americans are lying ... The dead are searched for something to eat. The soldiers are always hungry and the supply does not work at all. Regular meals have been a thing of the past for some time. Whoever finds anything eats it. The Americans had enough on them. Dry bread, tins of all kinds and even toilet paper are in the combatants' packages.

Everywhere around him Freund witnessed the randomness of death.

A direct hit struck the command and reconnaissance vehicle. Three men were killed at once. Private First Class Kessler was alive, but shaken. He stood there white as a sheet. Death can pass you by so fast.

Four men were sent to bury them.

The command and reconnaissance car was at the crossroads. The three dead soldiers were lying next to it. Han said, after he saw his killed comrades: 'They have had an easy death. Nobody had to suffer.' Shell splinters had cut off the head of Master Sergeant Preiss ... He was a good guy, but that does not count in a war. Corporal Wachter's head was smashed and there were lots of holes in his coat. The man had a foreboding about his fate ... On the night before, he had said: 'I will not see my family again, nor my Saxon home.' 'Why should you not survive the war? We all still have this hope at least,' Paul interposed. 'No, I can feel it.' 'It will turn out all right,' said another soldier. 'No, not for me,' was his point of view. He survived this discussion by a few hours.
   There was no time to mourn. The very next moment shell fire may start and then there would be even more dead and wounded ... In a small village graveyard the three soldiers dig a grave. They put the dead into it and have a short memorial. More ceremonies are not foreseen for front-line soldiers. The soldiers shovel earth back into the grave and the war continues ... One less day at the front. But how much is one day?

Obergrenadier Freund and his comrades now knew that they had no hope. Only horror awaited them.

The beaten troops move though a wood on the hillside. Suddenly, enemy tanks appear on the opposite slope. The soldiers move further into the woods where they will be fairly safe. At least the infantrymen think so, but it is a mistake. As soon as all the German soldiers are in the woods the shell fire starts. Screaming and crying for help is all over ... Second Lieutenant Fetten and Paul walk along a farm path. Then there is a terrible crack close by and everything is over. How long the two of them lay on the ground they could not tell. Paul hears the second lieutenant calling: 'Lange, Lange, do help me. It has knocked off my leg.' Paul struggled to his feet. He was hurt too ... The boy takes out of his coat pocket the extra leather belt he carried for the purpose and ties it tightly around the right leg just below the knee ... Perhaps the belt will save the life of the young second lieutenant...

'I cannot carry you any further,' said Paul. 'I am quite hurt myself.'

'No, just see to it you get away. I shall try to crawl to the village. Here I would freeze to death,' said the lieutenant.

Paul tried to get up and follow the other soldiers, but the front part of the shoe on his right foot is not under his control. The foot must be shot to pieces. There is no time to have a look at it and there is no medic available. Everyone is fleeing. After a few hundred metres, Paul throws away his gas mask, steel helmet and field bag. Everything is just too heavy. Since getting wounded he has not seen his rifle and has not even thought of it. A few soldiers take him and he puts his arms around their shoulders. Then they march on towards the next village. An SS unit is posted there ... As soon as all the wounds are dressed, Paul hobbled to a straw bed to wait ... The medics left him, saying that he will be picked up in the evening. If it is the Germans that come, everything is okay. Should the Americans come and find him, it cannot be helped either.

6
GÖTTERDÄMMERUNG: THE DEVASTATION OF THE HOMELAND

'In the last moment, by a miracle as it were, the Germans managed to stop the onslaught of their enemies at the very borders of their Reich ...' said Colonel Guethner Reichhelm. But it was a mere hiatus. The *Wehrmacht*'s stiffened resistance merely postponed the inevitable. As early as 23 December 1944, it was clear that the Ardennes offensive had failed. The Germans attacked again in the east on 12 January 1945. But in tanks alone they were outnumbered seven to one and on 20 January Soviet soldiers set foot on German soil. The V-1 and V-2 failed to be the war-winning weapons that had been promised. Now Colonel Reichhelm and his comrades had to face up to reality:

It could be foreseen that, as soon as spring 1945, Germany was to break down, if something extraordinary did not happen. But the German soldier went on fighting. He did no more cherish any ideal, but, in most cases, he seemed to have still a certain remainder of faith in Hitler. The point, however, that mattered most was this: the German soldier fought because he had nothing more to lose and because he was looking for his last chance. Already, by autumn 1944, there was scarcely a German family that had not lost one of their dearest relatives or that had not been bombed out and lost everything they had.

In Romania, Herbert Winckelmann could see only one possible salvation:

To me, only a political event – a change of government – could save us from catastrophe. But this had been an undiscussible subject due to the Nazis among us who still had the power to terrorize us even up to the last day. As a soldier, I fulfilled my duties just as my comrades did, convinced that one had to defend and save our country from Communism ...

Our army commander, General Schoerner, aware that we would not cross the American lines overnight, abandoned his command post and fled into Austria to avoid becoming a prisoner of the Russians. This was the man, or better Hitler's lackey, who had just days before ordered soldiers to be hanged for having tried to reach the American lines on their own. It was disgusting to watch how the Third Reich died. None of its leaders came to the foxholes to defend it to the last man as they had promised. They all abandoned their posts and fled, afraid of being held responsible, or cowardly died by suicide.

Winckelmann observed the collapse of morale:

> Some, unable to come to terms with the disastrous situation, broke and committed suicide. One example was Lieutenant Stolz, a squadron commander in his early 20s. He was the youngest lieutenant in our regiment and had grown up through the ranks of the Hitler Youth. He had been a good soldier as well as a comrade with a promising future. But he had been blinded by Hitlerism and now what he had believed in had fallen apart. In his desperation, he shot himself.

Eduard Bodenmüller was the commander of a Panzer Mk V Panther tank in Poland when the final German counterattack stalled in March 1945. His crew were repairing a track when Russian ordinance started raining down:

> Our driver, radioman and loader dived underneath the tank. I and my gunner got inside the turret. The crescendo of exploding shells rose to such an intensity that it was obvious that we were now deluged with shells [rockets] from a 'Stalin Organ'. Suddenly another terrific crash and our 49-ton tank shook violently. Either we had received a direct hit or a bomb had landed a few metres from us ... The enemy fire died down and it struck me as odd that we had not yet heard from our comrades under our tank. Then, suddenly a weak voice from outside cried out: 'Help! Help! We're wounded.' I grabbed the first-aid kit and box and with one leap I was behind the tank next to my wounded loader.
> I took my knife and cut open the back of his tattered and blood-soaked jacket. Shocked, I saw a wound 150mm long, very deep. With every breath he took, blood came gushing out. My gunner came

with all the wash-cloths he could find in the tank. I stuffed several of these into the wound to help slow down the loss of blood. We looked at him and knew that he had only minutes to live.

Paule stayed with him and calmed him, saying he had only been hit by a small shell fragment. I began to look for the others. Two pairs of feet stuck out from under the tank. I grabbed one pair, but to my horror I saw that it was only the lower half of my radioman's body. I had the urge to throw up, but overcame it. I crawled under the wagon, grabbed onto a meaty, bloody mass and pulled the completely mutilated body out. There was nothing I could do.

His driver was also dead, 'split in half from his head to his pelvis'.

When Bodenmüller radioed his commander, he was told to remove the radio equipment and destroy his tank. He and Paule, the gunner, decided to disobey orders and held off the Russians until a tank recovery vehicle turned up. On the way back to base, he spotted Lieutenant Grosse and his crew bailing out of a mechanized assault gun that was now on fire.

I ran over quickly to see if I could extinguish the burning vehicle ... Once I had gotten within a few metres of the assault gun, I noticed that only the camouflage netting, draped over the top of the vehicle, was on fire. Other than that there was nothing wrong with the vehicle. I took the fire extinguisher and put out the still smouldering netting. Then I climbed into the driver's seat, started the motor and drove at top speed following the route the recovery vehicle had taken ... My commander charged *Leutnant* Grosse with cowardice before the enemy and ordered him court-martialled. The rest of the crew was sent to a penal company. Then he turned to me and said that I too ought to be court-martialled for failing to follow his orders.

Instead Bodenmüller was awarded the Iron Cross First Class, promoted, and granted five days' leave in the Divisional R&R area.

I did not accept the latter offer and instead I requested that the maintenance section repair my tank and that I be given new crew members so that I could return as soon as possible back to action.

A day and a half later Bodenmüller was back in the thick of it. Meanwhile, the Fatherland was bracing itself for the final onslaught. This was witnessed by World War I veteran Wilhelm von Grolmann. In May 1943, he had been appointed 'president' of police in Leipzig, the proud home of the *Panzerfaust* anti-tank weapon, and director of air defence. At the time, the former Nazi stormtrooper claimed that there was very little 'crime and venereal disease' in the city, although some of the 80,000 'foreign workers' in the city had formed themselves into 'burglary gangs'.

> The smallest and, at the same time, the most important defence unit in the civil air defence was the house block, which might be compared to an infantry regiment. The children, old men, and women in the house block must be systematically trained to take prompt and courageous action, to treat injured persons and, especially, to handle incendiary bombs. Sufficient supplies of water and sand must be available in every house. Air-raid shelters with emergency exits, openings in the wall between neighbouring houses and attics cleared of potential fire hazards are obvious measures. Children who can run up and down stairs quickly and who know every corner of the house from their games have prevented many catastrophes by throwing burning incendiary bombs out in the street and by putting out smouldering fires. If several smaller fires are allowed to develop, there is danger of an area conflagration, and several such large-scale blazes may cause a fire storm. Once this happens, the situation is hopeless. Those who manage to escape death by burning or by being crushed under the masses of debris, simply asphyxiate.

His job was further hampered by the fact that Leipzig had only one waterworks. So if a water main was hit, the water system would fail citywide. Allied bombing raids also knocked out the electricity and telephone systems across the city. Grolmann's fire crews were sent to Hamburg in July and August 1943, when the RAF began the tactic of intense area bombing, which created fire storms.

> Anyone who has had a leading part to play in air defence operations, or who has been employed in any way after an air raid, will undoubtedly wish that no nation will ever again have to

experience the consequences of war. After the return of my reinforcements from Hamburg in August 1943, the commander of the fire-fighting police gave me a report of his experience; I interrupted him with the exclamation: 'For God's sake, what kind of a war is this.' Still under the impression of what he had gone through, he spoke with bitterness, 'General, this is not war – this is sheer madness.'

Although Grolmann was a committed Nazi, he dated the beginning of the end to 18 October 1944, with the call-up of the *Volkssturm*, or national militia, which included all men between the ages of 16 and 60.

For an officer who loves his country it is a difficult decision to admit that a war so successfully begun can no longer be carried to a favourable conclusion. The call-up of the *Volkssturm* brought me to full awareness of this fact. What madness it was to mobilize untrained cripples, old men and callow youngsters as a last bulwark against fresh armies provided with the most modern equipment, and to entrust the command of these forces to Party agencies operating under *Wehrmacht* regulations.

Grolmann saw that the increasingly intense and systematic Allied air raids would inevitably weaken German resistance.

This period saw the issuance of countless new ordinances and directives by the top-level agencies, most of which were patent nonsense, since they were out of touch with reality. Contact between the government and the country and people had been lost ... I remember receiving confidential instructions from Himmler in December 1944 to the effect that the units and organizations controlled by him should not become too deeply involved in matters concerning the *Volkssturm* because it had become an instrument of power of Bormann, that is for the top man of the Party, and the SS had no interest in it. Nevertheless, he implied that the *Volkssturm* would become the factor determining German victory.

In February 1945, Grolmann took charge of fire-fighting in nearby Dresden, as the merciless bombing of that city had put all municipal agencies out of action. Worse was to come.

When Russian armies reached German territory, a mass flight from east to west began for which neither urban nor rural authorities were prepared; the suffering endured by these refugees is indescribable. Party agencies in charge of caring for the population after air raids were flooded with requests for aid and bogged down completely. I assumed this task for the city of Leipzig on my own initiative and ... I entrusted my fiancée, who was working with the Red Cross, with the practical execution of our plans. In unwearying day and night work she succeeded in giving thousands of miserable people a feeling of being cared for again ...

However, their material conditions improved little.

US air bases moving nearer and nearer made rail and highway transportation very difficult. Food supplies from eastern areas stopped entirely and food could be obtained from other regions only in very limited quantities. Almost all males who were halfway fit even were drafted and sent to the eastern front with whatever weapons were available. The police had to release all men born after 1896 to the armed forces ... The power of resistance gradually collapsed.

THE WEHRWOLF

Other Nazi fanatics could not face the inevitable and there were calls for the establishment of 'Wehrwolf', a guerrilla organization that would continue the struggle against the occupying forces by terrorist action.

The beginning of the final phase of the collapse started with the call for the formation of the *Wehrwolf*. I heard it on the radio during the *Wehrmacht* communiqué on Good Friday, 30 March 1945. I regarded this as wholly wrong, since it was bound to give the enemy an opportunity to employ every means he deemed fit, even against the civilian population, in an attempt to protect his own troops. In clear recognition of the consequences for a city of such illegal combat I immediately ordered the criminal police to observe whether activation of partisan units had been planned or was already underway.

As it was, the resources of the civil authorities were stretched to their limits, as Grolmann described:

> Prisoners in the endangered eastern regions were moved to the west and almost always without prior notice in a state of complete exhaustion and near starvation after their stay in various prisons or concentration camps. Food was no longer sufficient, especially as the large ration depot in Gotha had been disbanded on 31 March ... On the second day of the Easter celebrations, the public prosecutor of Leipzig telephoned and asked for my help, stating that between 40 and 60 persons legally sentenced to death had arrived at his office. He had orders to execute them without delay. Since he did not have the facilities for this purpose, he asked me to place an execution detail at his disposal. I refused and asked the *Wehrmacht* commander to back me up, which he did.

In Nazi Germany such insubordination had an inevitable consequence:

> On 1 April I was suddenly relieved of my post as chief of the criminal police. It was taken over by the Gestapo, whose leader thereupon received the glorious title of 'Commander of the Security Police'. This agency, however, did not last long. Around 10 April, the Gestapo left the city ingloriously under the cover of night, after it had shot a goodly number of the prisoners entrusted to its keeping ... Chaos prevailed everywhere. In addition, there were orders from top headquarters that no city or town was to fall into enemy hands without having been defended, and that any subordinate was obliged to shoot his superior on the spot if the latter manifested a defeatist attitude in word or deed. Moreover, responsible officers were branded as cowards and their families made subject to arrest if they surrendered a town or position no matter how hopeless defence might be. Thus responsible leaders, already weighed down by other worries, became prey to feelings of mistrust and insecurity. One could not be frank with one's own subordinates, and much less with other agencies, nor was it possible to make the preparations called for by an objective appraisal of the true situation. This was my position from 6 April on, when US troops had advanced as far as Gotha, about 150 kilometres from Leipzig.

There was a meeting to discuss the defence of the city, where the representatives of the *Wehrmacht* present insisted that this was a purely military matter to be decided by the high command. However Nazi officials were not so sanguine.

> Paul Rudin, director general of NASG, attacked the generals present in a most unbecoming manner, demanding that the city be defended to the last, in accordance with the Führer Order and that the *Wehrmacht* commander, who was a sick man and inexperienced in service with field units, be replaced by another officer. The commanding general refused to discuss the matter further. Soon afterwards, however, General Reinhardt and Major General Kiegesar were removed from their posts and Leipzig was assigned to a new 'Combat Commander', Colonel von Poncet, an officer no one knew and who was unfamiliar with the city. A few days later Director General Rudin and his wife committed suicide with *Panzerfausts* – the first instance of a rapidly developing suicide psychosis.

Grolmann went to visit the commander of the 14th Flak Division, the only *Wehrmacht* unit in the area. His appraisal was grave. Although the Russians were being held on the Elbe, large, well-equipped, motorized American units were advancing from the west. The only heavy weapons his unit had were anti-aircraft guns. Besides, he was under the command of the *Luftwaffe*, and could offer no assistance in the defence of Leipzig.

> He did not know what action was contemplated for the defence of the city and stated that he personally regarded any military measures as madness. The new combat commander, who was not familiar with the local situation, apparently intended to fight, but he had not a single cannon at his disposal. Hence the city and its population were seriously endangered, and for no defensible reason.

Nevertheless, the district leader of the Nazi Party – the NSDAP – in his capacity as commander of the *Volkssturm*, drew up a plan for the last-ditch defence of the city:

> The *Kreisleiter* [county leader] pointed out that the enemy could only come from the west, so the city would only have to be

defended to that side. He went on to explain that the Hitler Youth, under its own commanders, would defend the city from a first defensive position 3km from the city limits. Its mission was to stave off the approaching enemy with *Panzerfausts*. At the very edge of the city was a second defensive position. Upon the approach of the enemy they were to fight a delaying action and slowly retreat toward the main line of defence, represented by the eastern bank of the Elster River. The bridges would be destroyed; preparations to blow them up had already been completed. The police were to open fire on individual enemy targets within their own precincts.

This estimate of the situation by the *Kreisleiter* of the NSDAP in his capacity of local *Volkssturm* commander and the defence measure outlined by him were the most incredible thing I had ever heard. They could only have originated in the mind of a man who had never been a soldier himself, and thus had no concept of military responsibility, or who was ready to die ... In fact, the *Kreisleiter* and his assistants, around ten in number, did commit suicide when US troops entered Leipzig.

In view of the general confusion and the unbelievable lack of responsibility, I felt obliged, in spite of the personal danger involved, to speak up against his appraisal of the situation and the use of tactics typical of those used by children playing cowboys and Indians. At first I protested about the commitment of untrained adolescents, calling it tantamount to the murder of children, and asked the *Kreisleiter* what he thought he was doing. He replied that German youth would be annihilated in its entirety anyhow, hence death under these circumstances would be the best thing. Further protest against this view was pointless, I could only call it madness. The other people present agreed with me ... I explained that it did not take much military knowledge to see that a strong enemy would not come into so large a city as Leipzig from one side only. He would be much more likely to encircle the city, and then converge on it when ready. I pointed out that it was quite within the realm of possibility that any attempt to defend the city might be met by an air raid, the consequences of which were inconceivable. In any case, our own forces were much too weak for effective resistance, since they were completely without heavy arms. Therefore efforts to defend Leipzig were incapable of achieving practical end, but the city itself and hundreds of thousands of men and women would be uselessly exposed to grave danger. I also protested vigorously against the police being employed without my knowledge by any other agency.

SAVE THE BRIDGES

Despite his protests, Grolmann said preparations for the defence of the city began, with Colonel von Poncet threatening to summarily court-martial anyone who did not obey his orders.

> I urgently requested Colonel von Poncet to save the bridges, otherwise the city would be divided in two and the western part could not survive since it would have no water, gas or electrical power. The combat commander promised to consider my request ...
> On Sunday 15 April, the encirclement of Leipzig began ... In Leipzig itself everything remained quiet. The *Volkssturm* contented itself with establishing inadequate anti-tank obstacles at the bridges by placing trolley cars filled with stones across their exits ... The government agencies ceased work and the larger shops were closed ...
> On 17 April the enemy converged on Leipzig and in part penetrated as far as the city limits. Sporadic shooting could be heard. It was accepted as inevitable that US troops would occupy the city the next day. No further defensive measures were taken. The city hall in the centre of town was occupied by about 500 men of the *Volkssturm*, headed by the *Kreisleiter* of the NSDAP and his staff. These men showed no evidence of enthusiasm for combat. The closer the Americans came, the more members of the *Volkssturm* departed by the numerous side entrances of the town hall. There were a great many *Panzerfausts* available, but hardly anyone had been trained in the use of this very effective weapon. Discarded, they lay about the streets and constituted a danger in themselves.
> On the afternoon of this day the combat commander came to my office in great agitation, accompanied by a strong military escort.

He had learned, he said, that the mayor, Dr Freyberg, was planning to sabotage the measures ordered by him. He asked me officially to tell him what I knew. I could only make the statement that I was not aware of any such plans. After the departure of Colonel von Poncet I immediately requested the mayor to come in. I had him escorted into my office by a security detail. After I had orientated him on what had happened I advised him to place himself under my protection; he refused, however, to do so. In unforgettable words, he described his present life to me and, in conclusion, seized the opportunity, as an old friend, to bid me farewell. After his only son had been killed in action, he said, life under the conditions to come no longer held any purpose for him. He, his wife and their 17-year-old daughter had resolved to take poison when the occupation of Leipzig began. Hence he was placing the fate of the city in my hands with the request that I exert myself to the best of my ability for the protection of the population.

To be able to effect anything at all, I had to try to find out the intentions of the combat commander. In the evening, therefore, I went to see him with a strong army escort, but could only gather that some operation or other still had to be carried out. It is grotesque to think that the two leading men of the city knew nothing of each other's plans, and that there was such mistrust between them that they met only after taking extensive protective measures.

That evening I spent with my fiancée and the mayor and his family in the town hall. His deputy, the municipal treasurer, was also there with his wife and 17-year-old daughter. I tried to get Freyberg to reconsider his decision to commit suicide, appealing both to his conscience and his duty to stand by his country as long as it was in danger. When I was called away towards midnight, I believed that I had talked Freyberg into staying alive. A few hours later the criminal police reported to me that both the mayor and his deputy, with their families, were lying dead in their offices.

Upon my arrival at the police presidency I found about 30 US soldiers who had been brought to me as prisoners of war, the combat commander having refused to accept custody of them. I

spoke to the soldiers and told them that I regarded them as free
men and as my guests. I advised them to remain with me until the
city was occupied, which they did.

When the Americans entered the suburbs, Grolmann contacted their
commander and offered to surrender the city, though Colonel von Poncet
and some 200 men continued their defence from a vault under the 'Battle of
the Nations' monument, commemorating the end of the Napoleonic wars.
Grolmann took over the administration of the city until a military government
was installed. Then he became a prisoner of war in France where, in July, he
heard that Leipzig was being handed to the Soviets as it fell in their zone –
'This is the most shocking news I have ever received in my life.'

INTO BERLIN

Hans Jürgen Westphal was just four years old when he saw the Russians
coming into Berlin in 1945. He had been born in the German capital on 11
May 1940 and his first memory, towards the end of 1943, was of his house
being bombed.

My father's driver and my mother picked me up and put me in this
little three-wheel transporter and took me to the railway station. I
remember coming out. It was a phosphor bomb, so there was
water all over the place and the flames skimming across the top of
the water. As we went down the street I saw the balcony coming
down. The next thing I remember was my uncle's farm in
Pomerania [now largely in Poland]. I remember very, very clearly
November 1944 when the Russians were approaching. I was
playing outside and my grandmother came and told me that my
father was coming to pick us up. You could hear the big guns
already in the distance, rumbling away. There was a level crossing
and I remember German lorries coming back with wounded
people and tanks going up to the front. And then my father
arrived and said we had to go that night. The Russians were
already near. We caught the last train. As we left a couple of shells
hit the railway station. The train went off. It was the last train that
ever left there. I remember being at the railway station at Frankfurt
an der Oder. There were only forces there. We had to wait a couple
of hours. Next to us was a train full of men in bandages.

But there was no escape from the horrors of the war as the Red Army pushed relentlessly on to Berlin.

> As the Russians approached Berlin, my father – he had lost an arm during the war – his driver and my mother were going up the street in his car and my mother covered my eyes all the time. This was because there were soldiers hanging from the lampposts – deserters obviously. Everybody tried to run away. Hitler had his death squads in the streets up to the very end.
>
> We lived near a railway station. It didn't handle passengers so much. There was a commuter station but next to it was a station for goods. This was the place the Jews were deported from, I found out later. Beside it was a big bunker. We went to this bunker when the Russians began to shell. Before the Russians came, there was an SS unit defending the railway station. There was fierce fighting. The bunker was divided in two. They put us all together in one room. It was very tight. The next room, they put the wounded soldiers. I still have that memory of the smell of burnt flesh – a lot of them had been heavily burned. They were brought there screaming. There was only one door between which was opened and closed all the time. And then one afternoon, the SS officers ran off leaving the heavily wounded behind. They were shouting: 'The Russians are coming! The Russians are coming!' Then a little later Russian soldiers came, had a look around and left.

There were still the terrible consequences of the Soviet occupation to face.

> My cousin, she was then 14, went missing. The Russians took her, raped her for four or five days, then let her go again. She was a broken woman for the whole of her life.

Hans was well aware that the war had destroyed the lives of other innocents.

> Where we lived there was this family. The father was Jewish and the mother was Christian. They had a daughter. One night the Gestapo came and arrested him. They were taking him down the stairs when the girl grabbed him and would not let go. One of these Gestapo men kicked the girl down the stairs. The girl broke her back and was crippled for life.

During the war the Westphal family had been bombed out twice and, by the end of it, they had found shelter in a house that belonged to the director general of the amusement theatre.

> Behind the director's house there was a beautiful house, undamaged, and the Russians took it as their headquarters. The Russians got drunk and came to rape my mother and the other women around. But my grandmother took a poker and hit the first Russian, breaking his arm. In the meantime, someone ran across to the headquarters. The commanding officer came and threw him out. The next day, the soldier came with his broken arm in plaster to apologize.

There were dangers for the men too and Hans's father was lucky to escape with his life.

> In the house we had before there was a family of an SS officer living above us. He used to have champagne and brandy, stuff nobody had. In 1943, he got drunk and started screaming and jumped out of the window. His wife gave my father his trousers and my father would wear them. The Russians looked at his trousers and wanted to put him against the wall.
>
> The Russians put people in charge of the local districts. Most were Communists. The others were well-known people who had opposed Hitler. We had this Jewish family who lived in the basement of the Catholic priest for two and a half years. Everybody knew about it, but nobody talked. My parents had a corner shop and when the housekeeper came shopping they gave her a little bit more to feed them. The man was a famous journalist before the war. My mother ran to get him. It was only two blocks. He came and stood in front of my father and said: 'If you want to kill this man, you have to kill me first.' So my father survived.
>
> A couple of days later, the Russians made a search of the shop. They found beer bottles full of petroleum on one shelf. They opened it, smelt it and they drank it. The next day, an officer and men came again and my father thought: 'Jesus Christ, now I am in trouble.' And they said: 'Have you got more of that stuff?'

Then the British came. There was a big Sikh guy sitting in a British scout car. We were children and we wanted a look. And we were allowed to sit in the car and he drove us around the block. A British major moved in. He spoke very good German. In summer time, he invited us children into his garden. We had cookies and he had a book of Grimms' fairy tales and read them to us.

There were other advantages of having the British around:

In 1946, the owner of my parent's corner shop came back. There was a shop over the road run by two women who were big shots in the Nazi party. The British took the shop off them and gave it to my parents.

HITLER'S TESTIMONY

By this time, Hitler was dead. He had committed suicide on 30 April 1945, at the age of 56. He left a 'Private Testimony' disposing of his property:

What I possess belongs, in so far as it has any value at all, to the Party. Should this no longer exist, to the State and, should the State be destroyed, there is no need for any further instructions on my part. The paintings in the collections which I had bought in the course of the years were never collected for private purposes, but solely for the gradual establishment of an art gallery in my home town of Linz. It is my heartfelt wish that this bequest should be duly executed. As executor I appoint my most faithful Party comrade, Martin Bormann.

Bormann died trying to escape through the sewers. Hitler also explained why he and his new wife, Eva Braun, chose to take what others would see as the coward's way out:

I myself and my wife choose death in order to escape the disgrace of flight or capitulation. It is our wish that our bodies be burnt immediately in the place where I performed the greater part of my daily work during the course of my 12 years' service to my people.

Hitler also left a 'Political Testament' in which he insisted that the war had had not been his fault – it was the fault of the British and, of course, the Jews.

And though he was dead, others should go on fighting.

> Many very brave men and women have resolved to link their lives with mine to the last. I have asked, and finally ordered, them not to do this but to take part in the continuing struggle of the nation. I ask the commanders of the Armies, the Navy and the Air Force to strengthen by all possible means the spirit of resistance of our soldiers in the spirit of National Socialism, with special emphasis on the fact that I myself, as founder and creator of this movement, have also preferred death to a cowardly flight or, worse still, capitulation ...
>
> I hope that my spirit will remain amongst them and always go with them. Let them be hard, but never unjust; above all let them never allow fear to counsel their actions, and esteem the honour of the nation above everything else in the world. Finally, let them be conscious of the fact that our task of building a National Socialist state constitutes the work of the coming centuries and that this places every single person under an obligation always to serve the common interest and to subordinate his own advantage to it ...
>
> Above all I charge the leaders of the nation and those under them to scrupulous observance of the racial laws and to merciless opposition to the universal poisoner of all peoples, international Jewry.

Both documents were signed by Hitler at 0400 hours on 29 April 1945 and were witnessed by Bormann and Goebbels.

In his Private Testimony, Hitler made provision for his family, including his younger sister Paula, who was interviewed after the war in an attempt to find out what had made her brother tick. As a child, she said, he liked playing cops and robbers with his mates and always took the leading role. This led to conflict with their father.

> Adolf always came home late. Every evening he got a sound thrashing because he did not come home on time.

Adolf, she admitted, had no feeling for his family.

> But it is inherited, I believe. My father never bothered about his relatives either. Only our mother's relatives were real relatives for

us. The Schmidts and the Koppensteins are our relatives, especially a cousin Schmidt who married a Koppenstein.

Their father died in 1903, then in 1907 they lost their mother.

Our mother's death made a deep impression on Adolf and me. After mother died, Adolf didn't come home any more.

Adolf disappeared.

Since my father had been a [customs] official, we shared an orphans' pension of 50 kronen. The money should have been divided between Adolf and me, but I could do nothing with 25 kronen. Then my guardian heard that Adolf was living in Vienna. He was located there and renounced his share in my favour ... I wrote a letter to him about it in 1910 or 1911, but he didn't answer it. He always hated to write. From 1908 to 1921 I never heard anything from him. I didn't know if he was still alive. It wasn't until 1921 that he came to Vienna to find out about me. I did not recognize him when he stood at the door ... I told him that it would have been much easier for me if I had had a brother [to help]. As an answer, he said: 'I had nothing myself and couldn't help you. And since I couldn't help you, I didn't get in touch with you.' My brother had actually just fallen from heaven. I was so accustomed to having no one. The first thing that made a big impression on me was that he took me shopping ... He looked me up again about a year later. We went to visit our parents' grave at Linz. He wanted to do it ... I myself went to Munich in 1923 and looked him up there. That was before the putsch of 8 November 1923.

She did not see him again for another six years.

Then I saw my brother Adolf at the Nuremberg Party Day in the summer of 1929. It was the first time he had invited me to a Party Day. I got my card to the events just like everyone else. He received me at the hotel, the Deutscher Hof. I saw him again in 1930 and once every year until 1941. We met once in Munich, once in Berlin, once in Vienna. I saw him in Vienna after 1938.

While Hitler made his life in Germany, Paula remained in Austria, working for an insurance firm in Vienna. However, his growing fame impinged on her. Her firm was Jewish-owned and Hitler's rabid anti-Semitic views eventually got her fired. Hitler compensated her with a pension of 50 schillings a month. When he took over Austria in the *Anschluss* of March 1938, this was increased to 500 marks a month. At his request she changed her named to 'Wolf' and retreated to a life of seclusion.

> He was already very serious in 1940. On one occasion I said to him, 'Whenever I see a chapel on a mountain, I go in and pray for you.' Then he was touched and said, 'You know, I am absolutely convinced that God is holding a protecting hand over me.' ... The last time I saw him was in March 1941 in Vienna. I must say in all honesty that I personally would have preferred him to have become an architect, which was what he originally wanted to do. The world would have been spared much sorrow.

During the war, Paula Wolf became a hospital clerk, but had to give up work through ill health. Then in the last weeks of the war came a surprise:

> One morning in the middle of April I saw a car in front of the door. A chauffeur came into the house and told me that he had been ordered to take me to the Obersalzberg. ... Half way to Berchtesgaden, the driver told me that he hadn't expected that I would be coming along ... I took my meals in my own room and didn't mix with the others. I knew no one there.

When asked about Hitler's death, she began to cry.

> His fate grieves me as his sister, more than I could ever tell you ... After all, he was my only brother.

A devout Catholic, Paula found consolation in her faith. And her brother?

> I don't think that my brother ever became an apostate. I don't know though.

The Allied officers who interviewed her concluded:

> It was not necessary to arrest Paula Hitler since she had had no part in her brother's triumphs, only in his defeat ... she was

connected to him only by the accident of birth, and not by temperament, ability or genius, either good or evil.

Some did not escape so lightly. At the end of the war Hebert Winckelmann had heard that Hitler was dead but, due to radio silence, nothing more was known. Even though they did not even have a map Winckelmann and five comrades decided to try to reach Austria and surrender to the Americans. But they did not make it.

> We were spotted by two Russians on motorcycles waving a large white flag. Without hesitation they rode up to us shouting, 'Comrades, *wojna kaputt – domoj, domoj*' ('Comrades, war is over – go home, go home'). They were young, friendly officers who were fluent in German. As is the custom among soldiers, when they meet, we exchanged cigarettes and sat down to chat as we had not done for a long time. Each of us was relieved that the horror of war was over and showed one another pictures of home. During our conversation we learned that Germany had surrendered five days ago ... They advised us to go to one of the gathering places to be sent home. I can still hear, 'Why do you want to get killed when the war has already ended days ago?' With these words, they jumped on their motorcycles and were off. The decision as to where we should go had been left to us. They hadn't even asked for our weapons.

Winckelmann and his comrades wandered around for a few days then, on the afternoon of 11 May 1945, they gave themselves up.

> At the gathering placed where hundreds of German soldiers who were scarcely guarded, we were once more greeted with the slogan, '*Wojna kaputt – domoj, domoj*.' The guards checked, correctly, only for weapons, nothing else was taken from us.

At first they were treated well, protected by Cossacks from harassment and plunder by other Russian soldiers. But soon they found themselves in cattle trucks on their way to labour camps in the Caucasus. There their personal possessions were taken and they were forced to work on starvation rations, though Winckelmann admitted that the Germans were treated no worse than the Russian inmates of the gulags. Many died.

While Winckelmann was away in the Caucasus, Germany was under occupation. When a 21-year-old Nazi supporter from the Focke-Wulf factory in Bremen was interviewed on 21 June 1945 and asked how she found life under the occupation, she had few complaints:

> I have had no trouble with the occupation government or the troops. My bicycle is gone; it was stolen by the Poles. I tried to enlist the help of some English soldiers and have the impression that they would have helped me except for their inability to understand me. By the time I made it clear to them what I wanted them to do, the Poles had gone ... I and all of us only believe what we were told in the newspapers, etc. I believed that all men up to the age of 65 would be taken to work elsewhere. I believed that we who remained behind would have to do hard manual labour in a slave status, breaking up stones, removing rubble and so on. I feared we would be moved about arbitrarily from one city to another. I feared we would not get enough food to support life. I feared rape and general violence and disorder. Also I feared severe limitations on civilian movements. I expected to be allowed out of doors only two or three hours a day. On the other hand, I expected freedom from air raids; that was a partial consolation.

PAY DOUBLY

The 25-year-old housewife from Duisburg who was interviewed on 27 July 1945 said:

> I had great anxiety when I saw the first Americans who came here. Although neither I nor any of my family was ever a Nazi, I fled out of the city into a village. I did not think that we who were not Nazis would be punished, but I was afraid nevertheless ... I thought that because the Jews had been treated so badly we would have to pay doubly. It has however gone very well. It is much better than before. There are no more fears of bombing attacks. Yesterday my sister and I went out in the fields picking berries. Some planes flew over and we remarked that it was so nice not to have to fear that they would attack us ...

Although bombing had destroyed her home, she had reasons to be joyful.

> My husband was a prisoner of war, but he had been released and now has his old job back at the telegraph office in Duisburg. At present we have no place to live and no furniture ...

However she was sanguine.

> It would not have been better if Germany had won the war. We would have had to work hard to built the cities again and there would have been no freedom.

Meanwhile a number of top German generals captured during the war in North Africa and France were being held at Trent Park in Hertfordshire, the former country home of the Sassoon family. There, British intelligence officers were able secretly to record their conversations to judge their reactions to the progress of the war. Here are General Wilhelm Ritter von Thoma and Major-General Gerhard Bassenge discussing the Holocaust.

> THOMA: I read in the papers today about the poisonings, the gassing business. I know very well it's true because I heard it from the men who actually did it.

> BASSENGE: I certainly didn't know about it, but I accept it a hundred per cent.

> THOMA: The SS and Gestapo, they were the boys who rounded up the Jews and got the stuff together, and since there were no specialists among them, they got chemists from the gas department of the Arms Office (*Waffenamt*) to work with them. One of them told me with horror that in Russia at that time it was absolutely appalling for him – I tell you, I wouldn't have done it ... As I have both the German and British intelligence reports, I can roughly work out what the truth is.

> BASSENGE: Quite right. Everyone tells lies in war, before marriage and after hunting! And here we have an equal opportunity to hear both sides.

> THOMA: We're better placed than the generals in command at the front.

> BASSENGE: We've never been so well informed as we are here.

Despite Germany's ignominious defeat and the revelation of the Holocaust, some German soldiers felt no shame. Fritz Langanke, who fought with the 2nd SS tank division '*Das Reich*' in the Battle of the Bulge, recalled:

> At Christmas 1945, having lost the war, almost all of us were detained in some PoW camp. We were deprived of our rights, confined, the scapegoats of the nation, some of us threatened with starvation, robbed of our belongings and many without homes. There is one thing, however, that nobody had been able to take away from us to this day: the constant awareness that we did our duty unquestioningly and to the best of our abilities, in good and bad times and situations. Christmas 1944 in the Ardennes may serve as an example. Neither do we allow our pride in our units to be marred; units with which we fought for Germany to the last day of the war and in voluntary obedience. Every defamation, all attempts to avoid or withhold the historical truth can only serve to cement our pride.

After three years in a Soviet labour camp, Herbert Winckelmann clandestinely refrained from eating his rations and starved himself to the point that he was found unfit to work. He was then returned to Germany – but not to his hometown, Berlin. He had given the Soviet authorities an address in West Germany, in Vilsbiburg, Bavaria, where his wife, Elinor, and mother had moved. For months after his return, they sensibly denied him rich foods, which might easily have killed him after such a long period of privation. But away from Berlin, Winckelmann found it impossible to start a new business, and local people were hostile to refugees from the east. He was forced to live on the charity of family and friends.

> The worst hosts were former members of the Nazi Party, all of Elinor's relatives had been party members. Many a time during Hitler's 'glorious' times, they had told me: 'You owe all this to our Leader.' But now they had forgotten that we also owed to the Leader the lost war, the destruction and the refugees.

Sickened by this attitude, Herbert Winckelmann and his family emigrated to the United States.

PART 2: VOICES OF THE JAPANESE

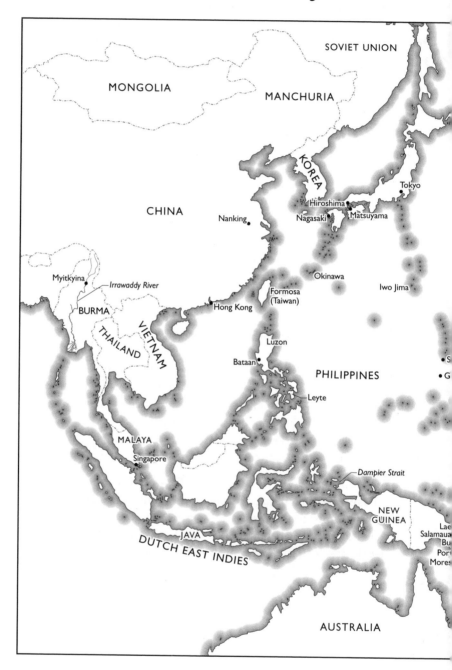

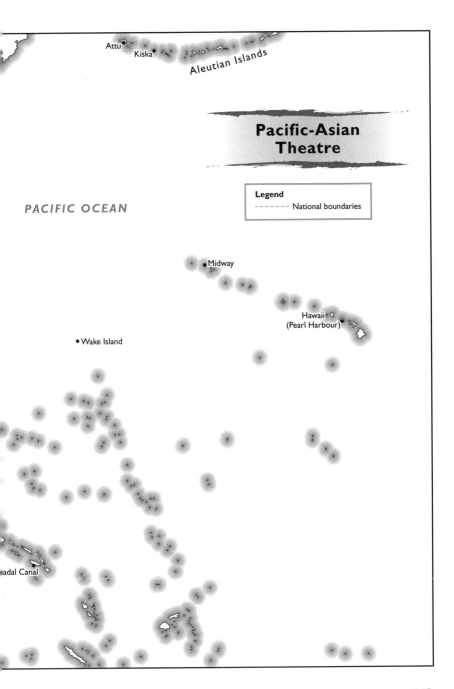

Attu
Kiska
Aleutian Islands

Pacific-Asian Theatre

Legend
------- National boundaries

PACIFIC OCEAN

Midway

Hawaii
(Pearl Harbour)

Wake Island

adal Canal

7
TORA! TORA! TORA!: ATTACK IN THE PACIFIC

For Japan there was no World War II. The Japanese fought *Dai Toa Senso* – the Greater East Asia War. Their primary enemy was not the US or Great Britain but China, and the war began, not in 1939, but in 1937 – though it could be argued that it began in 1931 with the invasion of Manchuria, or in 1910 with the annexation of Korea. Having gained a foothold in Manchuria, Japan's second attack on China led to the Rape of Nanking in December 1937, in which between 100,000 and 300,000 Chinese were massacred within a month in China's then capital. Then in 1940 the Japanese installed a puppet government there while the Chinese Nationalists, backed by the United States and Britain, established a rival capital at Chungking.

Japan signed the Tripartite Pact with Germany and Italy in 1940, in which they pledged to 'assist one another with all political, economic and military means'. Then in April 1941, Japan signed a non-aggression pact with the Soviet Union, which held until 8 August 1945, two days after the atomic bomb had been dropped on Hiroshima.

The Tripartite Pact did not oblige Japan to go to war against the Western Allies, alongside Germany and Italy. However, with the fall of Holland and France – and with Britain preoccupied with events in Europe – Japan was eager to take over these countries' colonies in Asia before the Germans seized them. Backing the Chinese nationalists, in 1941 Britain and America froze Japanese assets, embargoed trade and boycotted oil supplies. To continue the war in China, Japan now needed the oilfields in the Dutch East Indies (now Indonesia). The only thing that stood in their way was the US Pacific Fleet based at Pearl Harbor on Oahu, Hawaii. If that could be knocked out, Japan could also take the Philippines – a US possession since the Spanish–American War of 1898 – and other US territories in the Pacific to form a 'Greater East Asia Co-prosperity Sphere' – a Japanese overseas empire.

The crunch came on 7 December 1941 – the 'day that will live in infamy' – when the Japanese attacked the Pacific Fleet at anchor, the port facilities and the airfields at Pearl Harbor. But for Japan, on the other side of the international dateline, the pre-emptive strike actually came on 8 December.

That morning the 359 aeroplanes of the Japanese carrier-borne strike force were led by Captain Mitsuo Fuchida:

0740 hours – I gave the signal for a surprise attack. The dive bombers rose to 4,000m, and the level bombers hung just below the clouds.

0749 hours – I gave the order. My radioman tapped out the code 'To! To! To! to notify the whole squadron to plunge into attack!'

Later he cried '*Tora! Tora! Tora!*' – 'Tiger! Tiger! Tiger!' – signifying that they had achieved total surprise with their attack.

0757 hours – The dive bombers, led by Lieutenant Commander Tahahashi, attacked Hickam Field, Ford Island and Wheeler Field.

0757 hours – Lieutenant Commander Murata and his torpedo planes attacked the battleships in the harbour.

0800 hours – In single-file formation the fighter planes strafed the air bases.

0805 hours – The level bombers began to drop their bombs on the battleships. The Honolulu radio broadcast continued its normal programme. Then suddenly the ground below came alive! Dark grey blossoms of smoke-burst made my plane tremble. Suddenly it was jarred as if a giant hand had pushed it. We had a hole on the port side. A steering wire was damaged, but the plane was still under control. I looked down in the minutes that followed. Black clouds of smoke rose from the airfields. A huge column of dark red smoke rose a thousand feet into the air from the battleship Arizona. Its powder magazine had exploded. The Tennessee was on fire. I pulled the bomb release above the Maryland. The planes behind did likewise. Two direct hits! The target ship Utah on the western side of Ford Island had capsized. My heart was ablaze with joy for my success in getting the whole main forces of the American Pacific Fleet in hand. In the years that were to follow, I would put my whole hate-inflamed effort into conducting the war that ensued.

Alongside Fuchida was an anonymous pilot who later wrote to his brother. The letter was captured in New Guinea in 1943:

> In the attack on Hawaii on 8 December, I bombed the US battleship West Virginia, and made direct hits – it sank. Later on, I strafed groups of fighters on Hickam Field and Barbar's. Returned safely. The plane was hit by fragments of shells and anti-aircraft shells in two places and also received 18 machine-gun bullets. The fuel tank was hit by four bullets. I returned to the ship with only enough fuel for ten minutes more ... As it was the first battle for me, I was worried; nevertheless, I did it with considerable composure. As a result, I gained confidence in myself in the air raids that followed.

This pilot later attacked Kavieng in Papua, New Guinea, and supported the landings at Rabaul in the Bismarck Archipelago. He also bombed Port Darwin, conducted the operations in Java, attacked Chirachappu and Christmas Island, and raided Ceylon (now Sri Lanka), sinking HMS *Hermes* there. Then his combat career was cut short.

> While attacking the American Special Service Ship Picos in the course of Indian Ocean operations, I was hit by enemy 13mm machine-gun bullets in the left shoulder, and also received a slight wound to the left eye.

As a result of his impaired vision he became a flying instructor.

In the second wave to strike Pearl Harbor flew Chief Flight Petty Officer Juzo Mori, of the aircraft carrier *Soryu*, as part of a torpedo attack led by Lieutenant Tsuyoshi Nagai:

> The assigned objectives of the Soryu torpedo-bombers were the American battleships which we expected to find anchored along the wharf of the Oahu Naval Arsenal. We dropped in for our attack at high speed and low altitude and, when I was almost in position to release my own torpedo, I realized that the enemy warship which I was headed towards was not a battleship at all, but a cruiser. My flight position was directly behind Lieutenant Nagai, and we flew directly over Oahu Island before descending for our attack.

Lieutenant Nagai continued his torpedo run against the cruiser, despite our original plan to attack the enemy battleships. However, I did not expect to survive this attack, since I and all the other pilots anticipated heavy enemy resistance. If we were going to die, I thought, I wanted to know that I had torpedoed at least an American battleship.

The attack of the Soryu's planes was met with intense anti-aircraft fire from the enemy fleet, since the bombing waves from the Akagi and the Kaga had already passed over. My bomber shook and vibrated from the impact of the enemy machine-gun bullets and shrapnel. Despite my intention of swinging away from the cruiser, now dead ahead of my aircraft, and attacking the group of battleships anchored near Ford Island, I was forced to fly directly forwards into the murderous rain of anti-aircraft fire.

Because of this and the surrounding topography, I flew directly over the enemy battleships along Ford Island, and then banked into a wide left turn. The anti-aircraft fire did not seem to affect the plane's performance, and I chose as my new objective a battleship anchored some distance from the main group of vessels which were at the moment undergoing torpedo attack from the Soryu's aircraft. The warship separated from the main enemy group appeared to be the only battleship yet undamaged.

This was possibly the USS *Nevada*, which made a run for it, or the *Pennsylvania*, which was in dry dock.

I swung low and put my plane into a satisfactory torpedoing position. It was imperative that my bombing approach be absolutely correct, as I had been warned that the harbour depth was no more than 34 feet. The slightest deviation in speed or height would send the released torpedo plunging into the sea bottom, or jumping above the water, and all our efforts would be for nothing.

... I was hardly conscious of what I was doing. I was reacting from habit instilled by long training, moving like an automaton.

3,000 feet! 2,500 feet! 2,000 feet! Suddenly the battleship appeared to have leaped forward directly in front of my speeding plane; it towered ahead of the bomber like a great mountain peak.

Prepare for release ... Stand by!

Release torpedo!

All this time I was oblivious of the enemy's anti-aircraft fire and the distracting thunder of my plane's motor. I concentrated on nothing but the approach and the torpedo release. At the right moment I pulled back on the release with all my strength. The plane lurched and faltered as flak struck the wings and fuselage; my head snapped back and I felt as though a heavy beam had struck against my head.

But ... I've got it! A perfect release!

And the plane was still flying! The torpedo will surely hit its target; the release was exact. At that instant I seemed to come to my senses and became aware of my position and of the flashing tracers and shells of the enemy's defensive batteries.

After launching the torpedo, I flew directly over the enemy battleship and again swung into a wide, circling turn. I crossed over the southern tip of Ford Island.

To conceal the position of our carrier, as we had been instructed to do, I turned again and took a course due south, directly opposite the Soryu's true position, and pushed the plane to its maximum speed.

Now that the attack was over, I was acutely conscious that the enemy anti-aircraft fire was bracketing and smashing into my bomber. The enemy shells appeared to be coming from all directions, and I was so frightened that before I left the target area my clothes were soaking with perspiration.

In another few moments the air was clear. The enemy shells had stopped. Thinking that now I had safely escaped, and could return to the carrier, I began to turn to head back to the Soryu. Suddenly there was an enemy plane directly in front of me!

As my plane, an early version of the Kate carrier-based attack bomber, was armed only with a single rearward-firing 7.7mm machine-gun, it was almost helpless in aerial combat. I thought that surely this time my end had come.

As long as I was going to die, I reasoned, I would take the enemy plane with me to my death. I swung the bomber over and headed directly for the enemy aircraft, the pilot of which appeared to be startled by my manoeuvre, and fled! Is this really, I questioned, what is called war?

Fuchida and the rest of his men felt the same. Despite his pleading, Admiral Chuichi Nagumo issued an order cancelling any further attack and the *Akagi* hoisted a signal flag ordering a withdrawal to the northwest.

Fuchida was furious. 'Why aren't we attacking again?' he asked.

'The objective of the Pearl Harbor operation is achieved,' he was told. 'We must prepare for future operations.'

Below decks, disappointed torpedo ace Shigeharu Muroi said: 'Now all us pilots can live to be a hundred years old.'

As a result of this attack the United States and Britain – whose colonies of Hong Kong and Malaya had also been attacked – declared war on Japan. Then Germany and Italy declared war on the United States. The Sino-Japanese war and Japanese imperial expansion in Asia now became embroiled with the European hostilities in the global conflict that the Western Allies called World War II.

NINE HEROES OF PEARL HARBOR

While the Americans suffered 3,400 casualties, with 2,403 killed, including 68 civilians, at Pearl Harbor, the Japanese claimed they had lost only nine men, though the total was closer to a hundred. Twenty-nine planes had been lost, some in *kamikaze* attacks. However, the 'nine heroes of Pearl Harbor' were lauded in the press, and extracts from their letters home were published. One came from 27-year-old Chief Warrant Officer Sadamu Kamita of the Special Attack Flotilla, who wrote a note to his parents on the eve of his departure to Hawaii, which read:

Anything may happen anywhere at any time, as the situation is so tense. But please don't be flurried. Sailor as I am, I have offered my life to His Majesty the Emperor. For the sake of the country, I am determined and prepared to lay down my life. Your affectionate son, Sadamu, will never be disloyal to His Majesty, nor undutiful to his parents. Please set your mind at rest.

Twenty-one-year-old Chief Warrant Officer Kiyoshi Inagaki, from a rice-growing family in the mountains, also prepared a farewell letter:

Dear Father and Mother,

As parents of a naval serviceman, I believe that you are prepared for emergency. The international situation is changing rapidly, so anything may happen at any time. But please don't be shocked. I beg that you will be prepared for the worst possible eventuality so as not to become a laughing stock.

I will enhance the family reputation abroad, by giving full play to my activity through my abilities and determination which I have so strenuously acquired.

I will become the guardian deity of the country, even if I may die at sea, as my ill luck in arms would have it. There will be no higher honour in the family. Pray take care of things when I am gone. You may miss your children, who have all gone far away. Please pardon me for having given you lots of trouble for so many years.

Please take best care of yourselves. I pray that you may live long for the sake of my brothers and sisters.

Japanese submariners sent to attack US ships fleeing the onslaught showed similar fortitude. On the eve of his departure to Hawaii, 25-year-old Chief Warrant Officer Yoshio Katayama of the Special Attack Flotilla wrote a farewell letter to his parents:

Dear Father and Mother,

I am writing in full remembrance of your affection for me in the past 24 years. The clear sky in advanced autumn appears to bless my expedition. Your affectionate son, Yoshio, is going to lay down his life for the sake of his country, sharing the fate of his craft.

I am in high spirits. I will do my duty as a sailor. Man is mortal. Blessed is Yoshio, who can die in a place worthy of his death. I must thank you, father and mother, for bringing me up so healthy and so strong as to enable me to undertake this new assignment. When you, father and mother, receive the official despatch, reporting Yoshio's death, please praise his filial duty, which he had performed only once in his past 24 years. Services need to be rendered by me will probably not be made public, but please do not lose your heart. The secrets of the Japanese Navy are more important than a man's death. Dear father and mother, please take care of your health in the hot and cold days so as to attain longevity. It is my prayer offered to you both from my sea grave.

Special Sub-Lieutenant Shighénori Yokoyama, the 26-year-old son of a tenant farmer, told his parents:

My friend who joined the Blue-Jackets' Corps with me carried out self-immolation in mid-air in central China. I will offer my life to the State from the bottom of the sea. I will not be behind anyone in rendering service to the State.

It was his last farewell. Twenty-two-year-old Lieutenant Akira Hiro-o, born of a samurai family, left a note saying:

Man's merit lies in taking the right path and making endeavours in the right direction. It does not matter much whether man has a clear brain or not. Strive, and all things within the range of human possibilities will be accomplished. Otherwise, the cause for failure must be sought in lack of proper exertion. This is one aspect of my guiding principle in life.

Contemporary Japan, the journal of the Foreign Affairs Association of Japan, praised these nine 'human bullets' for their exceptional spirit of '*Bushido* – the unrivalled asset of the Japanese nation'. *Bushido* was the code of honour of the Japanese samurai warrior class, which valued self-discipline, courage and loyalty above life and was now emulated by all Japanese fighting men.

Lieutenant Furano painted the four Chinese symbols '*Chin Yu Ka Dan*' – 'Cold courage, harsh decision' – and left a poem for his parents:

The young cherry blossoms
    Fall from the branches
At the highest moment of their glory
    With no regret ...
Myself, like a broken pearl
    I will scatter my bones
In Pearl Harbor.
    The dawn is bright
With the joy of our reunion
    At the Yasukuni temple!*

* The Shinto shrine dedicated to Japan's war dead outside Tokyo. Visits by dignitaries to the shrine still cause consternation, as a number of convicted war criminals are buried there.

With the benefit of hindsight, Japan's decision to attack Pearl Harbor and take on the military and industrial might of the United States seems almost unbelievably foolhardy. Indeed, the Japanese Prime Minister Prince Konoye Fumimaro had been against it, but US President Franklin Delano Roosevelt had refused to meet him on 6 September 1941, the date set by Emperor Hirohito and his Imperial Council. On 12 October, Prince Konoye had called a meeting at his villa on the outskirts of Tokyo with his then war minister General Hideki Tojo, the head of military planning General Suzuki, foreign minister Admiral Toyoda and navy minister Admiral Okawa. According to an account of the meeting, heated words were exchanged between the prime minister and his minister of war:

> Tojo: Negotiations cannot succeed. In order for them to succeed, there must be concessions on both sides. Till now, it is Japan that has made the concessions, the Americans have not budged an inch.
> Okawa: We're precisely balanced between war and peace. It is up to the prime minister to decide and to stand by his decision.
> Tojo: It's not as simple as that. It's not the prime minister alone who counts, there are the Army and Navy.
> Konoye: We can contemplate a one- or two-year war with equanimity, but not so a war that might last more than two years.
> Tojo: That reflection is the prime minister's personal opinion.
> Konoye: I would rather a diplomatic solution than war.
> Tojo: The question of the prime minister's confidence in going to war should have been discussed in the Imperial Council. The prime minister attended, did he not? There can be no question now of his evading his responsibilities.
> Konoye: Not only do I have no confidence in going to war but I refuse to take responsibility for doing so. The only action taken by the Imperial Council was to determine the measures to be taken should all diplomatic means fail. I still have confidence in a diplomatic solution.

Later Tojo taunted Konoye to his face, saying: 'Once in his life, a man should know when to throw himself from the terrace of the Kiyomizu temple.' The Japanese expression 'jump off the stage at Kiyomizu' – a famous temple in Kyoto – is the equivalent of the English 'take the plunge'. Despite the prime minister's protests, behind his back plans for war were already well advanced. Speaking of the attack on Pearl Harbor, its leader Mitsuo Fuchida said:

> This was the culmination of my every waking thought since that day, 24 September 1941, when Commander [Minoru] Genda [who planned the air attack] had taken me aside at Kagoshima on the southern tip of Kyushu and said: 'Don't be alarmed, Fuchida, but we want you to lead our air force in the event we attack Pearl Harbor.'
>
> My heart was pounding with the excitement of the proposal when Genda took me on board the Akagi for a conference ... In that conference Commander Genda urged the use of torpedoes against the ships in Pearl Harbor.
>
> 'But that's impossible,' I protested. 'The water depth in Pearl Harbor only averages about 32 feet.'
>
> Genda insisted that if we could find a way to torpedo the ships in such shallow water, it would add to the surprise of the attack ... So at last I agreed to find a way. And I had only two and a half months. Indeed, less than that, because that day I learned that December was the month planned for the attack. Although officially we spoke of 'If we attack ...' we all thought 'When we attack ...'

EXCLUDE THE UNITED STATES

The military had the ear of the emperor and, on 16 October 1941, Prince Konoye was forced to resign as prime minister. He was replaced by Tojo – nicknamed 'The Razor' – who retained his portfolio as minister for war. However, when he was interviewed in Sugamo Prison in 1948, Tojo claimed that his original plan had not included the invasion of the Philippines – and he knew nothing about the planned attack on Pearl Harbor:

> I did not wish to drag the United States into the war. I became prime minister in October 1941 and called a conference of the chiefs of the Army, Navy and Government staffs ... I expressed the opinion that Japan should go to war with England and Holland, but exclude the United States. However, it was the Navy's opinion

... that to go to war with England and Holland would cause the United States to enter the war. The Navy further opined that if the United States was to enter the war anyway, that she should be included in the initial attack ... I did not know at the time that the Navy already had well-laid plans for the Pearl Harbor attack ... At a later conference, I believe in November 1941, I was informed of this plan. I thought initially that 'to go to war with the United States' meant an attack on the Philippines.

Tojo certainly seemed to be in a belligerent mood on 1 November when he summoned the chiefs of staffs of the army and navy, General Sugiyama and Admiral Nagano, and their deputies to a stormy cabinet meeting. However, foreign minister Shinegori Togo still urged caution.

Togo: It is unlikely that the Germans will succeed in effecting a landing in England, even with our assistance. And, in any case, we should not delude ourselves about the contribution that collaboration with Germany and Italy can make to our cause.

Sugiyama: We need the help of no one to achieve our objectives in our campaign in the south. Once that is over, China will be isolated and will capitulate. Next spring we shall turn our attention to the Soviet Union.

Finance Minister Kaya: We have confidence in a war lasting two years. But not beyond.

Tojo: Anyway, that gives us two years.

Togo: Why take such a risk? The western powers won't attack us, they have enough on their plate with the war in Europe. It is to our advantage to maintain peace.

Nagano: After two years at war, we shall have made all the conquered territory impregnable. We shall not fear America, however strong she is then.

Sugiyama: The first half of December is the right time to start active operations. We can temporize no longer with only a month to go. Let us break off diplomatic negotiations now and prepare unequivocally for war.

Deputy Chief of Staff of the Army Tsukada: The decision to go to war should be taken at once.

Togo: 2,600 years of Japanese history cannot be dismissed
so glibly.

Tsukada: The Army must have an immediate decision.

Deputy Chief of Staff of the Navy Ito: The Navy will be ready by
20 November. Why not continue negotiations until then?

Tsukada: The Army cannot wait longer than 13 November. I
propose that, as from 13 November, military action takes priority
over diplomatic action.

Shimada [for the Navy]: Why not continue negotiating to within
24 hours of launching an attack?

After 16 hours of heated debate, the date for military action to take over
from diplomacy was eventually set at 30 November. By that time Fuchida
was ready for war:

Early in November I licked the torpedo problem. We added more
fins to our torpedoes and planned to drop them from a height of
52 feet instead of the usual 300 or more ...

And now 7 December was here, and our air armada was airborne. We flew though heavy clouds for 45 minutes. Then I turned
on the radio-direction finder and picked up the Honolulu radio
statio ... I adjusted the antenna and found we were five degrees
off course. I corrected this. As I continued to listen I heard the
announcer give the weather report: 'Averaging partly cloudy,
with clouds mostly over the mountains. Cloud base at 3,500 feet.
Visibility good. Wind north at ten knots an hour.'

We could not have asked for better weather.

BRAVE SUBJECTS

After the attack was over Emperor Hirohito - whose chosen reign name,
Showa, means 'bright peace' - signed a formal declaration of war dated
8 December 2601 (the Japanese Emperor Era being reckoned from the
accession of Emperor Jimmu, legendary founder of the imperial line, in 660
BC). Hirohito's declaration of war read:

We, by the grace of heaven, Emperor of Nippon, seated on the
Throne of a line unbroken for ages eternal, enjoin you, Our loyal
and brave subjects:

We hereby declare war on the United States of America and the British Empire. The men and officers of Our Army and Navy shall do their utmost in prosecuting the war ... the entire nation with a united will shall mobilize their total strength so that nothing will miscarry in the attainment of our war aims.

To ensure the stability of East Asia and to contribute to world peace is the far-sighted policy which was formulated by Our Great Illustrious Imperial Grandsire and Our Great Imperial Sire succeeding Him, and which We lay constantly to heart.

To cultivate friendship among nations to enjoy prosperity in common with all nations has always been the guiding principle of Our Empire's foreign policy. It has been truly unavoidable and far from Our wishes that Our Empire has now been brought to cross swords with America and Britain.

More than four years have passed since China, failing to comprehend the true intentions of Our Empire, and recklessly courting trouble, disturbed the peace of East Asia and compelled Our Empire to take up arms.

Although there has been re-established the national Government of China, with which Nippon has effected neighbourly intercourse and co-operation, the regime which has survived at Chungking, relying upon American and British protection, still continues its fratricidal opposition.

Eager for the realization of their inordinate ambition to dominate the Orient, both America and Britain, giving support to the Chungking regime, have aggravated the disturbances in East Asia. Moreover, these two Powers, inducing other countries to follow suit, increased military preparations on all sides of Our Empire to challenge us ... Our Empire for its existence and self-defence has no other recourse but to appeal to arms to crush every obstacle in its path.

... We rely upon the loyalty and courage of Our subjects in Our confident expectation that the task bequeathed by Our forefathers will be carried forward, and that the sources of evil will be speedily eradicated and an enduring peace immutably established in East Asia, preserving thereby the glory of Our Empire.

The public reaction to the attack on Pearl Harbor was recalled by Dr Kawai, the chief editorial writer of the *Nippon Times*, who held a BA, MA and PhD from Stanford University:

> I do not think that the popular morale was ever very high, even in 1941 at the beginning ... I was surprised as I expected to see bands, parades, cheering ... It was in striking contrast to the Russo-Japanese War [of 1904–5]. The people had then been taught to hate the Russians and to regard them as enemies, so the war was popular. This time it was a matter of indifference and of shock. During the first few months this feeling changed to one of over-confidence as news of victories came in. But it was not a spontaneous feeling, rather one whipped up by propaganda. However, the over-confidence did not last long. The people did not know the true war news, but they began to feel the shortages from the second year of the war on. There was distinct dissatisfaction, though of course it was not open.

Some were more gung-ho. A diary captured in 1943 quoted the song of the military academy, which expounded the Japanese idea of *Hakko Ichiu* ('all the world under one roof'):

> We will plant the Rising Sun flag, dyed with our life blood, on a far desert with its twinkling stars; when the lion roars beneath the trees. We will drag the very crocodile out of the Ganges, where it flows at the foot of the Himalayas. The paper carp shall flutter high about the City of London. Today Berlin, tomorrow Moscow, and snowy Siberia will still be in our hands. Our grandchildren shall raise a monument to us in a Chicago purged of gangsters. And when our time comes to cross the Styx, we will wrestle with the Shades themselves.

The Japanese military were well prepared for war, and their initial victories were swift. On 18 December 1942, a diary fell into American hands in New Guinea that told of the run-up to war.

> 29 November: American has taken off the mask with which she had disguised herself until now. We are going to meet the enemy at Guam Island with ever increasing spirit.

3 December: It seems that the Japanese–American talks will finally break down.

4 December: Worshipped at the Imperial Palace at 0830. Gave three banzais. There was a speech. Japan–America war! It looks as though all the hardships we have borne until now will be rewarded. We have received life of Showa's reign. Men have no greater love than this. Convoy to sail at 0900. Now prosper fatherland ... The Empire has decided to go to war against America, Britain and Holland. The Southern District Army will quickly capture important regions in the Philippines, British Malaya and the Dutch Indies after the first attack on 8 December. For this purpose the first Japanese–American air attack will be carried out ...

8 December: War declared!

10 December: 0130 Begin getting into barges. 0230 Opposed landing [sic]. No sound of enemy fire. Landed without the loss of a single life. Passing the coral reefs was difficult ...

11 December: American and native troops surrendered.

Numerous diaries like this one were captured during the war. While British and American troops were told to burn personal effects before they went into battle, a surprising number of Japanese went to war carrying diaries and letters. When these were found in the possession of prisoners, or on dead soldiers, they were taken for translation by the Allied Translator and Interpreter Section (ATIS) as they were frequently full of invaluable intelligence material. In their diaries, Japanese soldiers often wrote that they were amazed at how good Allied intelligence was, when in fact they themselves were providing it.

KUBOTA'S DIARY

One captured diary belonged to Sub-Lieutenant Kumataro Kubota of Number 122 Regiment from the city of Matsuyama, the capital of the Ehime prefecture in southern Japan. On 1 November 2601, he and his unit were mobilized. Two weeks later they embarked at the nearby port of Mitsugahama, ready to go to war, though there were still over three weeks to go until the attack on Pearl Harbor. Kubota noted in his diary:

15 November: Start! To the Front where one marches over dead bodies, we start. The ship is already prepared to take us on our

way. Goodbye homeland. Goodbye, the moments of the busy life
of a human being. We are leaving Mitsugahama.

16 November: To the south the ship is speeding. On the blue sea
the white gulls are floating. Are they going to the Front with us?

17 November: The white clouds are streaming towards the
north. Where is the source of the Great Universe? Alas, there is
fighting among the men. Everyone wants to be a winner.

On 20 November, they landed on Formosa (now Taiwan) – a Japanese
possession since the first Sino–Japanese War of 1894–5. The other Japanese
soldiers Kubota met there bolstered his patriotism, though he had to wait
another ten days before he heard the earth-shattering news:

8 December: The news of the declaration of war against America
and England broke with the morning sun. At the same time
Hawaii, Guam and the Philippines were taken.

This was a little premature. Although Pearl Harbor, Guam and the Philippines
had all been attacked on 8 December, Japanese time, Hawaii was never taken.
Guam was not taken until 11 December and the Philippines were overrun the
following year. Nevertheless, Kubota was delighted.

9 December: The great order of the Proclamation of War by the
Emperor has fallen. People have waited; nations have waited; and
now men who have waited have the opportunity to bury their
bodies on foreign soil.

However, he would have to wait another two weeks before he could join in
the action. The night before they sailed, he recorded that 13 petty officers
from the torpedo boat *Takawo* went to see one last movie, noting that 'it was
their last pleasure in the human tragedies'.

23 December: Boarded the ship, the Shun-yo-maru, which is
leaving our Empire. Oh, Shun-yo-maru, I pray you reach your
destination safely. I pray to God for my child's health and
happiness. I think of this, the well-being of my child, before
I think of my safe return home.

The following day, his company was given a pep talk by its commander:

24 December: Today is the day after we joined the Greater East Asia war. We have lived safely in our own harbours and bays, but now everyone must realize that real struggle is before us. Now we are seeing victory after victory since 8 December and we are beginning to look on the war as one great sham. This attitude will lead us to disaster …Thinking of the enemy as a light one brings us to a most dangerous conclusion. The war has just begun and there are hardships before us.

Soon Kubota was preparing to go ashore, but he revealed no fear of the fighting to come:

26 December: Preparation for the Front is completed. Troops are on the boat. Warships guard us … one's great obligation and duty is to guard the Empire. Fight, my daring squad! Guard our Emperor's life! Advance towards the trenches. Die like a flower blown down by the wind! Advance with the flag of the Rising Sun! Thrust with the white blade of the Japanese sword! Forward with high spirit even though San Ferdinand beach in the Philippines is well fortified! The waves will be high and the fortifications long and strong, but we will always go forward!

The Japanese went ashore in the Gulf of Lingayen in three waves, protected by naval gunfire and an anti-aircraft screen, while torpedo boats saw off an enemy submarine:

30 December: Our convoy of transport with the protection of the 51st Torpedo Boat Group began operations at eight o'clock in the morning … Look at the ordeals of those brave torpedo boats which guard their land-based comrades. It is like mother birds caring for their young. She flies to the front, to the rear, to the sides, watching that the slow tottering babies come to no harm. And so the torpedo boats guard us from the attack from submarines. The waves roll over those arrow-like little boats, splashing their slender figures. I felt proud and the thought that we were the sons of Tenno [the heavenly emperor] increased.

But Kubota was held back aboard ship. He was saved from the first murderous onslaught and it was another two days before he could go ashore.

31 December: Tomorrow we will reach our destination ... Thanks for all of your efforts, my comrades of the sea! These are the words of the man of Shikoku [Kubota's home island], 'Goodbye brave comrade! I am going to Manila and give my last thrust to the enemy's throat. And may the flag of the Rising Sun electrify the air!'

So we exchange our thoughts. Good luck, those white sailors' caps waving at us and we returned the wave with our service caps. Goodbye Comrade! Thank you for the protection you have given us. The land is now ours. There is no barbed wire, nor forts nor shells to fear! We are the sons of the Mikado and ready with our bullets of human flesh!

Tomorrow is the New Year, the 17th year of Showa! Landing in the face of the enemy is due tomorrow ... the whole opening fire of the enemy is due tomorrow. Wait our people with good health, you will hear of the fall of Manila.

Then his big day came.

1 January 1942: The critical 16th year of Showa ended with storm and distress. Now we are looking at the mountains towards the south. The sea is calm and the morning quiet. I am writing with the feeling promoted by our Battalion Commander's talk: 'Go ahead with a friendliness among you and keep in good health and high spirits.'

The transport fleet swings into single file as I write. Friendly aeroplanes are flying over our heads. The New Year morning sun is very hot and our duties are important ones. I must spur on the men under me.

At around 2pm, the convoy rounded the peninsula into the bay. The captain of Kubota's ship came from Takahama, which was near to Matsuyama and Mitsugahama, so felt an affinity with the regiment. He was not going to let them go ashore without ceremony:

The captain is such a kindly man. He offered us saké for the New Year. He also gave us makizushi [rolled sushi] and zoni [soup traditionally drunk at the New Year].

It seems there had been plenty of boozing going on aboard ship.

> Saké and beer were served [on] alternating days to the officers, but
> none was given to those below the rank of warrant officer. I felt
> terribly sorry for the men, but at any rate they got saké for their
> New Year's celebration. But my conscience troubled me when we
> got beer and saké and the men got nothing.

There were other privileges.

> All officers have the privilege of taking hot baths every day, but
> not non-commissioned officers and soldiers. I felt terrible about it
> whenever I took my bath, yet I was thankful that I was of officer's
> rank. I will look for an opportunity to give the soldiers the right to
> take a hot bath whenever I can.

Then, at the end of his entry for 1 January 1942, Kubota recorded
dispassionately:

> At two o'clock in the afternoon, we landed without incident in
> Lingayen Gulf.

THE ENEMY IN RETREAT

Kubota had a gentle introduction into the war zone, though the initial
landing party had plainly had a hard time getting ashore.

> 2 January: I welcomed the second day of the New Year under palm
> trees. Strangely enough, my dream was not of home, nor of my wife
> and child. It was about 'K' who is an easy-going, self-willed person.
>   The soldiers of our company were already having a difficult time
> with fever. Today's report is that the enemy is retreating towards
> the south of Manila. There is no order for an advance …

He also got an opportunity to compare the attitude of soft, life-loving
American soldiers to that of his own men who were fired with *Bushido*.

> We got hold of an American soldier's letter. It was from the US
> barracks in San Fabian to a friend. It said: 'There is a report that
> the relationship between America and Japan is dangerous. If there
> is a war, don't worry. There is no chance of losing, nor any danger

to my life.' This soldier's letter most likely represents American thought. I wonder what they are thinking now. Our soldier's letter would be like this: 'The relationship with the USA is dangerous. Be at ease. We will never lose to a nation like America. Needless to say, we have made up our minds to die. We cannot meet you again in this life, unless you go and pay your respects at the Yasukuni Shrine and pray for the nation's safety.'

Sub-Lieutenant Kubota had 40 men under his command who seemed to enjoy sleeping under the palms on the beach at Lingayen.

3 January: ... The fruits from the trees hung like bells at the edge of the frame of an umbrella. Men were climbing up the trees with the joyous feeling of the native ... The sweet-juiced palm fruits and their peaceful shadows sway in the air, to protect and give joy to the tired traveller. Water buffaloes are strolling between the misty hills ... Summer is always here in the Philippines. The waves are beating and rubbing the beach and they visit with a white smile the gentle palms lining the white shore. They dance with the palms when the wind comes along the inlets of this strange land.

Even so, it was cold enough in the evenings and mornings to burn wood fires. But this reverie could not continue long.

4 January: Trucks from the main troop station arrived. Now the sky is protected by friendly aeroplanes. The truck drivers had a hard time because the bridge near San Ferdinando has been destroyed. They had to drive over the railway bridge which was still intact. They took away seven injured men and two non-commissioned medical officers. I felt sad at their departing and thought of the old saying, 'Just touching the kimono sleeve brings affinity.' The day after tomorrow the trucks will come back and pick up whoever is left and take them to Tarlac.

Kubota revealed the full extent of the Japanese losses in the initial assault.

Now we are sitting on the beach of Lingayen Gulf where our landing party was annihilated, save three out of the whole battalion. How great was our loss! ...

But he was not downhearted. He shared the belief that the Japanese Army was freeing the Far East from Western hegemony. This view was reinforced by a pamphlet called *Read This Alone – And the War Can Be Won*, prepared by Imperial Army headquarters. It was designed to be read in the cramped conditions of the troop ships, and 40,000 copies were printed and distributed immediately after embarkation. As well as practical advice on hygiene, the terrain they would be fighting in, fruits that could be eaten, snake bites, weapons, signals, tactics and the like, the pamphlet explained why they were fighting:

> Three hundred and fifty million Indians are ruled by 500,000 British, 60,000,000 Southeast Asians by 200,000 Dutch, 23,000,000 Indochinese by 20,000 Frenchmen, 6,000,000 Malayans by a few tens of thousands of British, and 13,000,000 Filipinos by a few tens of thousands of Americans. In short, 450,000,000 natives of the Far East live under the domination of less than 800,000 whites. If we exclude India, 10,000,000 are oppressed by less than 300,000. Once you set foot on the enemy's territories you will see for yourselves, only too clearly, just what this oppression by the white man means. Imposing, splendid buildings look down from the summits of mountains or hills onto the tiny thatched huts of the natives. Money squeezed from the blood of Asians maintains these small white minorities in their luxurious mode of life – or disappears to their respective home-countries.
>
> The white people may expect, from the moment they issue from their mothers' wombs, to be allotted a score or so of natives as their personal slaves. Is this really God's will?
>
> The reason why so many peoples of the Far East have been so completely crushed by so few white men is, fundamentally, that they have exhausted their strength in private quarrels, and that they are lacking in any awareness of themselves as a group, as peoples of Asia.

Japan, which had never been invaded, was going to put that right, the pamphlet said. But this ignored the atrocities the Japanese Imperial Army had already committed against Asian people, notably at the Rape of Nanking. Kubota would have known about this. He was a regular soldier and had served for two years in Manchuria. The pamphlet went on to complain that Britain and America were denying oil and other raw materials to Japan, though the very reason for this embargo was to get Japan out of China and stop the murder of Asian civilians there. Nevertheless, at this point in the war, Kubota felt a kinship with the Filipinos.

> 5 January: I sent Corporal Ishiki to the mountains for chickens. Four natives came along with twelve chickens, all for one yen, 50 sen [about 50 cents US]. All of the natives looked like one of us. I am convinced that they are the same race as ours and I wondered if they were thinking the same as I. I have always thought that dojin [natives] were a tribe that went about naked and wild. Now I know better. We should call them 'local people' from now on. They have the manners of Americans. They looked as if they were starving, perhaps because of wartime shortages. I gave them rice to take to their homes.

On 6 January, he received news that Japanese aeroplanes had destroyed 50 enemy vessels that were trying to escape from Manila Bay after the Japanese had sent a note demanding their surrender. Bases had been set on fire by 'bolting natives' – Philippine forces. 'There is a great difficulty in keeping the happiness of the natives,' he noted. He also heard that Manila had fallen on 4 January, though it was not occupied until 31 January:

> Oh, at last our enemy's capital, Manila, has fallen! Now we will draw out our swords and shout 'Justice!' to the world. It is the war for the Great East Asia! Fight, men, fight! Go and find a place for death. The dream of life ends with death – that is the life! The graves of our bodies are the trenches, the fields of skirmishes and the line of cross-fire!

The next day, news came that a military review had been held at Sasaki to celebrate the declaration of war on England and America one month before. But he also discovered that Manila had not fallen after all.

> 8 January: ... This morning's news report is that the Manila defence commander will meet our representative and talk over terms. What does the commander of a losing army ask of our victorious army? Now the flag of the Rising Sun is flying on the

land, in the air and on sea! Those nations of democracy – the lands of selfish principle – will fall when the flag of the Rising Sun marches on!

Two days later, Kubota tried to make contact with the main force and collect supplies, but it was a hot day and he was happy to get back to the beach.

10 January: ... I was glad to get back to the place where my men were waiting. After all this is our first home in a foreign land. This spot in Lingayen Gulf grows in our affection. The nights in the southern lands are always beautiful. Above our heads the families of stars are talking about the mysteries of the universe. And I recall those fairy tales about the stars which I read as a child ... Fireflies fly between the stars weaving the sky with their light.

That night, he received a message from the supply depot, saying: 'A hurricane struck at Tarlac and destroyed great quantities of war supplies.' He noted: 'The expected supply trucks have not yet arrived. Just waiting is a strain.' Again he attempted to take matters into his own hands.

12 January: I got in contact with San Fabian to find out about the supply trucks ... All of the trucks had left for the front and there was not one left to send to us. I felt disappointed. There is no way of communicating with headquarters. By now the soldiers of the third and fourth squad must be wondering where their platoon commander is and patiently awaiting my return. The wind has been blowing strongly since this morning and the white waves are rising on the sea. It must be hard going for the front-line troops. I wish we could join them.

Later native children came to see us again. All of them speak English so well and my men talked to them with their hands. I asked one, 'What is your name? Where do you live?' ... I watched those poor natives walking back towards the mountain, the leader with a white flag on his shoulder. I realized that a native should not lose in any wars and that the Japanese at home were very fortunate.

By the middle of January things were going very badly for the Americans.

13 January: Our force pushed an enemy force of 4,500 men, 40 tanks

and some fighting planes onto the Bataan Peninsula. Now there is fierce fighting going on. The enemy is facing our forces to the front and at the back of them is the sea. It is life or death. Justice makes the right destroy the wrong. If they have the spirit that there is so much talk about, those Americans must fight until the last bullet, then use their swords to take their own lives. What can one think of the high-sounding talk of President Roosevelt. He is not as big as his talk. Come natives, fall into our hands. I received news that our battalion was fighting at the front at Bataan. But we have no way of getting any automobile, so we must stay here and tell our regrets to Lingayen Gulf and rub our own arms as we anxiously wait.

A VERY PLEASANT TIME

Kubota was still having trouble obtaining supplies, but another lieutenant who was about to ship out for Java came by and 'we talked and had a very pleasant time'. He revelled in the progress the Japanese forces were making.

> 15 January: ... Our fighting forces are extending to the south. I can see the glorious figures of the Japanese advancing, while we are here among the palm trees, bathing in the soft breeze with nothing to do. What are we doing here when our comrades are fighting at the front?

It then dawned on him that the men at the front had completed their training, while his men had not – 'now I understand how important the drill is'. Meanwhile the tropical idyll continued.

> 16 January: ... The fruits of the palm trees are growing always. It shows how wonderful it is to live in a country that has summer all year round. This evening we all gathered together and talked about home. We exchanged stories of our children and our wives.

There was drill again the next day. Still no supplies turned up, though they managed to obtain six chickens and five aubergines. And with all this time on their hands there was a danger of discipline breaking down.

> 17 January: ...The military police came to report on the soldiers' conduct around Mabilao. Their conduct was not so good. Three cases of rape had been reported. I have been watching my men

carefully as we are all just a bunch of youths. I have warned them about their conduct ... Later in the day, we had a swimming contest. It is hard to imagine swimming in water surrounded by palm trees on 17 January.

Two days later the supply trucks brought bad news.

19 January: ... A Battalion tried to advance towards Fenerosa and lost some vehicles and some comrades. The Fukuyama detachment which took part in the frontal attack lost the battalion commander, two or three company commanders and the regimental commander was wounded. The transport group lost six men when shells from the enemy fort struck their automobile. The enemy is now at the edge of the peninsula and there is no way of escape for them. They are conscious now, of course, that this will be a hard fight. Bataan and Singapore are in the same position of importance. They are the life-line of America and England. There will be casualties among our forces taking over the important point of Bataan. It is a task for the Japanese Empire and her one billion people and it is for the honour of the army. There is a grave waiting for you where you jump over a dead comrade. The value of one's life is established by how one ends his life. There will be no question of social position or how much property one possesses. Death on the battle front is the most respectable possession one could hope to attain. The dead warrior becomes the son of the Mikado and becomes a god.

Kubota's men spent another fine day buying pigs and chickens, though he heard of heavy losses at the front. Still they received no communication from the main troop and Kubota grew increasingly frustrated.

21 January: ... Twenty-one days have passed since we landed. And I've heard only the sound of waves beating against the shore and occasionally the sound of shooting far away ... A transport arrived today. It may be in preparation for the next operation. Over three hundred enemy struck at San Fabian today, but here there is nothing to report.

22 January: Natives came with chickens and eggs and asked us

to exchange them for matches and soap. We wanted the chickens and eggs, but also needed the matches and soap. I offered them money but they refused. Now I realize they are living by primitive method of barter. I offered them food and they ate it with both hands. It is quite an unsanitary habit, but America has not educated them yet. What America wants from them is her own happiness. The countries like the USA, whose principle is individual freedom, will die because the coming force is the desire for one's national independence. There is great glory before us as we march for the independence of our country without the ambition of conquering colonies.

Kubota was an idealist, on paper at least, as Japan had already acquired a number of colonies – notably Manchuria, where he had served. Then, at last, news came from the front.

23 January: The last ring of Bataan's defence has begun to crack, according to last night's report. I am wondering about our Shiga Battalion at the front. Yet I should not be caught up in such personal feelings. Small personal feelings detract from the main objective. I am a regular soldier, not a reserve like the others. My service is not temporary. I am in this war and must do my best, yet I realize that I am a man and others under my command are men and we are all human. Fight! Fight! Well, anyway one must be careful about drinking. One who drinks for relaxation and to ease the day's duty is excusable. But one must be careful about the drink which annoys others. Anyway I have stopped drinking since I was at Kagi [Formosa]. I stopped for my own good as well as for my country. I wish I could study more of ethics and fulfil a more cultural life. There is no time when one thinks about things seriously as when one is facing death or life. One must think first of culture and truth, then advance and fight ... Again came a communication from the main troop. We are worrying about our battalion and the fighting at Bataan ... The sky is resting on a golden sea as the evening sun sinks in the distance. The sky is the colour of dark brass. The quiet palms stand above us to console our worry of tomorrow ...

25 January: I gave the platoon orders and sent Corporal Kawano

to San Fabian for supplies. Twenty-five days have passed since we landed. Here it is quiet and peaceful in spite of being in the land of our enemy. There are water buffaloes strolling and the snowy herons mingle with them on the ricefields. Natives are coming back to their homes gradually. Their faces are darker than ours, yet there is a likeness. I got my letter off for home. It will reach there about the middle of February. One can hardly believe that the people at home are facing the winter. Here one must be careful of sun-stroke. Here, I learned that there were as many deaths by sickness as death in battle. If I can help it, I do not wish to die through sickness ... I would like to go to Manila as soon as possible. Bataan is still holding out. I wonder what the result is of the general attack.

Kubota did get ill.

26 January: I have a temperature. I could not sleep all night long. Corporal Kawano and Private Tachibana took care of me. A medical lieutenant from the Omachi Brigade came to look at me and administered an injection ...

28 January: I still have a high temperature, but I feel much better. The medical lieutenant came to see me again. There are five more men as sick as I am ... Number 2 Squad are so busy taking care of sick men that they are no longer a fighting unit. It is regrettable that one man taking up everyone's attention should nullify the unit. Since I am commander of this platoon, I must decide which is more important – let one man die or make the unit unfit. In war, one must go on advancing and leave one man to die ... More sickness reported, Corporal Iishi and eight others. There is a need to train up non-commissioned officers. Their actions are worst of all. Some had been to school, but they lack knowledge and the ability to command ... Anyhow, they lack spiritual strength and the culture that a leader of men needs.

When he was well again, Kubota decided that it was time to join the action.

29 January: We have made up our minds to march to Tarlac. There is no report of the fall of Bataan. Our aim is to reach Tarlac and

send Corporals Iishi and Kawano to make contact ...

30 January: We begin our march to Alakan. Tomorrow Corporals Kawano and Iishi go to the railroad headquarters to report. Soon transports leave Lingayen Gulf for Java, I hear. Lieutenant Tamai came by. He is one of my hometown folk. We feel very near each other. At last we are moving! It is the end of one month's idle living.

1 February: Communication became better since the arrival of the Railroad Service Corps. There are 3,400 enemies remaining at Bataan and they are still fighting, according to the news. At last we are marching to join the men of the second camp.

In fact, there were some 80,000 men holed up on the Bataan Peninsula.

3 February: We left Alakan station at ten o'clock. We rested at San Fernando for three hours. At ten past three we left San Fernando for Tarlac. On the way we saw four or five destroyed automobiles. In 20 hours we arrived at Tarlac ... I ordered our belongings piled up at the station, put a guard around them and took a rest for the rest of the day. I prayed that our men do their best and thus deserve to be honoured as children of the Emperor. Our friends and comrades already wounded at the front need our assistance. Come warriors, and meet the great opportunity to do your duty for your country.

The first members of his company were injured when two trucks collided, rolling one into a deep ditch.

7 February: Unfortunately we left two men in hospital ... The whole day everybody rested. Tomorrow the 8th – 8 December was the declaration of war – we are advancing to the front. The men of my company and the truck drivers from the transportation corps eat together. Ten bottles of saké made everyone happy and gay.

After five weeks of anticipation and frustration since landing in the Philippines, Kubota was about to have his *Bushido* put to the test.

8
BUSHIDO: PUTTING THE MARTIAL CODE TO THE TEST

By February 1942 the Japanese had blockaded the Philippines, occupied Manila and confined the American–Filipino ground forces to the Bataan Peninsula, cutting off their lines of supply. However, they were meeting with fierce opposition from the defenders. Sub-Lieutenant Kumataro Kubota moved up to the coastal village of Maron on his way to the front.

9 February: I left Maron while hearing the roaring sound of the artillery. With the guidance of Top-Private Kurata, we climbed up a steep mountain. We got a terrific shelling from the enemy just as we reached a place where they keep horses for the field artillery of Nara Brigade. We were in hot pursuit by the enemy so we left that place right away. Took a breath at the place where they keep the food supplies of R Battalion. It was around six o'clock. There were so many casualties. It is a great tragedy to watch the wounded soldiers wobbling aimlessly along the paths. We received a shower of the enemy's bullets during the night. I could not sleep well. Bullets and shells were thundering in my ears like popping corn.

10 February: Today is Kigensetsu [the anniversary of the ascension of Japan's legendary first Emperor Jimmu, Japan's Empire Day]. We are near the front line. The personnel of the company are well and their morale good. Sergeant Kurata gave me four packages of cigarettes when he left. I distributed them among the squad leaders. I reached Ishimoto's brigade and reported to the regimental commander Watanbe ... Every soldier at the front is glad we have arrived. We met many old friends. Sergeant Nishimura, platoon leader, the company leader and others welcomed us with a smile ... Adjutant Fukuoa wants to hold my men back from the advance so there would be no repetition of the huge casualties sustained by the Tania Battalion.

11 February: I spoke to First Lieutenant Abe about the warning the Adjutant gave me yesterday. I sent our Kawano's Squad to

the three-forked road near the graveyard. Sergeant Yano who had already planned to advance with his squad has been shot in the ribs, so we sent him back to the rear.

12 February: Today we stayed at a place where Lieutenant Nakanishi is stationed. In the evening the enemy sent shells and bullets like rain. Private Shimiz of Inoue's squad was injured by a hand grenade. Sergeant Morita and one private came back today from a position which had been completely encircled by enemy forces. Everyone expected the complete annihilation of 3 Company, which had been encircled, but some came out of the trap. Two of them, an officer and a private joined our brigade – then later two sergeants and a private. There is a report that one officer and six soldiers reached Blagu. I am wondering about the lives of Sub-Officer Shimamoto and the company commander and all the others. They have been without food for 13 days. We were told this by the three soldiers who subsequently escaped and returned to us. I pray to God that help will come to this group of brave men. I pray for the good fortune of this encircled company.

But Kubota had concerns closer to home.

13 February: I had a stomach ache since the 11th, but today I went out with the Iishi squad. Sounds of rifles and artillery echoed all around. Platoon commandeered 4 Squad to cover the group crossing a stream and the Iishi squad reached their destination safely. Now I will have to fight. This is a war and I will help to annihilate the enemy if the opportunity arises. About 3pm a Top-Private from the communication camp was injured in his right leg and chest. Sent him back to the rear.

14 February: My stomach ache is better. At 8.40pm I got a scratch from an enemy bullet. I was at the side of Private Ninaviva's dugout. It must have come from a sharp-shooter. The men of our company are well and in high spirits. I am worrying about 3 Company and about the safety of 20 Regiment which is said to be retreating with her regimental flag intact.

15 February: No casualties so far today, but there has been a lot of shooting for about an hour. The enemy will start bombarding

us with artillery soon, as the exchange of bullets has stopped. I fell to wondering if I was near Hell when the bombardment was going on. Both sides stopped the bombardment when the night ended and the sun began to show her face. Occasionally an enemy sharp-shooter sent a barrage of bullets from his Tommy gun. I heard a bird singing while the shooting was going on. I wondered if Sub-Officer Nakamura and Apprentice-Officer Matsunaga, who had lost their lives, were hearing that bird singing. I could not help shedding my tears for their deaths. Now I am praying that the Sub-Officer is still alive ... The 20 Regiment flag came back with 300 men, all that remained of the regiment, along with 14 men from 3 Company. Some of 3-Company's men are badly injured, yet they withstood 15 days without food or rest. Then they broke through the enemy's encircling ring of iron. It is spirit that counts when it comes to life or death. Again I will spend the night hearing the roar of artillery and pray that my comrade Sub-Lieutenant Shimamoto is safe.

Eighteenth hour, 6pm: Tonight again begins with an exchange of bullets. Then came the fearful sight of a bombardment of shells, which became deafening. There are stars peeping through the leaves above our heads. Fireflies continue to fly as the shells burst along the valley and stream. I thought of my child and dream of home ... We must fight harder. We are for our country and our country is our home. The enemy's shells pass over our heads like a comet. They are fighting hard. Major Mizoguchi came tonight to take over command of the battalion. Major Shima's condition is improved, so he was sent back to the rear.

That day, 15 February 1942, the British stronghold of Singapore fell to the Japanese after a week's fighting, consolidating their invaded territory in resource-rich Malaya and giving them a strategic port. The victory was commemorated in a song, 'Singapore Has Fallen', the words of which were found among documents captured in the Buna area of New Guinea on 2 January 1943. Translated into English prose, they read:

Listen to the assault-tune of the century. The thousand millions imbued with the spirit of Asia are aflame and when the angry waves of the blood-tide raged, the American and British battle formations crumbled into dust. Ah, this deeply stirring triumphal song. Singapore has fallen.

We have won, we have won, we have reduced it. The virile roar of righteousness, echoing in the haunted jungle and winding through crocodile-infested creeks, breaks into the enemy's stronghold. Ah, this deeply stirring triumphal song. Singapore has fallen.

This day that we have waited and waited for. The history of aggression, blood-stained by the whip of America and Britain burning with selfishness. Look up as the sun sets on their withdrawal from their positions: the Sun of East Asia rises. Ah, this deeply stirring victory. Singapore has fallen.

Raise both hands high. Shouting the victory of East Asia, vowing the union of blood, the great march now goes on. May its rhythm echo through the world. Ah, this deeply stirring Greater East Asia. Singapore has fallen.

SONG FOR A DEAD COMRADE

On 16 February, Kubota wrote his own song for his dead comrade Sub-Officer Nakamura:

He was chasing the enemy when it happened;
The birds in the trees slowly stopped singing;
The sun's glare merged into darkness.

Through the darkness, enemy shells
Burst above his head. He drew
His sword and shouted, 'Come!'

That night of the 5th – the most
Memorable day of his life, the rain
Was falling on the jungle as the night
Covered all with darkness.

Shells from field artillery reared and
Splashed above his head. One struck a tree
Beside him. Together, they were scattered
Through the air like the petals of blossoms.

Alas, my friend is gone;
I call his name, but he answers not
Except the sound of rain.

Afterwards Kubota noted:

Again the bird is singing as I begin to pile the stones for his resting place. And it is a sorrowful sound to my ear. All the men at the front should realize that such a day as this will come to them. I am human. Losing a friend is a tragedy. I regret leaving you, dear friend, even though you will join the spirit of comrades at the shrine of Yasukuni. I left cigarettes on his grave.

He wrote another song for his friend Sub-Lieutenant Shimamoto, for whom he had been praying, then recorded more prosaic matters:

We received the order to move to the place where the brigade is stationed. We start at 23 hours. Private First Class Fusaichi Ono was killed at 11.30. He had such a nice personality and good character. The tragedy of the battlefield is deep and penetrating. We begin to retire from the front under cover of pitch darkness with 7 Company guarding our rear. The enemy feel their own strength and are shooting harder, due to the dead quiet of our front.

17 February: We begin our march very early in the morning. Kawano's squad, who remained behind to the last with two engineer squads, left the front and joined us at about 13 hours. Up to today, we have lost 20 men and the company commander. Sixty-six are injured. Second Lieutenant Akaboshi is among them. Twenty-six are dead through illness. The sickness is due to lack of sanitation. Ill men have difficulty going to the toilet when bullets are scattered around them. Most of the sick are staying at the front. I am among them. I must go out to relieve myself as often as ten times at night. And each time one does this, one's life is at stake ... Today is so quiet. I prayed, 'Please give good luck to our company.'

Although Kubota was ill and was out of the front line, there was no respite. On 18 February, he received a battalion order to go out and have a sign put up, saying 'Nara Brigade'. He took with him Corporals Iiwo and Ando, and Private First Class Kato.

18 February: ... All are brave and high-spirited. We came back at 8:30 (15.30 military hours). During the trip we faced shelling and bullets. Tomorrow our company goes to the front. Bad news – our troops at the front are retreating.

19 February: We started the forward movement. It is a difficult task. We must avoid being shelled by the enemy. As soon as the enemy see us, they shower us with bullets. During the march, I went out scouting and narrowly escaped the shells. Our company marches on. Everyone is covered with sweat and dust. Our force is only 85 out of the original 193 fighting men. But they are marching through the jungle paths. Their commander already killed and 20 under him, 67 disabled and 26 sick. There is always grief at the battle-front.

20 February: Our company are at last gathered at the bank of the Abuabua River. We will join Nara Division after four days of rest, and then engage ourselves in taking the enemy's possession around Kaplar. The enemy's shells are bursting all around us and bullets are passing above our heads day and night. The ground is shaking with explosions. The clear and ever-flowing Abuabua River, when will she become our friend?

Besieging the Americans now confined to the Bataan Peninsula gave Kubota time for reflection.

22 February: Two months have past since we landed. There is no sign of the raising of the white flag at Bataan. Our tactics against the enemy were just to fight and advance. We have paid a heavy price. Now we are blockading them. There will be fewer sacrifices, but a longer war than I can put down in this notebook. Bataan's fall? It will be April or May. Private Shimizu and Ishikami have been sent back to the base. Our days are becoming more normal, but still the shooting is going on. Only the river flows peacefully. We do not know what tomorrow will bring. We have a life today but not tomorrow. Even the life of the next moment is no longer in our control. Each time a shell hits a tree, the leaves and splinters fly down and we get more light. But, with the roar of artillery in our ears, it is not a comfortable feeling. Now we must answer their

call. We begin to fire. Firing becomes more fierce and through the smoke and dust we see our suffering comrades ... The enemy throws their shells furiously as soon as the sun is down. Those giant tree tops splinter like matchsticks and a shell passes by with a whistling sound and strikes something behind us. Then the dust and stones fall like a rain storm. After a few moments' silence, the word passes that everyone is safe and we heave our chests with a sigh of relief.

The next day, Kubota set out to get supplies.

23 February: ... Started out with the truck. The road was a difficult one. There were many places exposed to the enemy's artillery fire. We were shelled often, but there were no casualties. We were lucky. We arrived about five o'clock. I met Okura. He was suffering with a high temperature. I gave him medicine and cigarettes ... We stayed over the food storehouse belonging to the division and Private Nakajima made us comfortable. Eighteen of our aeroplanes passed over our heads. As soon as they passed, we heard their bombs explode all over the enemy's base. But the enemy is fighting hard. There is no let-up in their resistance. Yet it seems that their food supply is low ...

NEW LAND OF PEACE AND SAFETY
Kubota went to 6 Brigade to get filing cabinets for his command post. On the way back, he came across a lot of enemy vehicles abandoned in the mountains. This provided fresh inspiration.

26 February: Wrote a letter home, the first letter from the front line. Now we must advance towards our ultimate objective. Wherever the flag of the Rising Sun advances will be opened up a new land of peace and safety. Come, men of the Philippines, do not depend on others for your own development. Try to understand the true meaning of one's life and live independently. I went to your capital Manila once. It is a beautiful city. And she has escaped any serious war damage. I feel that new life will be put into her veins and she will come out more healthy and beautiful than ever before.

27 February: The enemy's shells are falling briskly at position 142. A sorrowful but friendly voice visited my ear through the telephone. He tells me that Kojima is dangerously ill and that he himself sent two men to the clearing hospital to care for him. Sergeant Yamada is always kind, but this is the front line and everyone's life is in danger. Yet Yamada has never forgotten that Kojima is my best friend and that I had asked him to look after him. I thanked Yamada deeply and told him I was thanking him for Kojima's father and mother. It is not the first time that Yamada has saved Kojima from death. On one occasion he ordered Kojima to guard a gun position and thus avoid actual combat. Another time he put Kojima in a safe position, while he himself went into danger.

The fighting has shifted from the east shore to the west shore. We are ordered to join Nara Division. I had the opportunity of seeing Kojima. He was pretty sick. I left word that he should have better care. Private Kojima must get well, come from his sickbed and fight with me side by side. I knew that his whole family would go to Wakamiya Sama [their local Shinto shrine] and were praying for him. Last night we went to put out wires at our front and met an enemy. He ran away and disappeared into a cornfield. After an hour searching, we gave up.

28 February: At last February is at an end. Two enemies appeared near the headquarters. Private Kameda saw them first. We exchanged shots, but I saw that they were in danger of escaping, so I ordered Iishi's squad to go around the enemy's left. But the enemy must have thought it wise to escape without more fighting. We could not find any of them. It was 16 hours. Two days we have found the enemy and each time let them escape. We must do better.

Allowing the enemy to escape had its consequences, but Kubota looked forward to a new offensive.

1 March: Once this morning the enemy's shells fell near our base. They must have found out our position. So far there have been no casualties. The date of the decisive battle is to be 10 March. It is

Army Memorial Day and there will be quite a battle because the enemy is almost out of food. Malbal mountain with its well-fortified defensive system will not stand against our offensive. No one can win a war by being continually on the defensive. March is the time for a total offensive. By that time, the cherry blossoms will begin to bud, but here in the Philippines it is now midsummer. It is just before the rainy season. The battle will be a hard one, but the men are in high spirits. I too must do my best so the men will be proud of me.

2 March: I spent last night at Sub-Lieutenant Hino of 2 Michin group. His trench is already completed, though ours is not. I received orders to go out and scout the right back of the Abab River. So I chose those brave men of Corporal Iishi's, Top-Privates Jinno and Ando, and Privates Ogawa, Shuda and Tanaka. It was night scouting so we went cautiously. We met about ten of the enemy, so we contacted the sentry of 6 Battalion. We started to attack at once, but the enemy fled. It was sort of fun and we enjoyed it.

3 March: I went to Elmarsa to pick up replacements. There I met Kondo and learned of Kojima's death. The last time I saw him was on 23 February and he died on 2 March. I do not know how to write to his parents. We came here together from Matsuyama. We talked and worked together ... We did everything together, yet I could not be with him when he went. I lost the best of my friends in Top-Private Kojima. I cannot stop crying. He was such a splendid character; he talked little, but possessed such a strong personality. I shall miss him forever.

4 March: I received an order to change personnel. I felt lonely all day by the loss of Kojima. Now the only way to make myself feel better is to go out and fight my common enemy, the Americans and the Filipinos and beat them to Hell.

5 March: Today, again, the enemy's shells are dropping around our trench. At last, attack and advance – our company is moving! Fight! Fight bravely!

6 March: Sergeant Tanaka and six men came back to join us. I felt more confident when I see such strong men come back to us. Soon we will start the all-out attack with the land and air combination.

7 March: I wrote to the parents of Kojima about his death. We are the supporting-post of the House of the Rising Sun. Our job is to keep the Mikado's Empire in safety forever. This is our duty and honour throughout our life. Therefore, our ending of life is the completion of our desire and duty. Soon there will be the all-out attack. Our lives are in the hand of God. We should have no fear of death.

But, again, more commonplace considerations came between Kubota and his dreams of glory.

8 March: I received new non-commission officers. They looked well and strong. We are moving out soon.

9 March: There is so much office work to do. I try to do as much as I can but never finish. I must go to sleep early tonight and start again in the morning.

10 March: Today is Army Memorial Day. Even if we start attacking today, we cannot win completely today. It is regrettable, but we need good preparation for an all-out attack.

11 March: I have a very bad stomach ache. It is dysentery. I am not accustomed to it, and keep on working. Trying to do office work amidst the bombing.

12 March: Office work! Fight! Office work! Fight! A sub-officer's life is not a glorious one. But it is war and one should not look for glory. Again, I spend the whole day in the trench.

13 March: Writing the diary of the battle is one of the jobs I assigned myself. Not being accustomed to this kind of work, it takes up too much time.

14 March: I spent all day in the trench doing office work. Every time I got out, bullets or pieces of shell strike near me, and make my stomach weaker. This is the important moment of one's life; I must keep up. The strong enemy base is at Marbenz ... We will attack from air, sea and land ... a three-dimensional fight ...

Then Kubota received some momentous news.

Today I received a letter from home. It informed me that my first daughter was born on 27 December. She was given a part of her father's name and called Chizuko. Chizuko, please grow strong and wait your father's return. Now, I can do nothing for you, but as soon as the war is over, I will come back with a nice present which you will like. Please grow up without anything happening to you. Good luck, my dear Chizuko.

But the war continued regardless.

15 March: Busy preparations to leave. So far, each day we have done well. From now on, we march in the rain of bullets and shells. Good luck, my men! Good luck, my child, Chizuko!

16 March: Kata is injured on the right side of his face. At 16 hours we gathered our company and went to the battalion station. We had an order to go there as a brigade because the enemy's attack is so fierce. In the meantime, I sent a messenger under heavy fire; we have begun to advance. The enemy's fire is getting heavier. At a point near where the Abuabua River joins another river, we crossed a bridge that the engineers had built. 6 Company came from the rear and went ahead, while our company took a short rest. Then we started to advance. The enemy's shells were dropping everywhere; one not 20m ahead of us – again 30m to our left. We got down flat on the ground each time, then got up and moved on again through the smoke and dust. Every inch we went ahead there was death waiting for us. Three men of 6 Company just disappeared with one shell! And the men who fell dead looked like ripe pomegranates broken in half. One of 1 Company's soldiers lay in front of me without the right side of his face. A lieutenant nearby is groaning from a heavy wound. I almost got buried with smoke and dirt when I advanced about 10m beyond where 6 Company's soldier lay dead. Sergeant Vand and Sergeant Nishimura report that Sub-Lieutenant Hino was surely gone. Well, I am still alive. I cannot afford to die. I must live and go on.

17 March: We began advancing towards the right side of the front line. There are so many points exposed to the enemy; but for some strange reason, we did not get much of the fire. The only casualty was a soldier belonging to 2 MG Battalion. I hear that we cannot do anything against the enemy's artillery. It is strong and

well protected. The only way to take them at all is to take the forts in an all-out attack. Our casualties from the enemy's artillery is so great ... We reached our objectives without any severe incident. Again we must sleep under the enemy's fire. Good night my dear wife! Good night my darling daughter, Chizuko!

18 March: Morning arrived. It is three days since we became a reserve. Top-Private Tachibana is always kind and helps me. Corporal Kawano is also very considerate. He tries to make me comfortable. For lunch, the men cook red rice for me ...

NO MORE FEAR OF DEATH
Red rice cooked with Indian beans is traditionally served by the Japanese to celebrate birthdays and the birth of a child.

I am sure that Chizuko will be pleased with the treat of red rice on the front line. As soon as I have the opportunity, I will send at least 100 yen to Chizuko. The all-out attack is waiting for us, but somehow I have no more fear of death. I believe that my life is dear and that I shall see my child, Chizuko. On the 16th, I witnessed our comrades buried alive by the enemy's fire. I am so disappointed in our artillery that I have lost faith in our artillery corps and its machines. Where is the proud army which called itself the first army of the world? Again and again, they are depending on infantry. Where are the field guns of R Battalion? They are always suppressed by enemy fire. Infantry again – because they can advance over the dead bodies of their comrades and fight to the last man. Where is our proud artillery? They are silent, always silent before the roaring fire of the enemy's artillery. I read the letter from home over and over again. It is darling and darling, forever.

19 March: All along, the enemy has not stopped firing at us. At night, they continue through fear of a night attack. Of course, they cannot win the war by firing at such a distance. We must do the all-out attack and take over the artillery before the rainy season. I am worrying about Corporal Kawano and his group who went after our food supply.

20 March: The sound of shells falling near my car. Can they be shells from Fort Mabell? We are standing at the corner of life

and death every time a shell bursts near us. We boast about our military strength, but we cannot do anything with it against the overwhelming artillery of the enemy. We are losing more and more men as the days pass. The enemy is having their own way with this artillery war. We are between two evils, the enemy fire and malaria. We are waiting here to die from sickness, or to be shot by the enemy. Come shell! I would rather face death through your fire than die of malaria! To live through this Bataan warfare, one must be very, very lucky. When I cannot write this diary any more, you will know that I am dead – Sub-Lieutenant Kubota is dead when this diary ends.

The next day, Kubota noted that it had been five days since they had moved up to the front, but still the offensive had not begun.

21 March: ...We get shelled from the fort, day and night. I try to recall those sounds of the big drum beating at the festival that I so enjoyed as a child. But the dream is broken by a shell bursting nearby. The more I think of it, the more I wonder how I am alive now ... At last the all-out attack is about to begin. Our life will be like a little candle light blown by a storm. However, we cannot stop advancing until we plant the flag of the Rising Sun on top of the evil mountain Malbal. The war is an unfortunate thing ... and the declaration of war by the Mikado is unfortunate too. But this war is here and it is for justice. We must fight it to its conclusion. Now our forces are in Malaya, Java, Singapore and Hong Kong! Now we are advancing to Bataan. We must fight.

22 March: The enemy's fire is as fierce as ever. Those trees and logs of the trenches are blown to pieces. Bodies of our comrades lie blood-soaked. All of these sacrifices are to make people at home safe. It is for our country and the people at home. My life is in God's hands.

23 March: At last we have men from the reserve. Among them were Corporals Taiichi and Hasegawa, who is the father of three children. Hasegawa should not be in the service with such a responsibility, but in the confusion of mobilization and conscription there was no time to look at the records of each man.

Today there was an order to go scouting. Corporal Hasegawa was selected to go. I know that his family, father, mother, wife and children are praying for his safety. Hasegawa never came back. He was killed. I cannot help thinking of his family. I saw his body where it lay all covered with blood. It is a tragedy, a great sorrow that this happened to him. Of course, this is war and no one knows who goes next.

24 March: The Maltic River is always beautiful. The water is clear. My admiration of this beauty increases through the tragedy of war. Little birds are singing and the cicada chirp shrilly in the trees. It is a strange feeling to face the beauty of nature while smelling fresh blood – here among men, where we are killing each other.

25 March: Flower-filled March is almost gone. The little water falls and streams are always friendly ... and my child, Chizuko is growing to be a graceful young lady ... This is the dream of a warrior who is fighting in a tropical jungle by order of the Mikado. Sub-Lieutenant Nakamura and Sub-Lieutenant Shimamoto are living in this world no more. Their spirits will return to the shrine of Yasukuni to be the guardians of our nation. But I know that their bodies lie in the jungle of a strange land. Also I know that their families are waiting their return ... not their spirits, their live bodies! It is my duty to write their parents, and their brothers and sisters. It is a difficult task, but it must be done ... Sama mountain and the Zambales mountains stand before us. The enemy is waiting there in well fortified positions. Soon we are going after them as waves of men who have made up their minds to receive death. It will be a fight to console our dead comrades. Wait, you Filipino and American troops who took our comrades' lives.

26 March: All day our aeroplanes have been dropping bombs on our enemy's fortifications. It must be as great a torture as we suffered under their artillery attack. At last, our artillery is ready to meet the enemy's might. We have held the air too and our infantry is waiting with their bullets of human flesh. We are determined. Our will is pitted against the enemy's fortified positions and superior materiel. But our will will come out on top. Thus we await the glorious moment. It is natural to think that one who

survives the battle front is fortunate. We have been watching so many of our comrades go – yet some come out alive. It is better to think that one will be dead as soon as he comes under the enemy's fire, because there is nothing to prevent death once one goes into the fighting. One's life is no longer under one's control, but up to the Supreme God.

I am now 31 years old. One's natural lifespan is 50 or thereabouts. Yet when one reaches 50, a man wants to live to be a 100. It is the natural desire of a man to want to live long. But here our lives are counted by minutes and seconds ... There is no present, past or future to a man at the front. So it is best to think one's life is death before one enters the attack. Yet I find myself suffering to live. How do I know this is the best place to die at the age of 31. How to live and how God is to judge whose life is to be saved is my confusion at this moment. Here is an old proverb: 'If there is a Hell below one's crossed sword, you may save yourself much by jumping into the depths of Hell at once.' It is true that one dies sooner or later, if one does nothing when the bullets are crossing in all directions. This is the philosophy one tries to find while looking at the half-blown-off bodies of comrades. It is the duty of an officer who possesses the spirit of Bushido to guard his homeland. To give the deepest respect to these fallen comrades on this jungle roadside, we must march on to fight to the death, believing there is a more important mission than just one's own life or death. This spirit makes enemies fear and respect us. It is called the Japanese wave – the wave of death until one gets victory. I have knelt and, with my clasped hands, paid my deepest respect to those dead soldiers who sacrificed their lives for their country by willingly jumping up and running forward before a shower of the enemy's bullets. It is done by just a word from their inspired officer. Now it is my duty to lead brave men who are advancing towards the mountain summit. It lays its evil shape across our front line. The Zambales fort stands at the height to the right. We must capture it and our waves of soldiers crush against it. There will be waves of Japanese soldiers piled high – dead – until we get it.

27 March: Men have disappeared like the melting snow to capture this high mountain fort. It is inevitable that it will fall sooner or later. It is hard to understand those Filipino native troops fighting so hard against us. General MacArthur has fled to Australia. Curson (president of the Philippines) is already dead. I know those natives have their families and they have no more leaders, yet they throw their deadly weapons against us. They do not understand our Bushido. As for me, I must fight against them, in justice to our fallen comrades. They will test our Japanese swords. The all-out attack is nearing.

Finally the order for the all-out attack came.

28 March: ... 6 Company of 122 Division is to advance on a line 1km wide to take the enemy's front line at night. Our artillery will fire with all they have to hand. The general attack will start at the 20th hour; the artillery will begin at the 19th. As I read the order from headquarters, I felt strongly the enemy's determination to live and defend themselves and their comprehension of what the war is all about. At the 16th hour, by order of 2 Battalion, we get reserve soldiers from the original division at headquarters ... The sun is going down over the western hill. Darkness is falling over the jungle. It is the 19th hour. Guns of every description have begun to roar. Our artillery is helping 6 Company advance. But enemy shells are dropping on our base long after our artillery stopped firing. I am praying for our success in getting the objectives without much sacrifice. Moonlight is shining strongly on the river and over the jungle. Those reserves we expected yesterday have not yet arrived.

29 March: The enemy's shelling has never stopped. The shells are falling all over us. 6 Company reached their objective last night. Again our group must wait here. Top-Private Makamura, Private Wamuki and Corporal Hamazaki stayed over night with us in our trench. I wonder when I am going to write about the fall of the mountain forts. As the evening sun began to fall into the Aboabo River, artillery started firing from both sides. There is skill and power in artillery battles. We must recognize the enemy's power and

their will, since they have resisted this long against our assault ... Those mistaken, misled natives! They are not defending their own country. They are playing the band with their precious blood for the American jazz song. What do they gain by fighting against us? Wake up, my friends, the Filipinos! We are fighting for a great Asia, the family of the yellow race. You should not be under the control of the white people. You must listen to our voice and become a strong nation. Follow the bell that your brothers are ringing.

30 March: At last the reserves have arrived. Most of them are from Matsuyama, and some are men who have been trained ...

REVENGE MY FRIEND

The bad news was that in order to pick up the reserves they would have to return to the confluence of the Abuabua River, where they had been badly shelled on the 16th.

> ... We received a terrific shelling when we marched along the upper stream of the Abuabua River. 6 Company, which was just ahead of us, became the centre of the enemy artillery's target and instantly four of our comrades were blown up. The next shot took two artillery men of our division, one from 1 Company and some from the supply corps. I received 58 men from the service base and proceeded towards our objective. Four shells were fired at us, but they dropped behind our position. We were proceeding carefully now. The enemy sent more shells, but they dropped near the base of the mountain artillery. We ran quickly to our stopping place. After lunch, we will start back to our base. It is lucky that we have no casualties among us ... I find that Top-Private Katuma Yamaguchi has been killed. Here, on the battlefield, it is natural for one to be killed at any time. But now I have lost both Corporal Hasegawa and Private Yamaguchi since we arrived at this river. We must watch ourselves more, for the great battle is approaching soon.
>
> 31 March: I got the report that Sergeant Kano has been killed ... He belonged to the educational department at Matsuyama and was liked and respected by everyone. He died on the night of the 29th. Of course, my life is as uncertain as others at this moment, but I will fight to revenge my friend as long as I am breathing ...

The battalion commander Lieutenant Nakanishi gathered together his officers to tell them that, during the night or at daybreak on 3 or 4 April, they were to take over a strongpoint that 'the enemy had been guarding diligently'.

3 April: It took us one hour and a half to reach this point. Soon our shells will be dropping on the enemy's position which has the benefit of natural protection. At 8 and 12 o'clock there was a terrific salvo from our artillery and the airforce was dropping their bombs on the enemy's position. Black smoke covered the enemy bases. The order to attack came at last. We faced the enemy as soon as we went down a valley and crossed a stream. We went forward and thrust into a hill which was the enemy base and took possession of their front line. The enemy snipers were very accurate and we had many casualties. We lost Top-Private Yano, Private Yamado, Private Kodama, Private Iida and Iwama, Tahara, Kato, Kinoshita, Yoshida – all of them injured.

4 April: The battlefield at night is as bright as day. It is strange that Yano is not around any more. He used to talk to me and like to stay near me. Now he is dead and I can no longer hear his voice. There is no sound of the bugler or other familiar sounds when the night was broken by day. We just fight, we front-line attackers, and go after the enemy when and wherever we see them.

5 April: Again pursuit. We went up a mountain where there was no path. But soon we found a splendid road and advanced. We went after the enemy and took a base, but we did not know what was to come the next day. We were trapped!

6 April: At seven o'clock the enemy began to attack. We are surrounded by the enemy. It is a hard fight. Our first squad is dying one by one. Fifty men in all are at the mercy of the enemy. If 1 Battalion had not come to our rescue, our company would have been wiped out. On this occasion we lost Tanaka, Sadavo, Kawabata, Kuniwo, Ogawa, Hirano and five men were injured. Under enemy fire 3 Company replaced our force.

7 April: We had joined 6 Company which was guarding the road on the morning of 5 April. We then followed 1 Battalion on the front line facing the enemy. We had pursued the enemy continuously, gained 6km and took a rest.

8 April: By order, we were to guard a point where three roads join. During the night, we suffered an earthquake, enemy shelling and malaria.

Kubota soon succumbed.

9 April: I am suffering from a very high temperature and am weak, but must advance. Our company took over again the point where the three roads meet. It was after midnight. I never felt such agony before. At last! The enemy has put up the white flag! There were about 800 prisoners.

10 April: Again 2,000 of the enemy gave up! We are smiling. I remind you that all of these enemies have a hand in killing our comrades and our brothers. It seems that no one is thinking deeply, just smiling. The enemy is giving up, but we must think of our loss. Our company alone lost its commander and 30 soldiers under him. One more breath and we will be in Manila. We are awaiting that day. At last the game is up. For this day, we went through our difficulties and suffering!

11 April: The enemy commander, Major General King, sent a declaration saying: 'Stop fighting.' Those soldiers who gave up fighting are coming down the mountain. Sixty, 80, 100 vehicles are coming down flying the white flag. Our dead comrades are now enjoying the sight from the other world. We have been waiting for this day ... we fought for this day ... and our comrades died for this day. This day is the fruit of our hard fight. Now the spirits of our dead comrades can go back to the shrine of Yasukuni and rest forever. There are 3,000 prisoners to be shot to death – those Filipinos who fought against us under the command of America. I felt sorry for the conclusion of their life. I suppose this is the end of the diary of the fighting at Bataan.

But it was not the end of Kubota's diary, as his suffering continued, though this was nothing compared to the suffering of those captured at Bataan. Some 70,000 starving prisoners of war were force-marched 100km (60 miles) under the tropical sun to a prison camp in Tarlac. They were kicked and beaten on the way, and those who fell behind were bayoneted. Some 7,000 to 10,000 died on the journey. But Kubota knew nothing of this.

German soldiers who had been sent to Russia recorded their sufferings in vivid detail. Some managed to requisition furs and felt boots from the natives, or steal them from enemy dead. It was not until the spring of 1942 that furs, warm underwear, gloves and ear protectors arrived from Germany. Even then there were not nearly enough to go around.

In U-Boats, petty officers shared bunks in their quarters immediately behind the control room, while officers had bunks to themselves. The U-boat commander enjoyed the privacy of his own tiny quarters opposite the radio room. Meals were taken with the officers at a table in the gangway but were constantly interrupted by crewmen going back and forth to the torpedo room in the rear and the engine room in the bow.

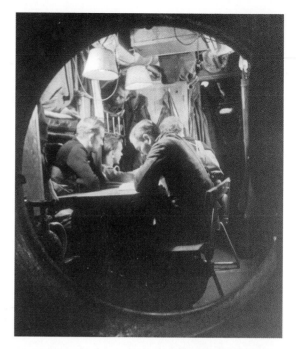

German submarines were metal tubes just 67m (220ft) long, into which were crammed four officers, three or four senior non-commissioned officers, 14 petty officers and 26 to 28 enlisted men. Around half the crew lived in the bow compartment, where the men ate, slept, serviced torpedoes and whiled away their free time.

The German people had long been told that the new 'Vengeance' weapons would turn the tide of the war. But when they saw the V-1s, most German civilians were too war-weary to be impressed. Some felt that the false promise they offered prolonged the war, preventing Hitler from bowing to the inevitable.

In the Ardennes, German soldiers regularly saw V-1s crash before they could inflict any damage on the enemy. Others were shot down by intense American artillery fire.

The Japanese believed that it was their destiny to remove European imperialists from Asia and the Americans from the Philippines, which they had occupied since their victory in the Spanish–American war of 1898.

Willing to give their lives for the Emperor, Japanese soldiers believed that countries such as the USA, which believed in individual freedom, would perish and that countries that believed in asserting their national independence would take over.

Kamikaze pilots (left to right) Tetsuya Ueno, Koshiro Hayashi, Naoki Okagami, Takao Oi and Toshio Yoshitake pose in front of a Zero fighter before taking off from the Imperial Army airstrip in Chosi, just east of Tokyo, on 8 November 1944. Of the 18 pilots who flew that day, only Yoshitake survived. A US warplane shot him down, but he crash-landed and was rescued by Japanese soldiers. He went on to see the 60th anniversary of the end of the Greater East Asia War at the age of 82.

General Kawabe insisted that kamikazes were not 'suicide attacks'. Pilots, he said, looked on themselves as human bombs whose aim was to destroy the enemy fleet rather than commit suicide, which would not be such a glorious thing.

Japanese soldiers were indoctrinated to die rather than be captured in battle. Lieutenant Colonel Toshikata Ohira complained that those who, in the later stages of the war preferred to be captured, had not received sufficient training.

The city of Hiroshima had no way of defending itself against conventional bombing, let alone the atomic bomb that hit it on 6 August 1945. Japanese newspapers had regularly reported the effect of carpet bombing on the solid stone and brick buildings of Germany. However, the wood-and-paper cities of Japan had no air-raid shelters, since the government 'did not want to unduly alarm' its citizens.

AP INDICATES AIMING POINT

Some children who survived the bombing of Hiroshima lived on into old age and had the opportunity of recording the nightmare they had experienced. They recovered from the horrendous wounds and from the trauma of seeing their provincial city being turned into a vision of hell and went on to become living witnesses to the horrors of this new type of warfare.

Despite seeing city after city destroyed by conventional bombing and shelling, as well as by the atomic bomb, Admiral Toyoda found that in 1945 the front-line forces were still 'raring to go', while Major General Miwa declared that: 'As far as the army is concerned, the termination of the war was declared by the Emperor and not by the army.'

'The Tai Commander has drawn his favourite sword... It glints in the light and sends a cold shiver down my spine. He taps the prisoner's neck lightly with the back of the blade, then raises it high above his head with both arms, and brings it down with a sweep.' These lines from a captured Japanese diary are graphically illustrated in this photograph.

For the Japanese soldier, to become a prisoner of war was shameful. Many preferred to sacrifice their lives in unwinnable battles, by suicide or by succumbing to starvation in remote areas. However, those who surrendered found themselves treated surprisingly well. One PoW even wrote a pamphlet in which he told his comrades that it was their duty to surrender and survive to become 'one of the rebuilders of the new Japan'.

12 April: We received orders to go to Baliugo or Bagio and we began to march at nine o'clock. Our division expected to reach there by stopping over at Hato Base which lay on the right bank of the Chawel or Jauel River. Again I had a temperature and a difficult time. Today we passed the place where they distribute the prisoners who are brought back by truck. There was a bloody wind blowing. We even smelt it with our nostrils.

13 April: Again I have a high temperature. It must be malaria. We will start marching to Guagua tomorrow. The diagnosis was malaria. Tomorrow I will be sent to the San Fernando clearing hospital. Thirteen of our company will go. I feel quite sick. I will depart with Kawano, Nishmura, Jinno. We had a nice farewell party because we had received additional supplies. We celebrated our victory over Bataan. At the same time we prayed for the repose of the souls of our dead comrades.

14 April: We arrived at the hospital by truck. I think it will take some time to get well because I am so run down. Today, I laid on a bed for the first time in months, it seemed, for we have been sleeping in the trench dugout.

15 April: Two days have past since I came to this hospital. Most of the patients were sent to Manila. I expect they will send me there around the 16th or 17th. I feel that my temperature is lower. There is so much perspiration while I sleep, Top-Private Ishikawa watching me has been a great help. Privates Hamada, Musui, Murakami and Kinoshito who are leaving the hospital to rejoin the company came to see me; also Lieutenant Suzuki. I will try and cultivate my spiritual side while I am in this hospital. For a long time it has been neglected. Now I am as weak mentally as I am physically. I recall many incidents while we were fighting. It was hard fighting. Our company lost its commander, 30 men killed and 100 wounded. At any rate, the enemy at last gave up at Bataan ... Since we arrived here on 1 January, we have slept on the beach, by the roadside, in fields, dugouts and on the mountainside. In pursuit after pursuit, we lost our comrades. Now I can hear the voices of those dead comrades and my blood begins to boil. I can visualize the fight on 5 Company on the river bank and the

enemy's artillery fire when we were crossing the Abuabua River on 16 March. 3 April was the attack on the enemy's base and on the 6th the assault. It is hard to stop thinking and seeing those fighting figures fall before the enemy's fire. Those shouting voices and bloody bodies. Those men who have gone as the many falling petals of the cherry blossom had now become glorified by Kudan* at the shrine of Yasukuni. Now they rest peacefully. It is so strange that I am alive. Such was my fortune to live through the battle and I cannot help but wonder how it happened. I know that my family are praying for my safety and that my wife and child are looking for my safe return. I look towards the sky where my family live and pay my deepest respect to them as I lay on this bed of the San Fernando clearing hospital.

16 April: This is the day I am to be sent to Manila. Lieutenant General Nara, the commander of the Nara Army, came to visit us at the 13th hour. He said to the sick men, 'You must take good care of your sick bodies.' Sergeant Major Utsuki came to report about our soldiers. I asked Private Tachibana to take my officer's public report. The price of commodities in San Fernando are so high that we find it very difficult to buy anything. I will buy rubber boots when I arrive in Manila. And I have no more shirts left. Also my gold filling is loose and the cavity in my tooth should be filled. I hope to be in Manila very soon.

17 April: The day passed as usual. There is nothing to write about, only that there are few cigarettes left. If I were at home I would smoke Homore [a cheap brand of Japanese cigarettes]. Here we can only get a few Piedmont, Commander and Circle. I will not smoke those cigarettes, but I will ask Lieutenant Kishi to get others for me ...

18 April: After the fight: There is no sound as the evening sun disappears behind the western hill. It seems like a dream. What has happened? Ten of my men are killed, ten injured. We buried the dead in the dugouts which the enemy built. There are the enemy's bodies too. Who will take care of them? It is a sorrowful sight. Again we will be marching tomorrow. Yesterday's soldiers

* The Yasukuni Shrine stands on Kudan Hill in Tokyo.

are no more today. There I was alone looking up at the moon, thinking. My emotions sink low.

19 April: Again the day. It is a lonesome existence at the hospital. Last night another soldier died. A lonely death for a soldier to die of sickness. Our company commander and Lieutenant Abe are on the hospital list. This fever is a greater enemy than the enemy itself. The nurse with whom I have become friendly for the last four or five days is leaving for Manila. The women of Japan are doing their part. They are working as hard as anyone ...

21 April: Another patient died ... died calling for Mr Orderly! Mr Orderly! His voice was restrained by army discipline. Why can he not shout out, 'My mother! My father!' Or call his wife or sweetheart's name? It is natural to call for one's nearest when one is dying. Why can they not supply nurses instead of those uniformed orderlies? A woman's voice after the death battle is sweet ... The soft voice, gentle manner, kindly words, graceful walk – all these we look for. Not for any physical desire, nor with worldly eyes towards the nurse. We only want their tender care and the feeling that we are at home. It gives us strength.

22 April: Again the hot wind is blowing. The sky is getting dark. Everyone is wishing for a downpour of rain and the breath of a cool breeze. Most of the patients are out of their minds with a high temperature. Their red eyes gazing aimlessly into the air. In the cellar of this hospital lay many patients. And they die, one by one, every day. It is the tragedy of this war. My pain in the heart is greater than anywhere else when I think of those who die by sickness after this glorious battle. Theirs is a lonely and sad death. We sick men must get well. We must fight against this fever as we fought against the enemy. We must not give up so easily.

LETTER TO CHIZUKO
Alone in his hospital bed, Kubota's mind turned once more to his daughter.

24 April: This is for my child, Chizuko:
Small, lovely girl, Chizuko!
I am your father who is lying on a bed in a white gown in a hospital. The hospital is in a town called San Fernando which

is 60km north of Manila in the Philippines ... As you know I am
a soldier, therefore, I do not know when I will be killed. This is
the life of a soldier. It is unpredictable whether one dies from
illness at any time, or when one is fighting on the front. I have
jumped over many death lines and been saved so far. But I would
like to tell you now, that I would like you to read this diary when
you grow up. And if you want to know more about your father,
ask your mother. Your father has been a quick-tempered and
simple-minded person. I have mistreated your mother by saying
unkind words to her and occasionally being violent. Your father
is untamed and ill-mannered, but I would like you to know I am
not an animal or a savage. With all of my shortcomings I have a
kindly heart and am considered manly. I have been admired and
respected by my soldiers ... and also my superior officers have been
friendly and liked my character. You will see those trophies and
the writings which are placed in the Tokonoma [a raised alcove in
a traditional Japanese home containing art or family treasures].
They are the records of my fencing contests. I have worked for
my training and won in such matters as fencing. I am sure that
you will be an athlete like me. I am also good at memorizing. I
was in the high school. And you will be good at memorizing too.
I am now training myself to be your good father, by correcting
my faults as I face them everyday. I was stationed in Manchuria
two years before I came to the Philippines. So I have been in
battle for two wars ... and three years engaged in office work at
headquarters. My characteristic is not liking to be inferior to other
people in my work. So I have worked hard to do as well as any
other person in a contest. Your uncle is a hard worker too. He has
studied and succeeded. He is a splendid person. I am sure that you
will be a beautiful young woman who will reflect all of our good
qualities. Your father has been a drinker of wine, and has given
much trouble to your mother by this. But I went to the army soon
after finishing high school and never had the opportunity to learn
the culture and manners of life which are learned through contact
and experience. In other words, I have never grown up with the
advantages that many men have had. Yet my heart is not so far

from your heart. My desire and wishes are still those of a child. I was raised in a family that had few difficulties through poverty and in happy and fortunate atmosphere. This good fortune of my family is due to your dead uncle's unselfish assistance. So I wish that you would keep up the best care of your uncle's grave. My mother rests there too. I have heard beautiful stories about my mother. I lost her when I was very young and my auntie raised me as her own child. She is the most kind and lovely person. I always thought that my auntie was a symbol of the Buddha. If you want to know more about your uncle and auntie, ask Aunt Moyo. She will tell you about them. My dear little Chizuko, you must listen to your mother. Learn from her and grow up to be just like her – a woman, gentle and kind, who is loved and admired by others. Just having beautiful looks does not make a good woman. You must be the possessor of a beautiful character and a good heart. And I want you to be a womanly woman. I always believed that a man should be manly and a woman womanly. This writing is for my daughter, Chizuko. I am writing this, dear Chizuko, from a bed in the San Fernando Hospital.

> Your father
> Sub-Lieutenant of the Japanese Army
> Officers Quarters, San Fernando Hospital

On 18 April General James H. Doolittle had launched an air raid against Tokyo, Yokohama, Kobe, Osaka and Nagoya. His 16 B-25s took off from the aircraft carrier *Hornet* and flew 1,000km (600 miles) to Japan. This mission had been thought to be impossible as the planes were unable to carry enough fuel to return to the carrier. But instead, they flew on and landed behind friendly lines in China. The raid did little damage, but the bombing of Tokyo was seen as a personal attack on the emperor and was a terrible warning of what was to come. Kubota's hometown Matsuyama, where his wife and newborn child waited, was over 650km (400 miles) from Tokyo. But it was just 65km (40 miles) across the Gulf of Itsuki from Hiroshima.

Meanwhile, the good news was that Kubota was recovering from malaria. He was not going to die ignominiously in hospital. He begged to be sent back to his company, and left San Fernando on 28 April, planning to visit Manila before returning to the front.

29 April: I met Higashiya. He seems well. He found a way for me to have a bath and made me comfortable in many ways. He gave me a watch in memory and in return I gave him a fountain pen made in the USA which has a gold nib. He accompanied me to Manila where I bought a pair of boots which cost me $23.00! I returned to San Fernando by automobile. Higashiya told me that he would probably be sent back to Japan to the main division base. I went to pay my respects to the grave of the late Shima Battalion commander. It recalled so many incidents that sorrow overcame me. We had both been well and in good health when we parted, but now he was in this world no more. At that last meeting we parted forever. I spent the night in San Fernando.

30 April: I went on to Tarlac and met Lieutenant Murai. I tried to locate my squad, but I could not, so I stayed overnight in Tarlac.

1 May: When I started out for Dalmolais, we changed trains and due to some trouble I had to walk 300m with my suitcase on my shoulder. Private Saito looked quite worn out and weak.

2 May: I took the train to Bagio. Many cedar trees were growing there and made me think of autumn at home. This is many thousand metres above sea level and quite cold at night and in the morning. I received supplies from 5 Company and was told that the commander had left here yesterday.

3 May: I took a sight-seeing tour around Bagio. It is a beautiful town. I learned that it had been a resort. The houses are lovely and the streets and gardens well cared for. There were cedar trees and cypresses and many familiar flowers blooming. It was just like home and I felt fine.

4 May: Today I went out shopping. I bought a sweater for my child, Chizuko. Mr Oniwa, who is an army doctor, is from Kurume and was our neighbour when we lived on Rvugae Street. He also bought a sweater for my child. Now she has two sweaters. I am going to put them in my office suitcase [a willow trunk] take them to San Fabian and leave them in the storing place there.

5 May: ... As I was resting on the road, someone put a hand on my shoulder. I looked up into the smiling, healthy face of a second lieutenant. We exchanged greetings and he went on. Not

long after I heard the sound of firing and about 300 soldiers passed me. More shooting followed. It was the sound of our light machine-guns. The fighting had started. 'To the left!' The order came through a straight narrow road from the jungle. I stood to the left of the narrow road as a stretcher with a man on it came down. The man's head was red with blood and he lay motionless. I asked the stretcher bearer in a low voice if the man was injured. He replied in a sorrowful voice, 'No, killed.' He was the X Company commander. Not more than five minutes had passed since he had put his hand on my shoulder and we had smiled at each other. I felt my hand and could feel the warmth of his when we had exchanged greetings. Now he was not with us any more. His spirit is somewhere and his dead body lay before me on the stretcher. This is the life of the front line, but how we men feel when one meets death so suddenly!

6 May: Sergeant Major Yazaki reported about the time of our leaving. Today I have a temperature and a headache. Mr Oniwa is having a difficult time with dysentery ... My picture has been developed, so I intend to send it home. Mr Fukuzaki wrote me that my daughter is getting big and that her eyes are large and round.

7 May: Seven o'clock in the morning we left Bagio. There is mountain after mountain. All of them stand several thousand feet high. The road cuts across the valley of these mountains and high cliffs hang below and above. It is the most dangerous road I have ever seen. One must shut one's eyes ... It has been made more difficult by the enemy's demolition work. It is 25RI [Japanese miles] long. We stayed over at the base of Towchi.

8 May: At 8.30 we left and walked about 5RI. We came to a place where a deep cliff invited our fall and death. If I miss one step, I will be at the bottom of the cliff. What makes it more difficult to cross at this point is that the enemy destroyed all the paths. Every step we took made us hate the enemy. We left five soldiers, Corporal Fujiwata and Private Junno to watch our supplies which we could not get through at this point. What would those Americans think if they could see 20 little Japanese passing this point under such a few men's command? We stayed overnight

at the lookout post at Tabatiko. Lieutenant Murai and Sergeant Major Yazaki stayed with us.

9 May: We left Tabatiko. On the way we faced the strong sun and a warm wind and it made us feel miserable. We marched 5RI ... and stayed overnight at a house belonging to an American. Many natives came to visit us. All of them were naked except for their red loincloths. I found one English-speaking native and we had a long and interesting conversation. I find that our cultural standards are far past theirs, but I believe that soon they will learn and accept our standards of culture.

10 May: We left at eight o'clock and I found a village after marching 2km. Our 7 Company was stationed here. The company is repairing a hanging bridge which the enemy destroyed before they left. I found Sergeant Major Nishimura healthy and strong. But I leaned that Sergeant Major Yano had become ill and died. A storm came and we got soaking wet.

11 May: We arrived at Bontock. I met Sub-Officer Hino and Private Ando. Both were well. Ando's duty here is head sentry. We stayed overnight due to the storm. We heard that Corporal Iishi and the soldiers who went to the hospital are getting better, but Yamaguchi is not critically ill. I fear more the malaria than enemy bullets.

12 May: Private Ando did me a kind service while we were staying here. Hirashi, a medical serviceman, and I left with two American prisoners to join the company, which is 5km west of here.

13 May: The company expects to stay here about ten days longer. The cost of a pig is about 35 yen and we have so little money. The sun is strong and every evening the storm comes, a sign that the rainy season is at the door.

14 May: We have joined the company and the storm has come again. At seven o'clock this evening the American prisoners must be taken to Sabanga. It is such an important task that I decided to take those prisoners myself. We started on the pitch-dark military road which had been damaged by the heavy rain. It was very dangerous from dropping stones and sliding dirt. The bridge had been washed away ...

15 May: We could not go on but came back to the Igot tribe. They are so black and wear only red loincloths. We cannot understand their language and we are having a terrible time. We have not eaten since yesterday and now we have to wait until the storm is over to proceed to Sabanga with the American prisoners.

16 May: I hear that a vehicle will come to take us to Sabanga. It has not come. We do not know what to do.

17 May: The Igot tribe, the Americans and our soldiers are living together at this station ... The rain falls for 16 hours every day and I am watching this power of nature with no feeling.

18 May: The red loinclothed native men and the under-skirted native women walk in on us. The life of these people is simple. They eat their food with their fingers and have no feeling for sanitation or beauty. Just living is their desire and nothing else. I am so surprised at finding people less sensitive than myself. I begin to feel that I, myself, am at the same level of these people who have no feeling but just to live. It is the feeling about myself since I came into the war.

19 May: Now I am living in the mountains. It is much easier for me to live if the river is clean ... Here the river is muddy and yellow. I hope we can leave with the prisoners for our garrison base soon.

20 May: I must stay at this Igot village to give the report to the coming squad. The coming squad has not come. Here I am with the American prisoners and a few soldiers and the natives. Suddenly, Lieutenant Sugano came in. He had been attacked and was being chased by the enemy. My heart understood his foreboding, and I felt sorry for him.

At this point the diary suddenly ends. Although the Americans had surrendered six weeks earlier, Kubota seems to have been captured. In the translated diary in the Imperial War Museum there are drawings showing the advance and the battles described, of the kind that usually accompanied the interrogations of prisoners of war. The translator also included information about Sub-Lieutenant Kumataro Kubota that would not have appeared in his diaries. So perhaps he survived the war. He may even have been reunited with his wife, son and little Chizuko, if they survived the bombing and shelling of Japan in 1945.

NEW GUINEA

On the day Kubota's diary broke off, Toshio Sato from Ikeda entered Saseho Naval Architecture Department. The following month he left for Truk in Micronesia, and from there went to New Guinea, to be employed as a translator of native languages attached to the navy. He wrote in his diary:

> 1 July: Reached Lae in New Guinea. In the harbour I saw a steam ship which was sunk, and heard that five others were sunk. Twenty-four of our men were killed by native troops. Many native spies were killed.

The Japanese forces in New Guinea were preparing for a big push on Port Moresby on the southeast coast, now the only remaining Allied base between Japan and Australia.

> 30 August: We moved into the jungle. I heard a shot. A few days ago natives captured an Australian second lieutenant. He was sentenced to be beheaded the day before yesterday.

More horrors were to follow.

> 8 September: ... A soldier told me that Tsukioka Butai that occupied Buna caught six or seven Australian men and women and cut their heads off one by one on the beach. There was a young girl of 16. She yelled and cried as they missed her head, but they cut her head by force. He said that it was a dreadful sight. The heads and bodies were thrown into the sea.

The captured diary of an unidentified Japanese soldier recorded yet more:

> 26 September: Discovered and captured the two prisoners who escaped last night in the jungle ... To prevent their escaping a second time pistols were fired at their feet, but it was difficult to hit them. Two prisoners were dissected while still alive by Medical Officer Yamaji and their livers were taken out, and for the first time I saw the internal organs of a human being. It was very informative.

A similar incident took place in Khandok:

> The man was tied to a tree outside the Hikari Kikan office. A Japanese doctor and four Japanese medical students stood

around him. They first removed the finger nails, then cutting open his chest, removed his heart, on which the doctor gave a practical demonstration.

And another unknown Japanese recorded witnessing what he described as a 'blood carnival' at Salamaua, New Guinea, on 29 March 1943:

All four of us (Technician Kurokawa, Nishiguchi, Yamata and myself) assembled in front of the HQ at 1500 hours. One of the two members of the crew of the Douglas which was shot down by anti-aircraft fire on the 18th, and who had been under cross-examination by the 7th Base Force for some days, had been returned to the Salamaua Garrison and it had been decided to kill him. Tai Commander Komai, when he came to the observation station today, told us personally that, in accordance with the compassionate sentiments of Japanese Bushido, he was going to kill the prisoner himself with his favourite sword. So we gathered to observe this. After we had waited a little more than ten minutes, the truck came along.

The prisoner, who was at the side of the guard house, is given his last drink of water, etc. The Chief Medical Officer, Tai Commander Komai and the HQ Platoon Commander come out of the officers' mess, wearing their military swords. The time has come, so the prisoner, with his arms bound and his long hair now cropped very close, totters forward. He probably suspects what is afoot; but he is more composed than I thought he would be. Without more ado, he is put on the truck and we set out for our destination.

I have a seat next to the Chief Medical Officer; about ten guards ride with us. To the pleasant rumble of the engine, we run swiftly along the road in the growing twilight. The glowing sun has set behind the western hills, gigantic clouds rise before the sun, and the dusk is falling all around. It will not be long now. As I picture the scene, we are about to witness, my heart beats faster.

I glance at the prisoner; he has probably resigned himself to his fate. As though saying farewell to the world, as he sits in the truck he looks about at the hills, at the sea, and seems deep in thought. I feel a surge of pity and turn my eyes away.

As we passed by the place where, last year, our lamented Han leader was cremated, Technician Nishiguchi must have been thinking about him too, for he remarked, 'It's a long time since we were here last.' It certainly is a long time. We could see the place every day from the observation post, but never got a chance to come. It is nearly a year since the Han leader was cremated. I was moved in spite of myself, and as I passed the place I closed my eyes and prayed for the repose of Shimizu's soul.

The truck runs along the sea shore. We have left the Navy guard sector behind us and now come to the Army guard sector. Here and there we see sentries in the grassy fields, and I thank them in my heart for their toil as we drive on. They must have got it in the bombing the night before last – there are great holes by the side of the road, full of water from the rain. In a little over 20 minutes, we arrive at our destination, and all get off.

Tai Commander Komai stands up and says to the prisoner, 'We are now going to kill you.' When he tells the prisoner that, in accordance with Japanese Bushido, he would be killed with a Japanese sword, and that he would have two or three minutes' grace, he listens with a bowed head. The flight-lieutenant [the prisoner] says a few words in a low voice. Apparently he wants to be killed with one stroke of the sword. I hear him say the word 'one' [in English]. The Tai Commander becomes tense and his face stiffens as he replies, 'Yes' [in English].

Now the time has come, and the prisoner is made to kneel on the bank of a bomb crater filled with water. He is apparently resigned. The precaution is taken of surrounding him with guards with fixed bayonets, but he remains calm. He even stretches out his neck and is very brave. When I put myself in the prisoner's place, and think that in one more minute it will be goodbye to this world, although the daily bombings have filled me with hate, ordinary human feelings make me pity him.

The Tai Commander has drawn his favourite sword. It is the famous Osamune sword that he showed us at the observation post. It glints in the light and sends a cold shiver down my spine. He taps the prisoner's neck lightly with the back of the blade, then raises it high above his head with both arms, and brings it down with a sweep.

I had been standing with my muscles tensed, but in that moment I closed my eyes.

Ssh! ... It must have been the sound of blood spurting from the arteries. With a sound as though something watery had been cut, the body falls forward. It is amazing – he had killed him with one stroke. The onlookers crowd forward. The head, detached from the trunk, rolls in front of it. Ssh! Ssh! ... The dark blood gushes out.

All is over. The head is dead white, like a doll. The savageness which I felt only a little while ago is gone, and now I feel nothing but the true compassion of Japanese Bushido. A senior corporal laughs loudly, 'Well, he will enter Nirvana now!' Then a superior seaman of the medical unit takes the Chief Medical Officer's Japanese sword and, intent on paying off old scores, turns the headless body on its back and cuts open the abdomen with one clean stroke. They are thick-skinned, these keto ['hairy foreigners' – a common term of opprobrium for white men] – even the skin of their bellies is thick. Not a drop of blood comes out of the body. It is pushed over into the crater at once and buried.

Now the wind blows mournfully and I see the scene again in my mind's eye. We get on to the truck again and start back. It is dark now. We get off in front of HQ. I say goodbye to Tai Commander Komai and climb up the hill with Technician Kurokawa. This will be something to remember all my life. If ever I get back alive it will make a good story to tell, so I have written it down.

The writer recorded that he wrote this account 'At Salamaua Observation Post, 30 March 1943 to the sound of midnight waves'. ATIS tried to identify the victim, and the translator noted: 'The prisoner killed today was an Air Force Flight-Lieutenant from Moresby. He was a young man, 23 this year, said to have been an instructor to the ATC at Moresby.' So the victim was not even a bomber pilot.

There were some displays of compassion too. On the morning of 18 May 1942, a Japanese soldier crossed the Ramu River in New Guinea. After attacking a village, only to find that the Americans had already fled, his raiding party got lucky.

Many natives from Waisha came to inform us that an American soldier was sleeping in a hut beyond the hill. With a determination not to let him escape this time, we advanced towards the hill. En route, we crossed a branch of the Waisha river. Since landing on New Guinea, this was the first time I've found such beautiful clear cold water. I washed my face with it. We had a native from Hoedei village guide us to where the American soldier was. By climbing up a steep hill and cautiously peering over, a small roof could be seen. Stretching my neck a little further, I saw a mosquito net and a rifle. At that moment, a native police boy got a glimpse of me and scurried headlong away. Immediately, the American soldier threw the mosquito net aside and began to flee like a bird. Just when I thought he had gotten away, Miike fired one shot, which hit the mark. We searched through the dead soldier's belongings and found a bible, a diary and a photo of his mother. Apparently he had malaria and was asleep. His mother is a woman with a very kind face. I don't know if he is her only son. How grieved she would be if she were to hear that her son was killed. Nevertheless, this is fate. A moment ago, he was probably reading his bible or thinking about his home. With one shot of the rifle which echoed through the Bismarck Range, he has gone to heaven. For many years he has been our enemy, but now that he has become a departed soul, we forgave him for the resentment we hold and buried him.

SUICIDE MISSIONS

Japanese soldiers were, of course, equally careless with their own lives. Suicide missions were common. At 0700 on 30 November 1942, Corporal Tanaka in New Guinea wrote a farewell note. It read:

To Giruma M.P. Tai members:
Thank you very much for your personal and public co-operation. Enemy attacks had been heavy from the 19 November. Today, 30 November, Battalion Commander Yamamoto and subordinates organized a suicide squad. Guard Leader Fujita and four men were included. Death is the ultimate honour. After my comrades and I are dead, please bury us in your leisure time. I ask this because it is

dishonourable to remain unburied. Please take care of your health and serve your country. I regret to say that Tai leader Nakayama is missing, and that we have no information regarding his whereabouts. The enemy trench mortar fire is increasing in intensity so I shall close. My best regards to you. Signed, Tanaka.

Those at home tried to keep up the troops' morale. The Voluntary Aid Organization of Hatano published *Home News*. The issue dated 6 December 1942 informed soldiers at the front:

Spring at home is just a farmer's spring. Bathed in the rays of the spring sun, the farming village awakens more and more to activity; the sight of the villagers swinging their hoes increases daily. The villagers, in the battle for production of the home front, are rising up to a man and putting their hearts and souls in the execution of the prefectual requirements.

The school principal's contribution reassured the soldiers that there would be plenty more to follow in their footsteps:

To the Officers and Men of the Imperial Forces.
It is now two years since the regulations covering National Schools were promulgated whilst four years have passed since the regulations covering Youth Schools became operative. In the case of National Schools, instruction is that the Imperial Way must form the basis of national life while in Youth Schools the order is that appropriate training must be given to the soldiers of tomorrow, but I fear that my ability has been insufficient adequately to carry out these instructions. However, with all due humility I send my congratulations for your brilliant military achievements ...
The sentimental feelings of the new instructors ran high over here. Lastly, in sending you this news, I pray for increase in national prestige and the continued military glory of you all. (Signed) Yamamoto, Minoru, School Principal.

But most news came in the form of personal letters. On 20 April 1942 Shigeru Nishimura's sister wrote to him about the Doolittle Raid two days earlier. He would not have got the letter for some time though. It was addressed care of the Central China Expeditionary Force, Shochiku Butai, Matsu, No. 4 Butai, Hachisuka Tai, but was captured in the Buna area of New Guinea. It read:

> To my dear brother:
> Are you in the best of health? I am worrying about you. On the mainland, the cherry blossoms have already fallen and mountains have changed to green and are getting darker after each rainfall. Parents, brothers, sisters and myself are in the best of health and maintaining our home as usual while you are away ...
>
> How is your malaria? I dreamed about you every two or three days for the past two weeks. In the dream, you were drinking tea with relish. In last night's dream, you were talking with me in the guest room ... However, I believe you are conquering the heat and doing well. Your picture is always looking affectionately at us from the Tokonoma. I would like to follow your footsteps and do something worthwhile.
>
> The test for our morale came at 12.30 on 18 April, when we received the first air raid since the Greater East Asian War began. It was on Saturday. Air-raid sirens sounded from hill to hill in Central Japan. The army and civilians, acting under unified command, put up such an effective defence that the enemy planes did not penetrate the Chugoku area. Enemy planes fled without causing any damage to our locality. Then the all-clear was given.
>
> Enemy planes appeared over Tokyo, Nagoya, Kobe, Yokkaichi, Miye prefecture and Wakayama prefecture. They dropped incendiary bombs on hospitals, schools and residential districts. Their immoral act is similar to the two attacks made previously on our hospital ships. I am very angry at them.
>
> But, there is no need for you to worry about us because the people on the home front are trained and well prepared against such attacks. Women, children and even old and sick men dashed to dispose of the incendiaries as they fell. Substantial damage was thus avoided. Bombs fell in only three places in the Kobe and Nagoya areas, but in Tokyo, especially to the Kawasaki area, many houses suffered more than five hits apiece. There were many instances of girls who put out fires and saved the district from disaster.

Students of the girls' school and university acted with great calmness throughout. The preparations we had made minimized the losses suffered. We shall seek revenge upon the enemy who made low strafing attacks and killed schoolchildren. We will share pleasure and hardship together, and prepare against further air raids. We are determined to win this Greater East Asia War at all costs, in spite of what the enemy thinks.

Anti-aircraft units shot down nine enemy planes over the Capitol. The enemy, suffering defeat after defeat, will attempt further nuisance raids. Therefore, it is obvious that we shall have to defend our country with a firm determination in order to protect our homeland of three thousand years ...

Please do not worry about us. We wish you to do your best. I pray from a distant fatherland for your success in war. I inquired about our relatives in Tokyo and Kobe and I believe they were well. I will write you again. Goodbye, your sister.

American-educated Dr Kawai, the chief editorial writer of the *Nippon Times*, also witnessed the Doolittle Raid and the bombing that followed:

There was a big change with the beginning of the air raids. There was real terror then. This, however, did not begin with the Doolittle raid which the people looked upon as a curiosity and they did not even bother to go to the shelters. At the same time there was considerable criticism of the army for letting the Doolittle raiders get through. The sirens did not even go off until the planes were over the city and the sky was full of anti-aircraft fire. I was out and saw the firing, but thought it was just practice, although it seemed strange to be practising with what appeared to be live shells. Then I saw the planes and realized it was a raid. Then finally the sirens were sounded. There was considerable criticism after that.

9
RETREAT TO YASUKUNI: DEFEAT ON THE ISLANDS

In March 1942, the Japanese had landed on the northeast coast of New Guinea at Salamaua and Lae. The next objective was Port Moresby on the southern shore, but to reach it they would have to cross the Owen Stanley Range, which rises to over 2,700m (9,000ft). In May 1942 Japanese newspaperman Seitchi Shiojiri joined them. He claimed to be the first war correspondent the Imperial Army had allowed to visit an operational area. Their advance, he noted, was slowed by the 'stubborn resistance of the Australians'. They also found themselves perilously low on supplies.

> When we were near the top of Mount Iaraba, the troops ahead were suddenly thrown into disorder and the pace of advance slowed down. The men scattered about in small groups, shouting at each other. Soon word came round that we had got splendid rations left by the Australians. When the soldiers came near what seemed to be the mountain top, they all left their path and started to run for their lives towards it. I found myself running too; the hungry man in me had got wind of something nice to eat. I was ashamed. I was fully aware how I was disgracing myself. But I kept on running. Nothing held me back. The soldiers I passed, one and all, had their mouths full of something delicious, their pockets bulging, their heads carrying all sorts of beautiful cans. The men coming up from below, dead tired from lack of sleep, suddenly came to themselves at the sight and rushed up the steep slope with amazing briskness. Soon I came out of the thick jungle into a small open place at the top. There stood a tall thatched Papuan hut, at the door of which I saw great confusion. Swarms of excited soldiers jostling and scrambling in and out. Evidently the hut had been used by the Australians as a storehouse. There were mountains of cans piled up – butter, cheese, milk, corned beef and everything. A number of cans of Arnold's biscuits were scattered here and there on the

bare ground. What a feast all those things were to us! It seemed
as though we had suddenly landed in fairyland. We had run out
of the meagre rice ration long before, and had trudged on day
'and night eating only tasteless army crackers with occasional
wild potatoes and papayas. The majority of the unit coming from
the farming villages of Kuchi prefecture had never seen or tasted
anything like this in their lives. I saw some of the soldiers who
had had their fill in the hut throwing away half-opened cans of
corned beef with evident distrust. I helped myself to Arnold's
biscuits and butter, thinking that I had not tasted anything so
fine for at least two years. Here in the Papuan mountains the
standard of living was higher than in Japan! I thought that I saw
something of the appalling power of Anglo-American civilization
that Japan had so recklessly challenged.

The feast was abruptly ended by an enemy plane, which strafed the hut. For
the next few days, they trudged on through jungle in the 'half light of dusk'
even at midday. 'The humidity was almost unbearable,' said Shiojiri. It rained
almost all day and all night until they were soaked to the skin and shivering
with the cold. Then they reached Efogy ravine, where the Australians and the
Japanese vanguard had engaged in hand-to-hand fighting.

There were about 200 bodies, Japanese and Australian, scattered
in the ravine. Here and there, on both sides of the path of blood-
red clay which ran through the cypress forest, I saw a great many
Japanese and Australians lying dead. One of them had a twisted
neck and broken legs, with his face covered all over with mud
and blood. Another was in a crouching posture, his face resting
at the foot of a tree. A third was lying on his back like a fallen
tree, and a fourth was shot through his forehead in a prone
shooting position, his gun left on the ground in front of him.
Another again was hanging on a tree over the edge of a cliff;
another lying with his upper body in a ditch; and another leaning
against a tree with his body bent forward – men in all postures
and conditions showing how desperately they fought and fell.

Shiojiri felt that if they had fought the enemy out in the open as they had
in China, they would have stood no chance, as their forces would have been

destroyed by Allied aircraft. As it was, they had numerical superiority over the Australian forces. They had more heavy weapons and, due to their low standard of living, were better able to withstand the privations of the jungle. These factors should have given them a decisive advantage.

> But when we reached Mount Efogybia, we had lost nearly 80 per cent of our men killed or wounded in action, or disabled by illnesses. Besides we had almost run out of food and ammunition. Our supply line by way of Buna had practically been cut off by enemy submarines and aeroplanes. We were indeed in a hopeless position. The only thing that kept up morale was the thought of Port Moresby.

Then came news that the Americans had landed on Guadalcanal in the Solomon Islands, denying the Japanese troops air support and further threatening their supply lines. They received orders from the area commander in Rabaul to abandon their attack on Port Moresby and withdraw to defensive positions in the mountains. That night Shiojiri saw the elderly commander, Major-General Noril, 'sitting solemnly upright on his bed, his face emaciated, his grey hair reflecting the dim light of the candle'.

> Lieutenant Colonel Tanaka, his staff officer, sat face to face with him, also on a mat. Two lonely shadows were cast on the dirty wet canvas.
> 'I'm not going back, not a step! Are you going back, Tanaka? How can we abandon this position after all the blood the soldiers had shed and the hardship they have endured? I cannot give such an order.'
> Noril grasped his samurai sword that lay beside him and, drawing a little closer to his staff officer, added in a biting tone: 'I will not retreat an inch. I'd rather disguise myself as a native of these mountains and stay here.'

But then orders telling them to return to the coast at Buna arrived from Tokyo, 'authorized by the Emperor himself – His Majesty's order had to be obeyed'. Nevertheless, Shiojiri reported, the army was close to mutiny.

> The order to retreat crushed the spirit of the troops which had been kept up through sheer pride. For a time the soldiers remained

stupefied among the rocks on the mountainside. Then they began to move, and once in retreat they fled for dear life. None of them had ever thought that a Japanese soldier would turn his back on the enemy. But they were actually beating the retreat. There was no denying that. As soon as they realized the truth, they were seized with an instinctive desire to live. Neither history nor education had any meaning to them now. Discipline was completely forgotten. Each tried for his life to flee faster than his comrades, and the confusion was worse than it had been at the supply dump.

The Australians were soon in hot pursuit. At every jungle clearing the Japanese were attacked from the air. The supply situation grew more critical. And there was no living off the land. Fields far to each side of the track were already stripped bare. Men lay by the wayside dying of starvation, but their comrades could not risk their own lives to help them. They plunged on over towering waterfalls and through the sunless forest, soaked with rain and humidity.

And in that eternal twilight lay numberless bodies of men scattered here and there – men so recently killed in action had already begun to rot. A nasty smell, like that of burning old cloth, filled the air, giving us a stifling sensation of nausea. It was the smell of dead bodies – rotting human bodies lying in all possible postures, some on their faces, some on their backs, some on their sides, some in a squatting position. What struck me as being very strange was that they all had on their bellies something like a heap of sand, black, glittering and wriggling all the time. I approached one of the bodies and found that it was a heap of maggots bred in the belly, where the rotting process seems to set in before any other part of the body. They were little creatures about an inch long, with numerous slender legs like those of a centipede and closely lined across their backs which glittered like black lacquered armour. They crowded in a heap on the belly, which had fallen in, pushing, fighting, dropping to the ground and scrambling up again, eager to bite into the rotten bowels. All the bodies had their pants lying flat on the ground, their legs having melted away. In one case, both hair and skin had gone from the head, leaving the skull exposed as a white birch split open. In another case all the skin and flesh had melted away from the chest and the ribs were gleaming like chalk in the dusky jungle.

When I was about to turn a corner, where the jungle cast a deeper gloom on the path, I saw something white among the trees moving noiselessly towards me like a ghost. Could it be one of the dead? I stood transfixed.

'Give me something to eat,' said the ghost in my ear in a feeble, whispery voice. 'Give me something to eat.'

I looked at him closely. Surely he was not a ghost; he was alive. His pale face, white as a sheet, was bordered sharply by black hair. His raw-boned, dark brown body was covered in part by a piece of white cloth. Probably he had been lying almost dead on the ground for some time and at the sound of approaching steps had risen to his feet by a superhuman effort and staggered out into the path.

'Give me something to eat,' he repeated over and over in his weak, husky voice, stretching out a thin hand which trembled like a piece of paper. I took a half-eaten rice-ball and a tiny taro out of my kit, put them in his outstretched hands and dashed away without ever turning my head ...

At last, after about ten days, we managed to get back to Mount Iarada which stood at the northern end of the path across the Owen Stanley Range. Here the narrow path was congested with stretchers carrying the wounded soldiers back to the field hospital on the coast. There were so many of them that they had been delayed here since before the wholesale retreat began. Some of them were on makeshift stretchers, each made of two wooden poles with a blanket or tent-cloth tied to them with vines and carried by four men. They had slow and laborious progress, constantly held up by steep slopes. The soldiers on them, some lying on their faces, some on their backs, emitted groans of pain at every bump. In some cases, the blood from their wounds was dripping through the canvas onto the ground. Some looked all but dead, unable even to give out a groan ...

As soon as we got out of the mountains into flat country we were exposed to more vigorous air attacks. We had a most terrible one by the Kumusi river, which flows along the bottom of Owen Stanley Range.

The river was 100m (330ft) wide but the bridge built over it by the Yokoyama Engineer Unit had been destroyed so often that they had given up rebuilding it. Instead, they slung a wire rope over the river and ferried supplies across with a basket and pulley.

> Some of the American fliers performed the wonderful feat of cutting this thin rope in the air with machine-gun fire.
>
> 'A circus in the air!' said a young engineer platoon commander, who was a student of the Engineering department of the Tokyo Imperial University. He spoke in pure admiration of the daring and skilful performance of the enemy fliers, without a shade of hostility in his tone. There was no longer the least suspicion of hostile feeling or fighting spirit in any unit or soldier. The only thing that occupied our minds was to get back to the coast as soon as possible.
>
> We were kept waiting for several days near the Kumusi, exposed night and day to air raids. Then, one dark night, we left the hut in the jungle and crept to the river. The engineers had made a big guide-light which illuminated the swift current. We waited in a long line and boarded a small folding boat which carried six of us at a time. When we got to the other bank, we pushed on through the darkness as fast as we could.

Soon after this, the Australians took the river crossing. The remaining Japanese tried to cross further downstream on rafts. Many, including Major-General Noril, drowned.

NOT A SINGLE LINE OF NEWS

Shiojiri made it to the coast and back to Rabaul where he met other newspapermen who had just escaped the fighting on Guadalcanal.

> We were not permitted to send a single line of news to Japan ... On top of that, I was told that the truth about the campaign in New Guinea would never have a chance of being recorded in the war history of the Army.

The journalists asked to be sent back to Japan. The Imperial government refused. The army did not want them in Rabaul, so they were shipped to Manila where they could be 'canned up', arriving just in time to enjoy the Filipinos' Christmas celebrations. The rest of Noril's force was left to starve on the beaches around Buna. Then American Marines landed and the survivors were pushed back into the jungle, where they perished to a man.

> While I was laid up in bed in a corner of Manila, trembling with malarial fever and morbid fear, and haunted by a vivid picture of Hell enacted on the coast of Buna, the whole city seemed to be intoxicated with the gay civilization left by the Americans, as if all were well under the sun.

Another survivor of the New Guinea campaign was Colonel Shigera Sugiyama. Interrogated after the war, he said:

> I am convinced that the result of the many years of military training of the Japanese from childhood was revealed in this New Guinea campaign. The suffering and hardship endured by the very last man, I know, can never be equalled by the Japanese people again – not for many years anyway. The reason that enabled these men to attain this result was the fact that every man was determined to fight, even to die, for the Emperor. It was life to the men. No man ever forgot the Emperor, even at death, and whenever they suffered, each man remembered that he was fighting for the Emperor ...

He also gave full credit to the Australians.

> The enemy suffered as badly as we did – not for food or equipment but there was the fact that they fought in the dark jungle.

Both sides also suffered from the same diseases, but being better supplied with food and medicines the Australians were better able to survive them. The chief medical officer of the 18th Army on New Guinea, Major-General Yoshio Niroce, found Japanese troops suffered from beri-beri, caused by malnutrition, as well as malaria. 'Since we did not have the necessary food for the treatment, the majority of malnutrition patients died,' he said.

> As for contagious diseases, we did not find any cholera and typhoid cases, but there were quite a number of amoebic dysentery cases (caused by stagnant water) and a few cases of bacterial dysentery. Many of the Japanese in New Guinea suffered from skin diseases such as scabies, tines, tropical ulcers, etc. Despite common medical conception that only the natives are susceptible

to framboesia, there was one case of this among our troops. The reason why we had many cases of skin disease was, I believe, that before the Japanese went to New Guinea, they had been accustomed to taking baths daily, but during the New Guinea campaign they could not take baths often enough to keep their bodies clean. It would have been difficult to make hot baths without being discovered by enemy planes and the Japanese were forced to take baths in the rivers. We did not find any cases of venereal diseases in New Guinea. This, I think, can be attributed to the fact that there were no women in New Guinea ... The Japanese soldiers who were seriously wounded in battle had to be left to die due to inadequate facilities for their evacuation. Many men who could have been saved by proper treatment had to be left at the battle front because no adequate medical treatment could be given. The majority of the patients in the Line of Communications hospital were sick ones rather than those wounded in battle, by an approximate ratio of 166 to one.

THE GUADALCANAL OBJECTIVE

It was clear that the Japanese had overstretched themselves. The navy had already been defeated at the Battle of Midway in June. As the US went on the offensive in the Pacific, its first objective was the airfield the Japanese were building on Guadalcanal. A captured diary described the terrible fate of the Japanese soldiers left to defend it:

24 December 1942: Since the 14th two officers of the 2nd Company have gone insane. They probably had become pessimistic about the war situation. There is no other change in conditions. We passed the day as usual.

25 December: Today is Christmas day. Therefore we had many presents from the enemy such as intense bombardment by artillery and naval guns. On the other hand, not one of our planes came from the new airfield which was completed on the 15th. Even the soldiers in the front lines have become very disgusted and do not even talk about our planes any more. The 1st and 3rd Battalion (strength 90 men), commanded by the Usui unit commander are looking forward to New Year's Day in the hope of getting supplies.

26 December: There are lice here and whenever we have time these days to hunt for these. My strength is exhausted and my ordinary pulse [at rest] is around 99, which surprises me very much.

A normal pulse rate is between 50 and 85.

28 December: My body is so exhausted that one go of rice is all that I can eat, and walking is very difficult. No relief comes for this unit. The army doctor will not even send us to the rear. At present we are very sick men. Even if we were relieved, not one of us may recover, in fact, we are left to die from exhaustion and malnutrition rather than from bullets.

31 December: Since the 28th not a single grain of rice has been distributed, and during this time three pieces of hard tack were issued. Today there were three cigarettes and only a bite of nutrition ration ...

1 January 1943: During these days of the New Year on Guadalcanal Island, we have lived on one piece of hard tack, and this morning got one go of rice. In the evening, one compressed ration was divided between two. Now we are eating rice gruel twice a day, and sleeping in trenches as we are not able to walk.

2 January: The enemy has finally become very active and the front lines are dangerous. I wonder if that relief will come about the middle of the month. It seems that friendly planes will be coming over after the 15th. Sergeant Sato Kame died of illness.

3–4 January: The enemy is getting extremely active and the front lines are dangerous. I wonder if that relief will come ...

10 January: Enemy bombardment becomes increasingly intense. We can hold out for one more week. My body is in such a condition that I can barely walk. Food is five shaku (half a go) of rice and some compressed rations. This makes one month that we have been eating just rice gruel.

13 January: At 5.30 this morning we received artillery fire. First Lieutenant Oyara. Superior Private Abe and Lance Corporal Senori were killed. Lance Corporal Watave was wounded. Kato and I were the only ones left from the 1st MG. Won't relief for the unit come soon?

Apparently not, as the Japanese had already taken the decision to withdraw from Guadalcanal. The diary of First Lieutenant Okajima, who arrived on Guadalcanal on 15 November 1942, was also captured.

24 December: Wakuda Noboru died of illness. That may be because he was unreasonably overworked.

25 December: Sawada and Uchida died of illness. In the end, those of us of weak will will die. He was always most eager to drink water.

26 December: Asabo Kasuo also died of illness. Malaria fever affected his mind and he acted peculiarly. After his meal he died suddenly. This death increased the large number of those killed in action and from disease to 18 men. This makes approximately the total of losses we received in the occupation of Hong Kong and Java. Even in the face of the enemy, the men's minds were entirely occupied with the thought of eating. We are waiting for the spring sprouts to come out, and we dream of the joy of reducing Guadalcanal. Moreover, the airfield is finished and friendly planes will come over in large numbers.

27 December: Oba Fumio died of illness. It was not that he lacked energy, but he was drenched by rains which come regularly every afternoon in this life in the jungle.

28 December: Yamamoto Kyoicki died from a wound, such soldiers with weak wills are not good, for they die from slight wounds. His wound was trifling with hardly any bleeding. Now the casualties are 25 men.

29 December: First Lieutenant Tammy died of the wound he got the day before. Without seeing the fall of Guadalcanal, his spirit slipped eternally into the jungle. My tears overflow.

30 December: By the 15th of next month transportation of supplies and troops will be carried out, and we shall again have air superiority. After the 16th, units from the rear will pass us, and after preparatory bombardments by planes and artillery will carry out a general attack. In two months all Guadalcanal will return to our hands. Then the enemy will not be able to hold Tulagai. Then our combined fleet will concentrate in the Tulagai area. I believe that the decisive battle between the US and Japan will end in a

complete victory for Japanese in the bright spring of 1943 and will be an everlasting light in military history.

1 January: Two officers of the company have died. One is ill and one is at the front. There is no one to be my rival as company commander. I went to see the company sergeant major and senior sergeant and had a long talk. I learned many things which I would not ordinarily have learned, such as the deficiency of ordinary training in recruits, deficiency of training in interior guard duties and lack of education. As company commander there is much of this that I can put to good use.

2 January: I am waiting for the battalion commander, Major Nojiri, and I am anxious to see what kind of person he is.

3 January: Rensio was ill, I stayed at battalion headquarters. The total of those who have died is 31.

4 January: Supplies are gradually improving and we only have to endure this for ten days.

5 January: In the evening the main force of the battalion arrived: although it is called the main force, it consists of only 59 men. The battalion must have taken a very serious beating.

7 January: Thirty-six more men departed for a battalion of Oke unit.

9 January: Hearing of conditions in each company from the NCO, it seems supplies are not coming in. Characteristics are revealed which are not known under ordinary conditions, such as the true nature of human beings. In a certain company it is said that the NCOs ate twice as much and the officers three times as much as the men. A certain battalion commander received 100 cigarettes to divide among his men but only gave one or two to his company commander and he lost almost all of his usual prestige. Thanks to my actions of equality like an ordinary soldier the NCOs of the company thanked me, as the supplies were starting to come in smoothly they brought me various extra things. There was good feeling all around.

10 January: Major Nishizura again drew men from the reserve unit this afternoon, although I am commander of the main force of the company there are only 19 men in all. It is terrible to see the electric lights go on at an enemy airfield ...

11 January: By artillery fire three were killed and four wounded. It is too much to receive naval bombardment also. In four days the 3rd is expected to land. The number of men is now 12.

16 January: I heard one of the enemy talking busily in Japanese over a loudspeaker. He was probably telling us to come out. What fools the enemy are. The Japanese army will stick it out to the end. This position must be defended with our lives. There was no artillery shelling because of the broadcast. The enemy is broadcasting something vigorously at a distance. It will probably have no effect at all.

17 January: According to the enemy broadcast, today they are to attack our positions. However, we have no fear. I went to battalion headquarters and saw the enemy propaganda sheets which were found in First Lieutenant Kasahara's area. The writing was poor. The enemy artillery shelling became fiercer and fiercer and the company's area is riddled with craters – like a bee's nest. The artillery stopped at 1500, and then we suffered from the rain leaking into the foxhole.

18 January: About seven o'clock a messenger from the Hachi company came and said that there would be a meeting of unit commanders. I should like to make a suggestion but the battalion commander would probably not make use of it. Sergeant Major Muri gave his opinion on some communication matters. I became angry and told him to just do his own duties. In the evening the battalion commander came to inspect the company, so I expressed the opinions of all of us to him at that time. He told us not to worry because everything would be all right.

19 January: Ants' nests are good to eat when one is starving ... I received some meat from Battalion Headquarters. My orderly is sick and I had to cook it myself. Artillery began to fire about 1100 and there was an enemy with light machine-gun, I believe they got a surprise. I felt dazed and semi-conscious because of my empty stomach. At 1330 I prepared my equipment to put in my haversack so that it can be packed at a moment's notice. It will be so heavy that I don't think I'll be able to carry it because of my run-down condition. Only my spirit will keep me going. A messenger from

headquarters reported that part of the 8th Company's position was occupied by the enemy and told us to be on the alert.

20 January: I heard that the 5th company commander died yesterday. The 8th machine-gun company has withdrawn a little and in the evening I prepared my equipment to be carried.

21 January: I'm sad at having to leave this foxhole in which I have lived so long.

And there the diary ends.

Things were just as bad for the Japanese all over the Pacific. According to a 1946 interrogation report:

> The average Japanese soldier eats about 700 grams a day ... The allowance of rice per man per day was approximately 200 grams.

However, in places where there was no fighting it was possible to live off the land. According to Colonel Kazuyoshi Obata on Hollandia (now Jayapura):

> We used flour from coconut trees and herbs from the mountains and fields. We dried salt at the shore and either detonated grenades ourselves off-shore or waited until after Allied bombings to gather up dynamited fish.

But few places had it so good. Out in the jungle, Mitsuo Ragino of the 29th Field Hospital wrote:

> 28 December: ... Enemy planes have been flying over frequently. Heard about Tabe receiving sweets and my stomach yearned for some. Received about eight shaku of rice. Due to lack of rain, the well dried up. Went to get water from the stream. On the way the jungles were full of dead, killed by shrapnel. There is something awful about the smell of the dead. The planes that fly overhead are enemy planes and the guns that roar day and night continuously are also those of the enemy. When considering these conditions, we must have hope for the future. Even though I know we are members of the Imperial Army, there are times when things look very black. I definitely have that feeling, but it is useless to think of these things. I must do my best to the last with the noble spirit of dying for the Emperor. Was a little late and could not treat Hagino and take care

of him. I cannot leave him behind. I have decided to stay. I do not think for a minute that this is the wrong thing to do.

At the present time, all officers, even though there is such a scarcity of food, eat relatively well. The condition is one in which the majority are starving. This is indeed a deplorable state of affairs for the Imperial Army. I took out the picture of my parents and looked at it. Ah, I wonder how things are at home. Artillery shelling commenced again towards evening.

29 December: Last night's gun-fire was fierce but at dawn we were still unharmed. As it grew light, enemy planes came. The sound of rifle-fire seemed very close. What a discouraging and miserable state of affairs – especially with the New Year just ahead ... What is going to happen to us? I pray to the morning sun that our situation of battle will be reversed. All of the patrol unit has fled and, at the present time, there are only four of us – the platoon leader, Makano, Hagino and myself. There isn't a single person who will come to help. I am in difficulty since I took over Hagino who is a stretcher case. I pray only for divine aid. I pray with the charm of the clan deity in my hand.

ATTACK ON DAMPIER STRAIT

Bunroku Yamamoto was an engineer on the *Uranami*, one of eight destroyers protecting a convoy of cargo vessels carrying some 20,000 men destined for Lae in New Guinea. On 2 March 1943 it was attacked by some 280 Allied aircraft in the Dampier Strait between New Britain and Umboi Island.

The attack continued for around 13 minutes ... The greater part of the Japanese destroyers and convoy were in flames and sinking. Those in the water were crying for help. At first, we lowered ropes and pulled them up. However, this method did not progress satisfactorily. We then used the boats which had been assigned to us. These were collapsible, made from two plywood sections, the bow and stern, which were joined. An engine was attached to the stern, which I operated. We were carrying out rescue work when another air attack occurred.

There were three Allied air attacks that day. The 20 Japanese fighters assigned to protect the ships were hopelessly outnumbered and the entire convoy, with the exception of two destroyers, was sunk. Of the 200 men on his collapsible, Yamamoto was the only survivor.

Another survivor from the convoy was Takeo Yamagisawa. With the help of a lifebelt, he made it ashore after 11 days at sea.

> The island was a place where walking was impossible due to the steep, stony cliffs. I was found by the natives who showed me where to get water. I had to eat the same food as the natives. They fed me enough but it was of no use as Japanese need rice, so I was in a weak physical condition, barely able to walk. I stayed with the natives for about half a year when the Allied forces arrived and told the natives they were not supposed to hide any Japanese. After that, they did not take care of me. I left the natives and went to an area that was grassy and slept there ... I was betrayed and taken to the Australians by the natives. I could not resist as I was weak and had malaria. They took me to a barter station. There I was given malaria medicine and had my hair cut and washed.

Uchiro Watanabe from Ikeda, Hiroshima prefecture, was also captured after being shipwrecked and in a diary written in a messenger's book taken in Singapore in 1942 he outlined his ordeal:

> 3 March 1943: Our convoy was attacked by 40 enemy planes in formation at 0800 hours. Almost all of the ships were sunk and the troops aboard dispersed in all directions. Seven of us were able to reach a collapsible boat, which was strafed by enemy planes two hours later. We gave up all hope of life then, but nothing happened.
>
> 4 March: The sea was very calm today. Checked the provisions carried by each man. We found that we had four canteens filled with water, six pieces of compressed food, eight cans, nine bars of sweet paste, four bags of condiments, four bags of dried noodles and one can of oranges. To avoid the danger of exposing ourselves to enemy air raids, we tried to get out of the tidal current. We improvised two oars, one with the shovel we had picked up.
>
> 5 March: We were hoping that we might be rescued by dawn but we were disappointed. We now faced a shortage of water. I ordered the others to drink some water if necessary. We sighted a triangular island on the horizon to the south. We did our best to

reach this island, but due to lack of water and the direct rays of the sun, we became weak as time went on. Two men at a time rowed in one-hour spells, day and night.

6 March: We neared the island considerably, after pulling hard since yesterday without rest or water. By this time, our mouths were so dry that the spittle hardly formed. And then, as if by the grace of Heaven, a squall came. We filled up the four canteens with water. A smile was now seen on the face of each man. We gave thanks to God, and gained confidence in ourselves that we might be able to land today. However we were afraid that it might turn out to be a hostile island or may be uninhabited, so we planned to land at night. Although we did our best to reach the island, we could not do so despite our hard work the whole night long.

7 March: We hoped to reach the island at 2pm. We met an enemy patrol plane, but nothing happened. We were surprised to meet Sergeants Makamura and Saikawa and others – nine men in total – on landing on the island. They all looked healthy, unlike we seven. The chief of the natives informed us that this island is located to the west of the strait between New Guinea and the island of New Britain. We gave unwanted things to the chief. He was so pleased that in return he gave us ten coconuts. Because of the strict want over the island, we planned to leave for the second destination five days later. In the daytime, we prepared for our next stop in the jungle and collected food.

But they were not to move on. That day, 7 March 1943, Uchiro Watanabe was captured and taken to Port Hennessy. He had been lucky. A Japanese soldier captured on Goodenough Island in March 1943 recalled being attacked while in the water:

Blast from bursting bombs was felt up to a kilometre away and shook the body heavily. Concussion from bombs bursting in water was much worse, as it travelled through the water and administered a sickening jar to the abdomen. Allied bombing of life rafts was responsible for many deaths from water concussion and was certainly a primary factor in lowering the resistance of men clinging to life rafts.

Making it through the Dampier Strait to New Guinea offered no safe haven, as another captured diary revealed:

> 26 May: Since our landing the enemy has had command of the air. It has been a tragic three months. During that period the enemy airplanes have dominated the skies over our lines appearing as often as ten times a day and never less than three times, either by daylight or by night. Many of us were exasperated to the pitch of cold fury at this and were thirsting for vengeance ...

Allied air superiority after the Battle of Midway was a constant scourge to Japanese soldiers in the Pacific. As early as November 1942, a diarist in Giruwa noted: 'Today's bombing was so terrific I did not feel as if I was alive.' And an infantryman on New Georgia recalled:

> I will remember this New Year under the title of the 'American New Year'! The unceasing Boeings, North Americans and Airocobras! Regardless of what one might say, the Boeing is the seed of trouble and agony. Three and a half hours of bombing during the night affected my nerves.

The strafing was just as bad as the bombing. A prisoner from Cape Wampun said that 'bullets seemed to search for a soldier until they hit him'. Another soldier recorded:

> The enemy air raids are terrible. I can't lift my head because of the fierce bombing and strafing. I eat potatoes and live in a hole and cannot speak in a loud voice. I live the life of a mud rat or some similar creature.

As the Allies tightened the noose around the Japanese air base at Rabaul on New Britain, the situation grew desperate. 'Every day we have raids,' wrote one Japanese serviceman. 'If there are none during the day, they come at night. It is becoming unbearable.' 'Everyone has a helpless feeling,' wrote another. And it was taking its toll:

> The majority of soldiers were rattled by air raids. As soon as the sound of planes was heard, all rushed to trenches and shelters and cupped their hands over their ears.

At Arawe Island to the south of New Britain, a private wrote during a raid: 'I expect this will be the end of my diary writing.' It was. And there was worse to come, as a superior private at Kamiri recorded:

> In preparing for enemy landings, we are conserving ammunition rather than expending it in fighting enemy aeroplane attacks; hence the enemy planes bomb and strafe us from very low altitudes. I would like to go back home once more, and in one piece. Many others have voiced similar thoughts.

In Burma, the RAF dominated the skies. A diary captured there said:

> Today the enemy aircraft came over twice. According to an old soldier, that is the smallest number of raids that we had so far in a day ... Today the weather has been fine and the enemy has given us no rest at all, bombing and machine-gunning divisional headquarters throughout the day. If this continues we shall soon want to be withdrawn. I started praying that all was well with the family at home ... Rain stopped play this morning, but the weather cleared up in the afternoon and the bombers concentrated on the steel bridge to our rear for four and a half hours. I have lost count of the number of times that the bridge has been bombed. If only we had some aircraft of our own we could ward off the majority of these attacks ... I get so scared when we are being bombed that I would do anything to get home to my wife and family.

Under constant air attack, those in the front line clutched at straws:

> Newspapers in Japan publish such slogans as 'one more plane', 'send at least one more plane to the front'. Being in the front line I realize the reason for this. I pray that people on the home front will exceed American and British production. Enemy aircraft have come again and are circling overhead. They will probably bomb us.

ISLAND CAPTURE

The Japanese had captured the American islands of Attu and Kiska in the Aleutians on 7 June 1942. The following year the US decided to take them back. On 1 June a diary was taken from the body of a dead Japanese medical officer, who had studied in California for five years to became a doctor. His diary records the fall of Attu.

12 May: 0155. Carrier-based plane flew over. We fired at it. There is a fog and the summit is clear. We evacuated to the summit. Air raids carried out frequently until we heard gun noise. It is naval gun firing. Prepared battle equipment. Information, American transports, about 41, began landing at Hakkai Missaki. Twenty boats landed at Massacre Bay and it seems that they are going to unload heavy equipment. Day's activities: Air raid, naval gun firing, landing of US forces.

13 May: Battle. The US forces landed at Shiba Deia and Massacre Bay, and the enemy has advanced to the bottom of the Misumi Yama from Shiba Deia. We have engaged them. On the other hand, Massacre Bay is defended by only one platoon, but upon the unexpected attack the AA machine cannon was destroyed and we have withdrawn. In a night attack we have captured 20 enemy rifles. There is mountain artillery gun firing. Approximately 15 patients came in the field hospital attached to the Arai Engineer Unit.

14 May: Battle. Our two submarines from Kiska assisting us have greatly damaged enemy ships. First Lieutenant Suy Uki died from shots from rifle. Continuous flow of wounded in the field hospital. In the evening the US Forces used gas but no damage was done on account of the strong wind. We took refuge in the trenches in the daytime and took care of the patients during bombardment. Enemy strength must be up to a division. Our desperate defence is holding up well.

15 May: Battle. Continuous flow of casualties in our field hospital caused by the fierce bombardment of enemy land and naval forces. The enemy has a great number of Negroes and Indians. The West Arm Unit have withdrawn to near Shitagata Dai. In a raid I was ordered to West Arm but it was called off. I just lay down from fatigue. The facial expression of soldiers back from West Arm is serious. They all went back to the firing line soon.

16 May: Battle. If Shitagata Dai is occupied by the enemy, the fate of the West Arm is decided, so we burnt documents and prepared to destroy patients. At that moment, there was an order

from the Sector Unit hospital to proceed to Chichagof Harbour by way of Unanose. At 0100 in the morning I accompanied patients. There was an air raid so we took refuge in the former field hospital cave. The guns of a Lockheed spat fire as it flew by our cave.

17 May: Battle. At night, about 1800, under cover of darkness, left the cave. The stretcher went over muddy road and the steep hill of no-man's land. No matter how far or how much we went, we did not get to the pass. We were rather irritated in the fog by the thought of getting lost and we sat down every 20 or 30 paces. Would have liked to sleep, dream and wake up again – and do the same thing over again. The patient on the stretcher does not move and has frostbite. After all the effort, we met up with Commander Colon Yamasaki. The pass is straight and narrow, falling steeply towards Chichagof Harbour. Sitting on the butt and sliding the feet, I slid very smoothly, changing direction with my sword. It takes ten minutes to slide down. We were straggling by the time we reached Chichagof Harbour ward. It took about nine hours. We set up a field hospital. Walking is now extremely difficult due to rheumatism in the left knee that reappeared in the pass.

18 May: Battle. At night, there was a phone call from the Sector Unit hospital. In some spots on the beach there were some friendly float-type planes waiting. I went to Attu village church, which seemed to be someone's home as there were blankets scattered around. I was told to translate a field order which was thought to have come from an enemy officer in Massacre Bay. I was ordered to execute a detailed sketch map of Massacre Bay and Holtz Bay which was in the possession of Captain Robert J. Edward, Adjutant of Colonel Smith. I got tired and went to sleep. First Lieutenant Hijio is also in charge of translation.

20 May: Battle. The hard fighting of our 303rd Brigade at Massacre Bay is fierce and it is to our advantage. We have captured enemy weapons and have used them to fight. We shot ten enemy closing in under the cover of fog. Five of our enlisted men and one medical NCO died. Enemy pilots' faces seen around Unanose. The enemy naval gun firing near our hospital wards is fierce and drops around 20 metres away.

21 May: Battle. We were strafed while I was amputating a patient's arm. It is the first time since moving over to Chichagof Bay that I moved into an air-raid shelter. The nervousness of our CO is severe and he has said his last words to his officers and NCOs that he will die tomorrow and gave all his possessions away. Hasty chap this fellow. The officers became desperate and things became disorderly.

22 May: 0600. Air raid again. Strafing killed one medical man. Akeyaki was wounded in the right thigh and has a fractured arm. During the night a mortar shell came awfully close.

23 May: Battle. Seventeen friendly medium naval bombers destroyed a cruiser off-shore. But naval gun fire hit the pole of the patients' tent and killed two instantly. From 0200 in the morning until 1600 we stayed in foxholes. Officers and men alike suffered in the frost. Everybody looked around for food and stole everything they could find.

24 May: Battle. It sleeted and was extremely cold. I stayed in the Hisume barracks alone. A great number of shells were dropped by naval gunfire, and rocks and mud flew around causing the roof to collapse. In a foxhole, about 5m away, Haysaka, a medical man, died instantly when shrapnel penetrated his heart.

25 May: Battle. Naval gunfire shook the earth when the Kisimi Barracks blew up. Consciousness has become vague. One tent burnt down after a direct hit by an incendiary bomb. My room looks like an awful mess from the sandbags that come down from the roof. Hirese, first lieutenant of the Medical Corps, was wounded. There was a ceremony of the granting of the Imperial Edict. The last line at Unanose was broken through. No hope of reinforcements. Well for the cause of the Imperial Edict.

27 May: Battle. Diarrhoea continues. The pain is severe. I took a number of pills, then slept pretty well. Planes strafed us. Roff broke through. There was less than 1,000 left from more than 2,000 troops – wounded from the coastal defence unit field hospital headquarters, the post office and the rest in the front lines.

28 May: Battle. We only have two days' rations left. Our artillery has been completely destroyed. There is a sound of trench mortar also of anti-aircraft guns. The company at the bottom of Attu has

been completely annihilated except one. I wonder if Commander Yenagawa and some of the men are still living. Other companies have been completely annihilated except for one or two men.

The 303rd Brigade has been defeated. Yenagawa is still holding Ananous. There are many cases of suicide. Half the Sector Unit Headquarters has been blown away. I gave 400 shots of morphine to the severely wounded to kill them. Ate half fried thistle. It is the first time I have eaten anything fresh in six months. It is a delicacy. Orders came from the Sector Commander to move the field hospital to the island, but it was called off.

29 May: Today at 2000 we assembled in the front of headquarters. The field hospital took part too. The last assault is to be carried out. All patients in the hospital were made to commit suicide. Only 33 years old and I am to die here. I have no regrets. Banzai to the Emperor, I am grateful I have kept peace in my soul. At 1800 took care of all the patients with grenades. Goodbye Taeke, my beloved wife who loved me to the last. Until we meet again grant you God speed. Misaka who just became four years old will grow up unhindered. I feel sorry for you. Tokika, born February of this year and gone without seeing your father. Be good Mataur, brother Kachair, Sukechen Masachan, Mitlicher, goodbye. The number participating in this attack is a little over 1,000 to take enemy artillery positions. It seems that the enemy is expecting an all-out attack tomorrow.

He died soon after writing this entry.

BIGWIGS ARE DOING FINE

As the war turned against Japan, a certain cynicism began to creep in. In October 1943, Lieutenant Yoshiro Kiroki, who had seen action on New Guinea, quoted in his diary the Chinese saying:

> To hell with the boys on the firing line,
> As long as the bigwigs are doing fine.

Another Japanese soldier, suffering malaria and constantly harassed by bombing and shelling, wrote:

> I wonder what they will say when we return to Japan safely.
> Probably: 'What a wonderful trip you had without any expense.'

During the fighting in northern Burma, Private First Class Hideo Fujino became detached from his unit. During the rainy season, he and a second lieutenant travelled down the Irrawaddy by bamboo raft and canoe and, pursued by the local Kachin, 'crossed jungle in fear of wild elephants and leeches falling on us from the branches and leaves overhead'. Finally, with the help of a Burmese priest and villagers, he returned to Myitkyina, near the Chinese border, which came under siege by the Allies in June 1944.

> There were only 700 Japanese soldiers there to defend the town
> without any aid, while four divisions of Allies with air support
> and modern equipment violently attacked the small base town
> about two square kilometres. Due to the extreme shortage of
> ammunition and food, battle casualties and other losses on our
> side mounted. In order to survive, I had to sip dew-drops from
> leaves, and eat dandelions and other wild plants. Even a wounded
> soldier with one arm and one leg has to fight with a gun and
> hand-grenades. It was only the high morale among men and the
> perfect unity of the whole army that made us cling so stubbornly
> to the defence of the town.
>
> The situation at Myitkyina gradually became deadlocked, with
> the Japanese unable to make a definite attack on the Allies, and
> the Allies unable to subdue the Japanese garrison. The Allies
> became irritated. To bring the campaign to a quick conclusion, the
> Allies attempted to blast the besieged garrison by digging their way
> underground towards our position. For two and a half months,
> the Japanese stubbornly resisted and held out in the town.
>
> Day and night, the US air force carried out air raids on the
> town and casualties amounted to a great number. In addition,
> the whole ground turned into mud on rainy days, and when the
> sun began to shine, the trenches were filled with the smell of the
> dead. We, the Japanese, were in increasing peril as the days went
> by ... Meanwhile soldiers were executing their duties faithfully
> during the 80-day siege.
>
> However Major General Mizukawai, commander of the Tatsu
> [Dragon] Division, could not allow his unit to be annihilated, and
> so he decided on his own responsibility to retreat from the position
> ... The invalid and the wounded were the first to be transferred to

Bhamo [130km (80 miles) downstream] by bamboo rafts floating on the Irrawaddy. The next to be evacuated were the all the members of his unit. He ordered his men to start for the opposite side of the river at midnight on 1 August and prepare for a fight there.

In thick darkness, dozens of bamboo rafts on the river struggled to reach the other side across the wide and large river. With the others our raft began to start in the same direction. Soon afterwards, some of the rafts were upset and sank in the strong current, while the others were carried down the river. It was monsoon season and owing to the heavy rainfall, the Irrawaddy had risen a lot. Moreover, the rafts of undried bamboo were too heavy to carry the eight or more people on each. We tried hard to get to the opposite bank, and I had to take the lead by swimming in the extremely cold river. Nevertheless, we failed. Our raft began to be carried down the river and it was soon capsized. In the morning, as the sun rose, I found myself alone. All of my colleagues must have been drowned.

I was on the raft all by myself. It drifted into a small village on the riverside where I found a canoe. I stole it to continue my journey to Bhamo. It took five days to reach there alone. During those days I could find nothing at all to eat or drink. Moreover, I could not escape the danger of being sniped at, or being drowned in the furious rapids in the gorge at the next turn of the Irrawaddy. Hovering between life and death, I happened to find grains of gold at the riverside, but at the time it meant nothing to me.

He eventually reached Bhamo and survived the war.

Yoshio Shioya was in Malaya in 1944, where they suffered few shortages.

1 July: Arrived at Dama Village at 1400 hours. Had a few drinks with the village chieftain and had a gay time hearing phonograph recordings for the first time in quite a while – Chinese recordings only. Left for Galela with a cane as a souvenir. When I awoke the ship was entering the harbour. It was 2350 hours. After unloading had a sugar drink and returned to ship at 0230 hours.

13 August: My daily routine is breakfast, dinner, afternoon nap and supper. This may not be believed by others but it is so.

As usual in the evening I gather the children together and teach them how to drill. Tried to teach them to about face. Had them try it a hundred times but they still can't do it. Ichiro and his younger brother Kumosuke [the ATIS translators noted that the native boys had been given Japanese names] have the best minds of the children in the village. Kumosuke is only seven or eight years old but at times his sayings are very mature. Their father has been imprisoned in Djailolo for nine months and has not yet been released.

Allied planes regularly bombed nearby villages, but there was plenty of fish in the sea and the local inhabitants gave them fruit. Shioya was also impressed by the beauty of the Malay women.

27 September: Heard that a native in Dowongigila village found a small bomb. Not knowing that it was a bomb and wishing to make a tobacco container of it, he began to saw it in two. It exploded and killed three men instantly and wounded a fourth.

28 September: At 1000 hours I sent a prau [a small sailing boat] to village chief of Apulea with 14 cases of canned beef which I wanted him to keep for me ...

29 September: Two mysterious vessels went northward though the mist. At 0800 hours the Apulea-bound prau departed. Sent my trousers to a Chinese in Fitako for repairs. He returned them at 1500 hours. Aeroplanes appear intermittently one at a time. Heavy seas caused me to delay my departure. The mysterious vessels were heading south off shore at night.

30 September: At 0600 hours two mysterious vessels entered Dama and after ten minutes left, heading north. At 0800 hours left directly for Ngadjama. The prau was tossed like a leaf. The surf was so rough at Ngadjama that we could not go ashore, so we went to Doroeme. The natives had scattered and the only remaining things were pigs and chickens. On the 25th an enemy vessel had shelled this village and had killed one native. On the 21st five Japanese survivors had drifted into Doroeme, it was reported. It is rumoured that the Navy is going to withdraw from Soefoe. Cooked my own meal in a native hut tonight. Felt grateful for

portable fuel. The Kedi-bound prau departed at 2200 hours.
Gave the natives some rice for encouragement ...

20 October: All I worry about nowadays is concealment. I can't
even hang my washing out to dry. Nevertheless, my present location
is fairly safe, so I guess I'll stay here a couple of days. There was a
set of dishes and bowls, pots and pans, under the floor so I'm using
them. The hut belongs to the Doroeme village chief.

21 October: Enemy aeroplanes were strafing this area even before
sunrise. Four Lockheeds strafed for about ten minutes before
leaving. After breakfast decided to move farther back into the
mountains. Will stop overnight in an abandoned hut. I went down
to reconnoitre the village and found it in miserable shape. Houses
were knocked down and some burned. I was surprised at the size
of the bomb craters. The beautiful church was also demolished. I
wonder why the enemy bombs villages where there are no Japanese
troops. Then bombs were dropped and there are two bomb craters
of about the size of 50kg bombs.

The diary ended on 25 October with enemy planes circling overhead.

VICTORY!

Some soldiers managed to maintain the spirit of *Bushido* to the very end.
Among the papers of Fuzuko Obara was a diary that began with his
battalion being posted from Manchuria to defend the Philippines 'with
treasured memories of five years as soldiers and friends'. Their spirits were
high:

> 'Victory!' be our cry! Comrades in arms
> Of the South Seas, shall we all soon meet in Yasukuni?

This was written on 3 August 1944, less than three months before General
Douglas MacArthur returned in triumph to the Philippines. Just three days
after leaving Manchuria, Obara was already suffering from dysentery:

> My physical condition continues to worsen. By nightfall it has
> turned to diarrhoea. Since the freight train is completely without
> toilet facilities, and to make matters worse, since I never know
> when nor for how long the train may stop, I am very soon fasting
> and petitioning the gods, 'Please, cure me quickly ...'

On 21 August, they set sail from Pusan harbour in Korea.

> Suddenly something is spotted in the water that looks like the wake of a torpedo, and this is turned into an impromptu lesson on anti-submarine observation.

After stopping briefly at Ariake Bay on the west coast of Kyushu and seeing the homeland once more, they headed for Formosa, then journeyed on to the Philippines.

> 5 September: As we reach the middle of the Bashi Strait, there is a submarine alarm. Bombs and bullets from the skies, depth charges from the escort vessels and ships of the convoy, combine to produce a series of bone-jarring blasts ... Blasted by concerted attack, a stricken Anglo-American submarine plunges to the bottom.

Another submarine was spotted the next day and 'to avoid the dangers of the Manila area, we stop at San Fernando'. They landed the following night.

> The realization that we are now finally here fills my head with emotion. Among the loyal comrades who bravely marched forth from our old base camp to take part in the building of the new Philippines, there are probably some who, rather than treading this soil, lie uselessly on the bottom of the sea. When I think of them, I marvel to find that we are safely here. It is divine providence. It is by the grace of the gods, nothing else.

They noticed how cold it was at night, but as the dawn came up everyone was eager to sample coconut for the first time. Soon there were other weather problems to contend with:

> 12 September: We have been in a violent rainstorm since evening, a downpour as if the heavens burst. I suppose this is one of those squalls characteristic of these southern regions. It is impossible to see 10m ahead. The surf is violent. The palm trees seem about to fall under the lashing of wind and rain. We had been on night manoeuvres, and had to return to our tents in the midst of this great squall. Unable to change into dry clothes, we strip and sleep naked in our blankets, mosquito nets and gloves.

On the way to Lipa by train, they were attacked by enemy aircraft. It was a worrying portent.

'Not one of our planes went up?' one asks with a puzzled look.
'And not one of theirs went down.'

The following day they were attacked again, this time by a formation of 25 or 26 planes.

And now, I say to myself, the heroic battle in the sky begins, as our planes tangle with theirs. Not at all; no such thing happens! Their planes continue to soar the skies about in formations of four or six. I think perhaps half of them are ours, but even as the thought forms I can see that all the planes are enemy.

There were enemies on the ground too. The Filipinos, whom they assumed to be their friends, killed Private First Class Awaji Shoji.

The guerrilla who killed Awaji is soon caught and laid out smeared with blood at the feet of Awaji, along with two other guerrillas also seized and thrown down. While they are being interrogated about the killing of Awaji, I try to grasp the idea that this man is the one, this young man of 22 or 23, trembling, blood-smeared and prostrate before us. But then he speaks, saying, 'I am a captain of the American-Philippine Army guerrillas.' Had others not been there, I wonder if I might not have instantly slashed at him.

24 October: The dawn sky is filled with the rumble of great formations of aircraft. It is our 'Arawashi' on their way to strike the enemy. We pray for them to achieve victory in memory of Awaji. About seven o'clock we recover his ashes and put them in a proper new Japanese box. Each man sheds his tears within himself.

But even while the funeral was still under way, US carrier-based Grummans continued to dogfight overhead.

10
KAMIKAZE: THE LAST DESPERATE DEFENCE

The Japanese term *kamikaze* means 'divine wind', and it was originally used to describe the typhoon that dispersed the Mongol fleet as it threatened to invade Japan in 1281. However, in World War II the word acquired a new sense, when it was applied to the Japanese pilots who flew their planes into enemy targets, usually ships, in suicidal attacks. Though suicide attacks had begun earlier, *kamikaze* attacks were first employed as a deliberate tactic during the Allied landings on Leyte in the Philippines in October 1944, as Fuzuko Obara recalled:

> 30 October: 'Newspapers have come!' I hear the shouting and, starved for news, jump up to have a look. It is a one-page Manila paper, and the smell of ink strikes the nose. It is so black with large type, but the headlines that greet the eye are not about the number of enemy warships or enemy divisions invading Leyte Island, nor the appearance of enemy planes, rather the big type tells of our Special Attack Forces' fierce onslaughts. Ah, those words, 'Kamikaze Special Attack Force, Manila Attack Force!' Who could have foretold the story of these men? Only Imperial Japan can boast of such headlines as these. All around, all of us reading in this pool of electric light are as one struck dumb with deep emotion, and tears stand in every eye. If only my pen were able to express in unadorned grandeur the dignity, the immortality of the Special Forces ... These gods of the skies who have chosen this path to glory are generally young men, about 22 or 23 ... However, the newspaper also reports: 'So inspiring is the example of these gods of the skies that there are now many dedicated 16-year-olds graduating from primary training.' 16 years old! 16 years old! I think of how it was when we were 16 years old, how many years ago.
>
> It is of course a matter of pride to be Japanese and then in addition belong to the Special Attack Force. Thus it is that in

the present situation in the offshore area of the nearby island of Leyte, one plane after another turns itself into an inextinguishable fireball to strike like an eagle from the skies an enemy warship dead on target! Ah! Who would not declare such to be the Eagles of Heaven.

In the 16th year of life to have attained such self-control, such enlightenment, is sure to have attained the sublime heights of the gods. This is Japan! This is Japan! Divine winds blow! Kamikaze fly! Annihilate the American forces and send them to the bottom of the sea. And should the enemy come here, we who are the surface forces, in concert with the Eagles of Heaven, will all adopt ramming tactics, one man destroying one tank, and so kill the enemy until not one remains. Thus will we leave the Land of the Gods in the tranquillity of a secure Greater East Asia. It is the sacred duty of warriors such as we, though we lack wings, to achieve this. It is our paramount responsibility not to fail to achieve this. Let them come! We shall slash with lightning attacks! We shall hurl our bodies at them!

My feelings as I am writing this in the dugout by the weak light of a coconut-oil lamp are such as to stop my breathing. This is Japan! This is Japan, that our holy warriors fly, fly, fly, while we also prepare to hurl ourselves at the enemy.

Staff Officer Lieutenant Colonel Jin explained why the tactic was adopted:

I think there were four main reasons:
1. There was no prospect of victory in the air using orthodox methods.
2. Suicide attacks were more effective because the power of the impact of the plane was added to that of the bombs, besides which the exploding gasoline caused fire – further, achievement of the proper angle effected greater speed and accuracy than that of normal bombings.
3. Suicide attacks provided spiritual inspiration to the ground units and to the Japanese public at large.
4. Suicide attack was the only sure and reliable type of attack

at the time attacks were made (as they had to be) with personnel whose training had been limited because of shortage of fuel.

However, the *kamikaze* did not prevent the Americans landing on the Philippines, and an attack on Luzon at Tayabas Bay was expected on Christmas Day. But on Christmas Eve Obara noticed that the twin-fuselage Grumman P-38s and the four-engine Consolidates normally flying overhead mysteriously disappeared.

> Through the front of the palm grove, we see the beach, relatively well-lit by the moon, but in the shadows all is dark. A quiet surf sparkles in the brilliant moonlight as each one of us in his defensive position maintains a steady surveillance clear to the horizon. Any landing craft, no matter how small, would be detected by watchful eyes of soldiers staring at the surface of the sea ... Until recently there would have been lights visible from the fishing villages around Tayabas Bay, but tonight there are none to be seen. Apart from the sound of waves lapping at the shore and an occasional cry from fowls in the dwellings nearby, it is completely quiet.

While the lookouts strained to hear the sound of approaching landing craft, Sergeant Major Sado was shot by a guerrilla during a local round-up and died of his wounds.

> He had been given a blood transfusion and everything possible had been done for him, but because the colon had been severed, all was in vain. He was a man fond of kendo, rather taciturn, yet ... Some time ago, Nagasawa Sempei of HQ was similarly shot and killed by guerrillas while on a terrain reconnaissance mission. In his case nothing remained that could be done for him except to recover the body. These wretched Filipinos! Forgetting all gratitude for the gift of independence, they yearn only for the soft pleasures of American-style hedonism.

There were also the Americans to worry about. Having secured Leyte they were now preparing to invade Luzon.

Soon after welcoming the New Year, we were urgently pulled out of
the Tiaong area of Tayabas State on the 15th and sent to the
mountains near Montalban, northeast of Manila ... It will be our
mission, following the example of classic ancient stratagem of Lord
Kusunoki, to prepare in these forested mountains fortified
positions more inaccessible than this Chihaya Castle on Mount
Kongo. Our transfer from Tiaong to Montalban was accomplished
by motor vehicle entirely by night because the impossibility of
suppressing enemy air attacks caused us to be concerned that
travelling by daylight would result in excessive casualties ... As when
a bee's nest has been disturbed, all these mountains are swarming
with activity. Not only Army units are assembling here, the Cyorotai,
Navy units and all the other forces here are engaged in the work of
carrying supplies deeper and deeper into the interior ... Here and
there along the road we had come upon the sad spectacle of
overturned vehicles with fresh bullet holes, the victims of air attacks
... In the villages around Marikina, we see mingled with the
inhabitants refugees from Manila who have been savagely burned
out of their homes and have fled there. On both sides of the road
lay extensive farmlands, and the fragrance that arises from the
verdant fields of daikon [Japanese radish] and bananas remind me
of home, fragrance that since coming to the Philippines I have
known only in dreams ... After that is a thick forest and cliffs that
have never known motor vehicles ... a place of terrifying cliffs and
dams where haunted crags are lapped by sparkling clear water ... I
wonder if it is true that there are monitor lizards up to two and a
half metres long living here? I am told that some of the soldiers
have seen them.

As they crossed this difficult terrain, the Japanese were bombed and strafed.
In the heat, they sweated 'like a downpour of rain'.

Soldiers of the Divine Land! That is a good name for them. In
truth they seem godlike, supernatural figures ... Their faces seem
illuminated by an inner glow. I am struck with the thought that
they resemble the Imperial Guard of Sakimori in ancient times
who dedicated themselves to the protection of the grandson of the

Sun Goddess. When the enemy swoops and wheels overhead, we take cover in the shelter of the trees ... the drops of sweat little by little begin to dry, and as they evaporate, leaving the salts, our bodies appear white ... Our food ration is 400 grams of uncooked native rice, some salt, and leaves of the wild sweet potato.

Eventually they camped in a grove beside a river.

Immediately we are enveloped in humidity as in a cloud of steam ... The hot moist air in the grove is seething with mosquitoes. You only have to clap your hands to crush five or ten of the insects. They come at you from all directions. Each day's work lays out one or two with malaria.

But they were not downhearted.

The bond of affection among comrades-at-arms is a noble feeling. I wish the people at home could witness this, and I wish especially they could see the contrast with the selfishness of American individualism. This nobility of character, this highest love! Amid steaming heat and clouds of humidity, and the invisible poison of the striped insect.

Under constant strafing, they had to deal with scorpions and poisonous snakes, and 'no matter how frequently you handle a thing, shortly afterwards a green mould has appeared on it'. But there was a worse problem.

Everyone has contracted athlete's foot on both feet. It makes us really miserable ... the infection is so bad for some that walking becomes difficult ... every step hurts like fire.

They were also suffering from ringworm and dengue fever, but for Obara the athlete's foot was worse.

Certainly when the day comes to order 'Attack!' and I myself cannot move because of this fungus, I could never forgive myself.

And always there was the humidity.

The air is so saturated with humidity that water falls in a steady precipitation, drip, drip, dripping onto the bamboo leaves ...

The word 'dew' evokes the language of poetry, but this dripping is not the dew of poetic tradition ... Our biggest problem is cooking. If we allow the least wisp of smoke to rise, immediately planes are overhead, not attacking targets but dropping bombs at random ... Swarms of lizards eight or nine inches long make rustling sounds as they skitter over dead bamboo leaves ... At intervals when the sun happens to emerge, it is not much good for drying anything since it cannot effectively penetrate the foliage. Soon everything is soggy again. The whole camp smells mouldy.

EVERY GRAIN OF RICE

But their major concern was food. The men were now living on less than half the wartime ration.

We should learn from the battles of Saipan and Guadalcanal that the enemy must be crushed and exterminated. It is for this that we need every grain of rice. Each grain therefore has its part in the purposes of Divine Will. And what of the needs of the women and children at home? Think of children with empty bellies! It is a piteous thought. One wishes, though it were for only a day, that they might once be able to eat all they wanted. But no, for the purpose of all this is to assure victory ... we must swallow our tears and sharpen our anger ... each grain plays a part in the final destruction of the enemy ... Our seasoning is limited to a little rock salt ... Our broth is made of potato leaves, and comes out a clear, thick, greenish-black, flavoured with brine ... Fare such as this 365 days a year and not a word of complaint. Even so, there are times when one remembers the aroma of miso with longing.

And now the enemy was on its way.

4 February 1945: Manila is on fire. The tempo of gunfire is increasing. The shelling is averaging about one report a second. There may be some naval bombardment from enemy ships that may have slipped into Manila Bay. Enemy planes have intensified their disruptive raids. Now with my own eyes I see enemy ground forces, armoured units. I see for the first time enemy vehicles on land. I look at them and think: 'Those are the enemy's. Those

tanks are enemy tanks. There is the long-awaited enemy.' Suddenly one of our automatic cannons on a neighbouring hill is seen to belch an intense burst of fire. An enemy Douglas light bomber emits a fierce spurt of flame and appears to be falling. As I am thinking, 'We got him', the falling plane, manoeuvring desperately, is seen to be making progress towards his own armoured units until, just before it appears about to crash, a parachute suddenly is seen to unfold and comes drifting down. 'The bum made it,' someone says, and I hear the disappointment in his voice.

Now came their baptism of fire. Obara recorded feeling 'exaltation' when his unit was ordered to make an infiltration raid on the enemy's armoured units. But first a libation was made.

We receive with gratitude the Imperial gift of o-saké [rice wine] ... When it becomes quite dark, we begin a stealthy advance towards our objective ... The stars are shining and the sky glows with the fires still burning in Manila, but in the tall grass and gullies it is so dark that we can see scarcely an inch ahead. It becomes difficult to keep a sense of direction. We are among the enemy now, so it is essential to avoid making the least sound ... Completely baffled as to the best way to proceed, we seem to have fallen into a queer world of illusion ... The ravines are choked with thickets, principally bamboo. Our progress is as little as a single metre in five minutes ... As dawn approaches, we are able finally with great difficulty to infiltrate to a position at one corner of our objective area. I send out a patrol. They discover a Filipino guerrilla ... I put my field glasses to my eyes, and there they are. I count ten American soldiers in khaki, accompanied by five or six guerrillas in white shirts, guarding a mobile 45mm cannon. To see enemy soldiers with my own eyes affects me deeply. These are enemies of the Divine Land and they must pay dearly ... Perhaps tonight we will launch and attack to destroy this enemy we now see ... With the coming of daylight, an observation plane hovering in the skies seems almost to tease by threatening to fly over us. All this time I am nervously wondering, 'Now will we be seen?' ... At 1430 hours on 9 February, orders come authorizing us to attack the enemy position at 2400 hours. The reaction of my men is simply this: they begin to check and recheck their arms and equipment. Scanning their faces, I find them calm and unruffled, scarcely changed except for a look of anticipation ... The captured guerrilla has been killed. Sunset is near. Without conscious will or interest, I find scenes of the distant past flashing through my mind like so many lantern slides. 'Still attached to worldly desires,' I scold myself, but the more I try to shake off these memories, the more they crowd in on me, memories of childhood, of my mother, of my wife ... 'What is this,' I say to myself. 'I am a living, breathing man, who should be directing his thoughts towards a clear view of present realities.' ...

By 2400 hours we have safely penetrated the enemy's security perimeter without being detected ... From here on, each squad is to proceed on its own. The 3rd Squad, which I attach myself to, has proceeded about 50m when we discover an enemy infiltration warning trip-wire and communication line, which we promptly cut. As we resume our advance, I hear what appear to be four bursts of static from an infiltration warning device speaker, followed by four violent blasts, probably the explosions of landmines buried in the area. Now there can be no delay. I blow the whistle for the assault. The results achieved are the destruction of 12 or 13 men, three medium field shelters and two 45mm mobile guns with their vehicles. We continue the advance, still seeking the enemy. Recovering from their shock, enemy soldiers one by one commence firing from the ridge line extending in front of us. Undeterred, we continue to advance ... At this time we begin to receive intense fire from a variety of weapons ... Before me, about 5m away is a machine-gun, and there is another about 30m to my right. Good ... I take a hand-grenade and throw it. In the violent explosion that follows, one machine-gun and seven or eight men are destroyed at a blow. Meanwhile the enemy is receiving fierce fire frontally. However bullets from all directions are beginning to fall like raindrops around us. The concentration of fire produces a surprisingly beautiful effect with its tracers. Ricochets arch into the sky. The danger of encirclement is increasing, so I order a withdrawal to the first assembly point, during which we are subjected to enemy pursuit fire. At the assembly point, I find that three men are missing.

The fire was so intense that they were forced to withdraw without them.

They do not return. At the time we were under enemy fire, it seemed to me that no one was hit. Still, were they, after all, killed by those enemy bullets, or wounded, or fallen victim to guerrillas? Such are the unpleasant thoughts that float unbidden through my mind.

But eventually the three men made it back, uninjured – 'then there is a warm lump constricting the throat and suddenly hot tears begin to flow'.

This was our baptism of fire under American bullets. It has been good experience, and serves to reinforce our determination that they shall be destroyed without loss to ourselves.

A STORY WRITTEN IN BLOOD

Despite the success of the infiltration raid, the enemy hit back harder than ever with bombing, shelling and strafing. Obara's men were forced to dig in. They no longer dug fortified trenches as they had earlier in the war. Instead they dug 'individual "spider-trap" foxholes or cave-type tunnel dugouts'.

The Greater East Asia War, especially since Guadalcanal up to the present, is a story written in blood. The design of our present shelters has been drawn in the precious blood of countless war dead. In these dugouts which we dig with only pick-axe and shovel, and in these arms streaming with sweat, there lives the blood and sweat of veteran officers and men who have gone before us. It is these spirits of heroes who died in defence of the fatherland that inspire us.

On 2 March, they were ordered to recapture Yamata and Shikishima Hill, which had been overrun by the enemy.

At 2400 hours on 4 March, as ordered, we attack Shikishima Hill, recapture and hold it. However, in spite of the success of our assault, the enemy comes rolling back as irresistible as a landslide, penetrating our positions and compelling our withdrawal to

Mount Mukyu. Their assault is indescribably ferocious, both in mechanized force and artillery fire.

The enemy were quick to press home their counterattack.

Since 9 March we have been besieged on all sides by the enemy, encircled and cut off from reinforcements ... Meanwhile, the enemy's lavish use of shot and shell and incendiaries has to an amazing degree denuded the mountains and even the marshes of the surrounding area ... Our telephone lines to the rear have at last been cut. We must from now on fight completely on our own initiative: if we are to get back, we must break through the enemy ... Of the men in the units who were dug in among the surrounding hills and valleys, the greater part has already died a hero's death ... When I think of what we could do if only we had aircraft, or if only we had artillery comparable to the enemy's, I taste tears of anger. We are few, but we will fight on with whatever weapons and ammunition we have left. The enemy continues to destroy our positions one by one with deluges of shells and bombs, lavishing many thousands of rounds on the capture of each little hill. In the attacks on Mount Shori and Mount Mukyu, they blasted each with about 50,000 projectiles. It was a weird sight in full daylight to see these mountains become obscured from view by the intensity of the bombardment ... From the skies overhead, bombs follow shells in a continuous rain as the intense bombardment continues. Meanwhile we behold roads constructed regardless of the steepness of the gradient, followed by a flow of vehicles, one after another bringing more ammunition to the summit. No matter how unpleasant it is to admit it, I see before me with my own eyes the enormous strength of mechanized power. It is said that at Saipan, the shelling attained a rate of about one ton per square metre. I really believe what we are seeing here exceeds that.

Some of the incoming whistlers end in a tremendous explosion, while others produce nothing at all because they are streaming over our heads to pour down on our positions in the rear ... Three or four or even five of our men are lying dead out there, and it affects me deeply that, because of the intensity of the fighting, we cannot recover their bodies. I pray the gods to send us some planes. Even one plane would help ...

Each time a barrage is heard coming closer, each of us in this dugout wonders, 'It this it? Is this it?' I think this feeling must be how it feels to mount the steps to the scaffold one by one. Regardless of how one feels mounting the scaffold, the steps must be climbed. Simply stated, one climbs without faltering because it is in the defence of the noble land of our ancestors ...

We have gone through all undestroyed dugouts gathering and sorting everything edible from the inedible ... By tomorrow night they will all be consumed. When our supplies are finally gone, then will come the time for each of us loyally to offer up his blood for Emperor and country.

17 March: Another day and I am still alive. I say to myself, I am still alive, and yet it is strange, such a thin line separates death from life. There is life beyond death; is there not also death in life? We live from moment to moment, and while we live, we live only to fight the enemy. It seems that beyond the smoke of battle, I can see a broad highway extending to the limits of heaven, and it leads to the Yasukuni Shrine. It is in my thoughts that this is the place and this is the time of my death.

Obara did not die. Instead he watched a bird in the treetops. Its feathers were bedraggled, but 'when it sings, its voice is quite lovely'. Then the thought struck him, 'This ordinary patch of trees may be my home for eternity.' Meanwhile, 'Today three of my men blacken their faces and cheerfully set out to find and attack the enemy.' But he himself began to reveal misgivings:

One mission certain of achievement is the command, 'Forward to death!' I cannot conceive of myself as the person who might have to issue such a tremendous order. 'Go die!' 'Come die!' Short words that carry an eternity of meaning. One speaks readily enough of right of command, supreme authority and so forth, but am I, upon whom this role has fallen, a person who could issue orders of such finality? Our mission, in any event, is to strive for victory, Whatever comes, we must win and win and win again.

Nevertheless, he conceded: 'Sooner or later, we must take the road that leads to Yasukuni Shrine.'

Despite the overwhelming odds, the Japanese counterattacked and returned to their positions on Mount Hoshuku. Even so, shells and bombs continued to rain down on them.

> Let them come. We will destroy the enemy with one blow. Our morale is extremely high ... Somehow we will triumph. Yes! For the sake of victory, we will endure all.

And there was plenty to endure:

> Shells from heavy guns, medium guns and light guns, mingled with white phosphorous incendiaries, are falling incessantly. In a period of 30 minutes, the area of the mortar squad and my command bunker was hit by approximately 750 to 800 bursts, of those about 80 or 90 close to my command bunker ... I tried counting them. After five or six minutes I had reached 170, but then had to give up because shells seemed to be exploding three, four, five at a time. We were hit, not by one shell per square metre, but by three or four. Even in the side hole of my bunker I was stunned by the excessive ferocity of this shelling. All around us, the air is filled with shell fragments, bursts of dirt, the flaring of phosphorous incendiaries and smoke. Inside, there is darkness and the choking stench of phosphorous. I think, this is the end, and put on my gas mask. The concussion that follows the explosions shakes my anti-blast curtain and makes it flap, and then the pressure seems to stop my breathing. I keep wondering, 'Is this the end? Now? Now?' I have lost all feeling of being alive.
>
> This intense barrage continues for about an hour and then seems to taper off, but the shells continue to come in at a rate of 200 or 300 an hour. After about two hours, the rate of shelling had diminished. I creep out of my side hole, through the crumbling foxhole, and stick my head out to survey the situation. The hillside into which we have dug our position now appears ploughed and harrowed beyond description. Directly before me are trees torn out by their roots. Even our reserves' foxholes are mostly crumbled or buried.

However, a miracle has come to pass – no, not a miracle, it is divine aid. Not one of my men has even a scratch. Wonderful! Wonderful! The men, all plastered with dirt, cannot help laughing as now here, now there, another blackened face pops out of the ground ...

This afternoon an attack using flame-throwers is mounted against our Futaba Hill positions, but is repelled by the spirited fighting of our reserves supported by fire from our main force, and the enemy retreats in confusion. We prepare to repel attack but have nothing to do but observe as the enemy retreats in disarray with loud howls of pain. No matter how they are hurt, what a disgrace to bawl like that. Several of their voices sounded incredibly like babies who have burned themselves. Grown men crying as they ran away! It is a farce, ridiculous in the extreme for the enemy to bawl in view of the Japanese Army. It is too much even to speak of it. After watching and waiting for a worthy opponent, it makes one feel as if a treat had been snatched away. We feel puzzled and let down.

A GREAT VICTORY

Repeated attempts were made to take Futaba Hill, each of which was fought off with high American casualties. Then the Japanese heard of the 'unprecedently great victory off Okinawa'. On 1 April, US troops had landed on Okinawa, the first of Japan's home islands to be invaded. But on 4 April, 700 *kamikaze* pilots attacked the invasion fleet, sinking 13 ships. In the Philippines, the Japanese were feeling bullish.

Judging by information gleaned from enemy classified documents, the bulk of the enemy forces now facing us on the Philippines battle front apparently consists of draftees who were called up in America around January and immediately put on transports ...
May the time be soon at hand when they will all be dealt with ...

With such an inconsequential enemy on its way, there was time to appreciate the natural world:

The sky is so blue it hurts the eyes. There is not even a wisp of cloud.

The Americans resumed their tactic of heavy shelling of the Japanese positions, killing or wounding many of Obara's men – though his troops had some successes of their own.

> Our raids on the 8th killed nearly 50 of the enemy, and yet ... the stream of shells continues unabated and by ones and twos our number continues to diminish. Rank upon rank of the enemy is spread into the distance before us. We are day by day, moment to moment, on the steps between life and death.

Nevertheless, the news from Okinawa lifted their spirits, along with the hope that this might herald the return of Japanese fighters to the Philippines to challenge the US in the sky. It did not on dawn on Obara that the *kamikaze* attacks were, in fact, depleting their stocks of aeroplanes.

> If only it were not for the enemy planes, no matter how intense their shelling, their land forces would be no great problem for us. It angers me to think that these wretches, who howl when struck by bullets, are able unceasingly to deluge us with an astronomical number of shells, while we are barely able to reply. Sometimes I pick up enemy propaganda and look it over, but generally it is so childish, it is as painful as it is funny. 'Final Surrender Proclamations' are stuck up on trees, telling us to come and give ourselves up, but to come in daylight, not at night, and not in large groups, but a few at a time, so that they, the American soldiers, can see us coming. It is utterly ridiculous. From this we see all the better just how much the enemy fears our night raids. To me this is an admission of weakness.

Every so often the guns fell silent.

> The extraordinary stillness at such times ... gives one an indescribably weird feeling. But just as one had begun to wonder, can this really be the field of war? the interlude of some ten or 20 minutes is again shattered by the same maddening roar.

On 13 April, Obara came down with malaria and lay shivering in his dugout while P-51s bombed and strafed it so intensely that he began to worry that his foxhole might crumble. Even the elements seemed to be against them:

Last night this field of battle was deluged by heavy rain. It was a terrifying chaos of thunder mingled with the roar of guns and the explosion of shells. Water collected two or three inches deep in our foxholes, so that even in the midst of the downpour of water at shells, men found it necessary to get out and bail.

But then came more good news.

News from abroad tells us that our great victory at Okinawa has led to greater consequences, and our hearts leap up ... Roosevelt has dropped dead of a stroke, most likely brought on by the shock of having so many ships sunk. It serves him right.

President Franklin D. Roosevelt had indeed died on 12 April; he was replaced by Harry S. Truman. US troops again tried to take Futaba Hill and were beaten off with heavy casualties. They then withdrew completely, leaving Obara time to write a long poem hailing Japan's inevitable victory. More men were killed and wounded, but Obara's spirits were raised once again on 22 April:

More details of the great victory off Okinawa have been announced. At least 400 ships were sunk. Estimating over 1,500 men per ship, a total of almost 800,000 men were sent to the bottom off Okinawa. The faces of our men light up with joy.

Despite this 'great victory' the Americans still had the wherewithal to shell, bomb and strafe the Japanese on the Philippines, causing inevitable casualties. Obara recorded how much he admired his comrades who died with 'Banzai!' or 'Long live the emperor!' on their lips. There were attacks and counterattacks, both equally costly, and the endless shelling had completely denuded the mountain.

How many thousand shells will they hurl at Mount Hoshuku until they are satisfied, I wonder?

Obara reckoned that 20,000 or 30,000 shells had pounded their position, along with enough incendiaries to burn off the jungle covering.

Whenever there comes a break in the shelling, we emerge to beat out the fires around our foxholes.

On 28 April, increasing enemy reconnaissance missions led Obara to think that an attack was coming.

> Two female guerrillas infiltrated the area of our company positions, but are quickly captured. Both rather plump females, they were about 40 years old, more or less. We exchanged some words in a mixture of broken English and Tagalog and they tried to appear innocent, saying they had come from Montalban to dig up roots. After plying them with various questions – ha! they were nothing but animals – they are killed in the bush.

Again he berated the ingratitude of the Filipinos.

> Naturally American soldiers are our enemies, but we are beginning to think the Filipinos are even worse enemies. They, too, were born and reared, as were we, in the Orient, and we are the ones who gave them at last their long-sought independence. How incredible that in spite of this they should be aiding foreign devils against magnanimous Japan. It is generally recognized that Japan is a just country, and the Imperial Army a just army. It may be that in the first stages of the war in the Philippines, we were a little too indulgent with them. Japan seeks only co-operation, while the coming of the American forces has brought to the Philippines the misery of war, and yet they turn solidly to the enemy. But the day will come when we have annihilated the American army, and we must then exterminate these Philippine beasts until not one remains. It would be incalculably easier to fight this war if the Filipinos were our comrades-in-arms, or even if they did not become our friends but just did not take the side of the enemy ... It makes me angry just to think about it.

The next day, 29 April, was the emperor's birthday.

> Many are convinced that on the emperor's birthday we shall resume the offensive and begin an advance on Manila, but right now it seems to me to be an empty dream. It appears unlikely that our aircraft are coming. The word is that we are nearly out of rations and no one knows how long this may continue ... Each man must survive on a daily ration of about 200 grams, but after

no great number of days one must expect that even this will dwindle down to nothing ... Day by day, not only provisions grow less, but also the number of our men diminishes by ones and twos. This is warfare bitter in the extreme.

The supply position made Obara reflective.

How many days, I wonder, will I begin making the battlefield jottings? How many times have I thought, today is the last! That I have been able, in spite of all, to go this far with these notes is to me a matter for grateful wonder. Yet, in all honesty, what good is it to continue such a thing as this? I realize I will probably never be able to take it home, and I don't know how often it has occurred to me to give it up. I must confess it seems strange even to myself that I have kept on and even now go on jotting down one thing after another. If fate is kind, perhaps someone will come along who will find this diary and take it to my home; otherwise, I suppose it will in the end just rot away here in the depths of a Philippine mountain forest. Well, whatever the reason, although I probably should put it aside and forget it, I go on writing. Bullets rain down all around me and still I go on writing. It cannot claim to be literature, so it must be because this diary has become like a child to me. In any case, this journal records the names of my men who, having fallen, have gone to join the pantheon of spirits guarding the nation. Crude though it may be, when I think of these men, it is precious to me.

The emperor's birthday dawned, not with an advance on Manila or the arrival of Japanese planes, but with 'an artillery bombardment such as to seem to turn day back into darkness again'. It ended with a thunderstorm that rivalled the intensity of the artillery bombardment. Then the month changed with no sign of an offensive and there were other things to worry about.

The sun of May beats down upon the battlefield, and as the atmosphere grows ever more oppressive, the sweat begins to flow so fast, it drips ... The men are being disabled in rapid succession by the high fever that accompanies malaria. In a critical situation such as this, this problem is an especially perplexing one. I note with anguish that, not only are our remaining medicines inadequate for our present needs, but supplies such as syringes are completely exhausted. Yet these are men who will pour out their last drop of strength in the effort to destroy the enemy. Standing guard day and night with 40°C fevers, a fever high enough to blind them, still they managed to maintain battle readiness even under the broiling sun. It is painful to witness.

The general good order of the Imperial Army was also affected:

Our hair and beards are growing thick and long, so that we begin to look like wild men, but we will put up with anything until at last every one of the enemy has been destroyed.

NUMB WITH GRIEF

On 2 May, the enemy attacked with tanks. 'After nine hours of bitter fighting, we succeeded in repelling them with heavy losses.' But there was also a cost to Japanese morale.

Our military strength is now so diminished, I hardly have the heart to write about it. Pen and paper are too frail to convey what it was like to receive the enemy's main attack full in the face ... Numb with grief, I write the names of my fallen men. And while I write in this frail, tattered notebook, I, too, step by step approach the abyss of a depth so blue it shades into black. Pain will follow pain until fallen, until the last man, and a single ... banzai!

Even so, the following day another attack was repelled, at great cost to the Americans.

In relation to the enemy's losses, ours are perhaps only one to their ten. Still, each one is a priceless sacrifice. Will tomorrow bring the tenth enemy attack? Well, whether the tenth or the 100th, we will continue to hold this ground and let them fell the strength of the Imperial Army until at last they have had enough! Flying our banners in the name of Akita Danjiro ['the youth of Akita' – a city in northwest Honshu], we shall endow them with a glory that will make them shine forth all the more gloriously. In this way we shall perform the ultimate service for our country.

Boy's Festival Day, 5 May, was celebrated with good news: 'Fifty of our aircraft are in action in the air over Marikina.'

> We have so long wished to be able once again to look up and see wings emblazoned with the crimson sun. Just hearing of this report brings such a look of relief to the faces of the men. If only we could see them with our own eyes, hear them with our own ears, how much the more joyful would be these faces.

Then the Army newspaper turned up for the first time in a long while.

> There are articles on the American populace in crisis, the strong resistance put up by the Germans ...

(but Berlin had already fallen and Germany was two days from surrender)

> ...and news from Okinawa as recent as 17 April describing our great victories there. The enemy lost all of 390 ships sunk or damaged. A minimum estimate of their losses in men is 800,000, of which 210,000 were killed. Our Shimbu Group battle results also appear. We are 56,000 strong. Just a little while longer, the time for a general offensive is perhaps at hand.

On 7 May, while under attack in something like 'a shooting contest', news came that: 'The enemy on the island of Okinawa is annihilated (confirmed by the Army).' In fact, General Ushijima, defending Okinawa, had made one last attack, which failed at the cost of 5,000 men. 'Now you see the fix you are in,' wrote Obara, addressing the Americans. 'We have been concerned for the homeland, but this news has relieved our minds.'

> Somewhere far from this charred mountain exists the spirit of Corporal Asano, who fell in the defence of the homeland and who must have been greatly concerned over its welfare. May he find heart's ease in this news. He was denied the joy of hearing this news in his lifetime, and we are powerless to tell it to him now.

Asano had been sent back to the front line even though he had a shell fragment in his leg.

> One cannot remember him without a sense of regret. To men generally, it is a matter of concern where one may meet his death,

but for the soldier, neither the place nor the manner in which death may come should occupy his mind. Yet all our men who have fallen have died splendidly ... May those of us who remain hope for a splendid death.

The opportunity was soon at hand.

8 May: Today is Imperial Rescript Day ... at last the great order of the offensive is received!! The date for X-Day is imminent. How we have waited for this, the order for a general offensive! The order that we have exhausted our patience waiting for ever since we first heard of the enemy landings! And now this order has been received. X-Day!! X-Day!! ... It is now no longer a dream, we will be coming back, and with flags flying ... I feel tears unconsciously welling up. I don't know how I keep from weeping. The men are similarly affected.

Plans were laid to retake Manila.

'Can it be coming true at last?' is the thought that goes through my mind. We have waited so long for this order, day after day, clinging grimly to this crumbling mountain while being blanketed by a deluge of shells. No matter how impetuous our spirit, all we were able to do was to grit our teeth and swallow our tears and hold on ... Now this is dispelled and my heart is light. I feel I cannot remain quiet – I want to sing. I look up at the sky and I see the gleaming of machine-gun bullets as they stream over our heads. I lean back and gaze through them at the clear bright sky, and feel my heart as clear and bright as the sky while I watch the white clouds silently passing over the violence of the battlefield ... Beasts, pour on the shells and bombs as much as you can! You have just a little longer to shoot and die – X-Day is coming. Night has ended.

What actually happened was a redoubling of the American shelling.

I stuff my ears with rags, but even so it seems any moment my eardrums will be broken. The violence of the explosions is such that with each explosion my palpitating heart seems to skip a beat.

I crawl into the side-hole of my command bunker, but the concussions follow me there and continue to shake my whole frame. The roof seems about to cave in. It is a terrific shelling. It is as if they will not be satisfied until they have fired in one day all the shells their trucks had spent the whole day in hauling up. They blast away at random like madmen. These mountains are now altered beyond recognition from what they had once been. If you were to tell a visitor now that these mountains had formerly been covered with forests so thick it was dark even in broad daylight, who could believe you? ... As shells continue to fall around my command bunker, I curse and cling to the wall, worrying whether the enemy is now advancing, and whether I should stick my head out, and almost sweating blood as I stay there and take it. I feel as if blood would flow from my hair-roots if I rubbed my skin.

Listening to the shell bursts, it sounds as if the worst of the shelling is falling on the positions of the men further down. I wonder how they are making out, and who may have caught it, and will the rest be buried in their dugouts.

Spontaneously, I begin to pray, 'Oh, gods, protect us.'

Soldiers under shelling often unconsciously touch with one hand the good-luck banner they have wrapped around the belly, and naturally they may also touch and make sure their talisman is on them where it belongs. Then when the shelling subsides, and they assemble in a dugout and greet one another, their faces are a blend of laughter and soberness, and their words will be casual and simple, yet to me somehow noble.

A SOLDIER OF THE EMPEROR

Unfortunately, Obara had forgotten to put on his talisman and the good-luck banner given to him by the people of his home town. Instead he comforted himself with the thought: 'Forget the gods, rely on yourself' and 'He whose time it is to die, will die; he whose time it is to live, will live.' Afterwards he grew pensive.

When I gaze around our raked, harrowed and ruined position, it comes to me, what a strange place for me to be. Soldier by the grace of the Emperor, yet also a living human being, feeling instinctively like any man the desire to live. Somehow I have been able through all this to repress these impulses to weakness. Because I am a man? No. Because I am a soldier? No. It is because I am Japanese, a son of Japan, a soldier of the Emperor.

He took advantage of an intermission in the shelling to poke his head out of the command bunker and look over at the enemy.

There, as if to mock us, more and more men are perching on the northern slope of Shimbu Hill. I curse them as mongrel curs, but for the moment all I can do is grind my teeth. It is unbearably bitter. Thinking of my men being opposed by these beasts, any anger rises. But we shall soon see! We will destroy you. In the end not even one of you will be left.

Sudden downpours indicated that the rainy season was about to begin. The rain brought with it new life:

Here and there on the burned and blasted surface of the mountain, grass has sprouted. Growing serenely in the little spaces between one shell hole and another, it has reached in places heights of seven or eight inches. But then, having with great persistence achieved this growth, it is in the end blown up by a shell or cut down by a shell fragment.

But Obara was more concerned with hatred and death.

For the past two or three nights, searchlights have been frequently observed probing the sky over towards Manila. I wonder if it could be that our aircraft have been making night raids. May they blow Manila to hell! Whenever we find Americans or Filipinos now, we must simply destroy them. In plain language, even those who surrender cannot be kept alive. How could we have overlooked the fact that these are beasts worse than the great predators?

There was more shelling and more American attacks, again repelled with heavy casualties on both sides. Finally on 12 May, X-Day arrived. But no Japanese aircraft turned up. Without air support, the Japanese were forced to endure another day's shelling as usual.

> The mountains endure and the clouds drift by. We remained
> clinging to our positions, yet the tears one by one trickle and fall.

On 17 May, the enemy infiltrated their positions, but 'we used our mortars to give them a blood-letting'. Obara heard that, after the victory off Okinawa, the Imperial Navy had gone on the offensive. In fact, what was left of it did not have enough fuel to sail. He was also convinced that the Japanese counteroffensive was progressing elsewhere and that, somehow, the enemy was in difficulties.

> The enemy must be short of men. They are now pressing Filipino
> women into the front lines. We hear reports that women soldiers
> account for about one-third of the total.

And of course, Filipino women would be no match for the men of the Imperial Army.

> But is the counteroffensive succeeding? This bombing and
> shelling is so excessively intense that I wonder if it is not just a
> question of time before these positions and the mountain with
> them will not simply crumble away ... I cannot bear to think so. I
> will continue the fight and I will resist even if I should be the last
> survivor, and yet ... When the counteroffensive shall have
> prevailed, then we will leave these positions and pounce upon
> the enemy! Ah, ah! I cannot wait.

They were short of rations and ammunition, but there was still hope.

> An M-4 type medium tank overturned with a loud explosion and
> burst of fire. 'We got him! We got him!' I said to myself, and felt
> from the bottom of my heart a sudden thrill of triumph. It looked
> like an A-T close attack – leaping the boundary between life and
> death, a son of the divine land, a sacrifice to the nation! An
> explosion was perhaps this message – this is a soldier giving his
> life. Ah, ah! How like a god, that soldier! Come then, enemy
> tanks! We shall all of us turn into human bombs, and all of you
> will be destroyed.

However, he had noted that his men were becoming less and less talkative.

'Hold on, it will be just a little longer,' I say to encourage them. 'I hear the Navy is now in pursuit off Okinawa!' Eyes fixed on a point in the distance, they fall silent my men.

Fukuzo Obara's diary ends on 19 May 1945. A US naval analyst noted:

Despite the firestorm that Obara described, it was estimated that 60 to 70 per cent of casualties on the Philippines were caused by disease rather than injury. Lieutenant Colonel Shigeo Kawai of the 2nd Tank Division reckoned they lost 95 per cent of their infantry – 'At times during the fighting along the mountain ridge of Salacsac, we lost a total of 180 men a day.'

A STARVATION DIET

It was now clear that no amount of *Bushido* could win the Greater East Asia War. Lieutenant General Tadasu Kataoka, commanding the 1st Division on the Philippines, recalled:

We received orders from the 35th Army headquarters that we were to resist until the very end, even if it took two or three generations ... Once, during a lull at the front lines, men of the 57th Regiment, which had been fighting up front for days, were brought back to the rear area divisional headquarters for a short period of rest. To show them our gratitude for their efforts, we fed them rice, which had been carefully nurtured and grown by our field hospital patients. However, these men had been on a starvation diet so long that their stomachs could not handle all the food and consequently, there were a great number of vomiting cases ... Later, as the intensity of the fighting grew, our food supply became so low that dead horses were a welcome addition to our diet. My personal horse, which was used by my adjutant to maintain liaison between our troops and divisional headquarters, was one of the last horses to be killed. He was fatally wounded by enemy artillery fire and his carcass passed around to our men.

Morale had already suffered a crippling blow. According to Major Chuji Kaneko, a junior staff officer with the 102nd Division on the Philippines:

In our unit, the morale was exceptionally good until after the Leyte operation. The men in our division at the time were sure that our troops on Okinawa and other areas would repel the enemy and turn the tide of battle. The morale at this time was astonishingly high. However, after the fall of Okinawa, our morale wavered to its lowest ebb and few men remained who were confident of victory.

By then the homeland was in peril. On 27 March 1945, American B-29s began mining the Shimonoseki Strait, which connected the Sea of Japan to the Inland Sea. This was used by ships carrying food and raw materials from mainland Asia, and handled 40 per cent of all Japan's maritime traffic. Some 1,250,000 tons of shipping a month were funnelled through a waterway less than 750m (half a mile) wide. Over the next four months, 12,000 mines were dropped. Captain Minami of the 7th Fleet explained the disastrous effects:

> Due to the fact that the United States did not use mines extensively during the first years of the war, the Japanese allowed their research efforts to relax and consequently were in no way prepared for the saturation type of attack that was delivered in Japanese waters in the spring of 1945 ... Frantic efforts were made to counter the mining of the Skimonoseki Strait ... [but] at times the traffic in the straits became so jammed that it was necessary to force ships through regardless of losses.

According to Commander Tadenuma, a staff officer of the Kure Mine Squadron, which was responsible for sweeping mines from the Inland Sea:

> Large warships did not attempt to use the Shimonoseki Strait after 27 March 1945 and were forced to use the Bungo Strait.

There they were vulnerable to attack by Allied submarines. Captain Tamura, head of the Mine Sweeping Section of the Japanese Navy, told his captors:

> The result of the mining by B-29s was so effective against shipping that it eventually starved the country. I think you could have shortened the war by beginning earlier.

It was clear that the homeland could now be defended only by suicidal action. After the war, Lieutenant General Tazeo told his captors how the *kamikaze* were to play a vital part in the defence of the home islands:

We expected an Allied invasion of southern Kyushu or of the northwestern coast of Kyushu in September or October ... The airforce plan was to attack the Allied fleet with kamikaze planes, and for that purpose the full airforce led by the commanding general was made ready to destroy the Allied ships near the shore. We expected annihilation of our entire airforce, but we felt it was our duty. The army and navy each had 4,000–5,000 planes for this purpose. Of that force, waves of 300–400 planes at the rate of one wave per hour for each of the army and navy would have been used to oppose a landing on Kyushu. We thought we could win the war by using kamikaze planes on the ships offshore; the ground forces would handle those which got through. The army could not put out effective resistance without the air arm, but we intended doing the best we could even if we perished. The entire navy and army airforces volunteered as kamikaze and there was sufficient fuel for these attacks.

General Kawabe explained the irreducible logic of this strategy to his American interrogators:

I know that you in the United States found it more difficult to manufacture crews than planes and did everything possible to rescue the crews, but our strategy was aimed solely at the destruction of your fleet and transport fleet when it landed in Japan. It was not difficult to manufacture second-rate planes, that is, makeshift planes, and it was not difficult to train pilots for just such a duty; and since pilots were willing, we had no shortage of volunteers. At no time did we run out of pilots to man these planes, but our big difficulty was rather a question of manufacturing than a shortage of crews.

But I wish to explain something which is a difficult thing and which you may not be able to understand. The Japanese, to the very end, believed that by spiritual means they could fight on equal terms with you, yet by any other comparison it would not appear equal. We believed our spiritual confidence in victory would balance any scientific advantages and we had no intention of giving up the fight. It seemed to be especially Japanese.

Also, may I point out another thing. You call our kamikaze attacks 'suicide' attacks. This is a misnomer and we feel very badly about you calling them 'suicide' attacks. They were in no sense 'suicide'. The pilot did not start out on his mission with the intention of committing suicide. He looked upon himself as a human bomb which would destroy a certain part of the enemy fleet for his country. They considered it a glorious thing, while suicide may not be so glorious.

Captain Rikihei Inoguchi of the 10th Air Fleet, a veteran of the Philippines, was in charge of training *kamikaze* pilots for the defence of Okinawa. According to him:

At the time of the Philippines campaign, men were very anxious to get into the kamikaze and volunteered in great numbers. They felt that to die for Japan was not only honourable, but their duty. About the time of the Battle of Okinawa, they became more reluctant to volunteer, particularly inasmuch as the outcome of the war did not look too favourable for them. However, fearing that they would be called 'slackers' or told they were not 'true Japanese citizens', they did volunteer ... I knew that in case of invasion of the homeland, I, as well as the other men who conducted this type of training, would be called upon to fight for the defence of our homeland. For this reason, we did not hesitate sending out the pilots. Before the loss of Okinawa, they still thought the war could be won ... Even after the loss of Okinawa, they were still willing to die as kamikaze pilots. Only when the Emperor broadcast that the war was over did they willingly lay down their arms.

On 23 May 1945, the eve of his sortie, *kamikaze* pilot Captain Masanobu Kuno wrote his final letter to his five-year-old son Masanori and his two-year-old daughter, Kiyoko.

Dear Masanori and Kiyoko,
Even though you can't see me, I'll always be watching you. When you grow up, follow the path you like and become a fine Japanese man and woman. Do not envy the fathers of others. Your father

264

will become a god and watch you two closely. Both of you, study hard and help out your mother with work. I can't be your horse to ride, but you two be good friends. I am a cheerful person who flew a large bomber and finished off all the enemy. Please be an unbeatable person like your father and avenge my death.

Lieutenant Masahisa Uemura left a letter for his baby daughter, Motoko, asking her to pay a visit to the Yasukuni shrine:

When you grow up and want to meet me, please come to Kudan. And if you pray deeply, surely your father's face will show itself within your heart ... Your uncle and aunt will take good care of you with you being their only hope, and your mother will only survive by keeping in mind your happiness throughout your entire lifetime. Even though something happens to me, you must certainly not think of yourself as a child without a father. I am always protecting you. Please be a person who takes loving care of others. When you grow up and begin to think about me, please read this letter.

P.S. In my airplane, I keep as a charm a doll you had as a toy when you were born. So it means Motoko was together with Father. I tell you this because you being here without knowing makes my heart ache.

11
ENDURING THE UNENDURABLE: THE UNIMAGINABLE END

By the end of May 1945, the situation on the Philippines was untenable. The diary of Commander Tadakazu Yoshioka of 26 Air Flotilla, who was hiding out on Luzon, recorded:

31 May: We can find enough to eat, but my conscience bothers me. I don't know if it is right to live on stolen goods.

8 June: Will the American and the Filipino armies spare us? The fact that they shoot at us every day and kill almost anything they encounter leads me to believe that they have no desire to spare us. I certainly want to live. I cannot die without knowing the situation in the world. I want to become a Christian. Amen.

9 June: Rained for three days. I guess nature cannot be conquered. Talking about sailing last night.

10 June: Rain. Are we considered worth taking alive? Or will we be killed? Hatagoe came. He promised to be with us from now on. Illness and hunger – no one cares. I have nothing to do with the world situation. Nevertheless, I will live a life worthy of a human being.

11 June: I asked Iio for his opinion on surrendering. He replied that he prefers death to capture. However, there is no other plan worth considering. Does the nation still prohibit us from taking free and independent action when the situation is absolutely hopeless as it is now? No food and no rice. What should I do as a human being? Die? Death can be achieved at any time. I shall wait.

12 June: Went to get tapioca last night in the rain. Discovered a booby trap in the adjacent field. Should we leave here before the mopping-up commences? Kudo insisted on taking a boat from north of Masinloc even if he had to go alone. I have no confidence in this place. But we must leave the hiding place if we want to live. Rain, sickness and no food. How many months can we live on tapioca? Will the enemy forgive us? Will he forgive us if we collect

stragglers and work for him? I want to go back alive and analyze why Japan acted so foolishly. Never before in history was anything so foolish done.

Sato's condition is bad. If he does not leave now while he can still move, he will die, but it is no use dying unnecessarily. Humanity insists that I at least cultivate farms for the Filipinos.

13 June: Saw B-29s in flight heading north. Is the war still on? As a human being, is it right to assemble troops in the area and persuade them not to give any more trouble to others?

14 June: All out of tapioca. Will war end by 8 July? If there are some people in Japan with common sense, I think an end can be brought to this war. However, if they are all lunatics, it is another matter. Relying on America and Britain to rebuild Japan is the far-sighted national policy. The concept that a nation will perish when losing one war is erroneous. Still, to rely on Russia would lead the nation into danger. We must depend on America. I do not think that America will annihilate all the Japanese. Kudo disagrees with me on the '8 July theory'.

17 June: I hope the war will be over soon. Ate the last grain of our dried rice. Rice is truly good. I want to eat rice after I become a prisoner of war. Three of us talked about food at night. We haven't had meat for six months now.

18 June: Takahashi died of stomach illness. Muramatsu returned without any food. Tonight we will depart. I pray that the war will come to an end. I will become a Christian. I will be a good citizen. I will not steal. I want to do something for the Philippines for the damage caused by the Greater East Asia War.

The following day Yoshioka was captured at Botolan in Zambales province, Luzon, and his diary was taken from him.

A Japanese soldier captured on the Indonesian island of Biak told of the appalling conditions there in 1945:

The Japanese forces, who took pride in their superb discipline and high morale, were completely bereft of those virtues by the advance of the enemy's mechanized forces and by their lack of food. Never in the history of the world's warfare has an army met

with so tragic a fate as is the lot of the present Japanese force on
Biak Island, whose members continually roam the jungles in
search of food; all will inevitably die of starvation. I should like
to recount to the world our deeds in the Biak campaign, and for
posterity, the trials and tribulations we have suffered.

I would note a few incidents from the tragic tale. At first there
were four deserters from our unit, all members of the colour
guard. Their number subsequently increased. Things were stolen.
Men were killed. The sick were put to death. Those who could
not keep up with the unit were held near the billeting area and
callously murdered with sabres or bayonet. Men died of fever.
Some of the sick, who had not eaten for a month, as they died,
pleaded for a pinch of salt.

Graves were opened in the night and the bodies of the malaria
victims were exhumed. The human flesh was dried and carried
along as rations. Some, while seeking food, were killed by the
enemy, some by the natives. Even the innocent are deceived and
killed. The strong are those who kill men and eat their flesh.
Even a lowly private, if he is strong, never heeds his NCOs or
officers. Even the force commander, Sudo, had to dig in the
gardens for potatoes, gather kindling, fetch water and worry
about his dinner. The men have neither hope nor discipline.
They wait only for someone to die, or dream of finding a garden
with potatoes.

Front-line soldiers ignored Allied leaflets urging them to surrender. They
were told by their superiors that they could expect no mercy, as the Americans
were barbarians. One captured Japanese said:

The promise of kind treatment was doubted and the men laughed
outwardly about the general contents of the leaflets. However,
inside their hearts, men were wondering if the conditions
described in the leaflets were true.

When they discovered that they were, Japanese captives were shocked, even
outraged. One Japanese officer captured in Luzon, who had been well treated
by US troops, said indignantly:

The Japanese Army is murdering the Japanese race by the lies they are telling their people concerning the progress of the war and the barbarianism of the Americans.

For most Japanese soldiers, being taken prisoner was not an option. Lieutenant Colonel Toshikata Ohira, of the Personnel and Training Section of the 8th Army, said:

The Japanese soldiers had been indoctrinated to die rather than be captured in battle. If troops were well trained in the Japanese Army they would have chosen to die. The Japanese troops that fought in the early stage of the New Guinea campaign were mostly well trained, but those who were sent there in the later stages of the campaign did not have sufficient training, consequently, more Japanese soldiers preferred to be captured rather than die as the battle situation became unfavourable to the Japanese.

Minoru Yamo, the commander of the landing party at Milne Bay, New Guinea, agreed:

The Japanese soldier is taught that, if he has six grenades, he should throw five and then kill himself. That is why my soldiers killed themselves when it appeared they might still have done some damage to the enemy.

However, one Japanese soldier who was captured in the Philippines realized that his comrades' situation was hopeless and prepared a pamphlet called 'Become the Foundation of the New Japan'. It read:

I who was born in Japan and am a soldier of the Imperial Army know only too well the feelings you must experience who are still hiding in the mountains, lacking food and water, and continuing the fight against every difficulty. Indeed right up to the present I was myself wandering about the mountains almost without food or drink ...

The American Army is approaching Japan and with succession of night and day bombing attacks is reducing our people to the depth of misery. Our parents, our wives and children, our brothers and sisters, are compelled to pass a wretched existence ...

Resistance in the mountains is quite senseless. The Army has to choose between a wretched death from starvation and being taken prisoner ... but let us be sure that the choice of present death is to the country's advantage. Is it anything more than a mass death? Japan today desperately needs young men to bear the burden of the forthcoming period. At all costs there must be enough young men left alive.

The denunciation is made: 'Why not choose to die? You are a man false to your country who has forgotten the Japanese spirit and the military spirit.'

But now such narrow modes of thought should be revised.

The home country cannot be protected by your death ... To become a PoW is today not at all shameful. A PoW that is one of the rebuilders of the new Japan ... So, free yourselves from the old way of thought, and follow the path of national service.

Lastly, the American Army, which announces that no one need be frightened of them, is in fact kind. What you have been taught up to now is the direct contrary of the truth.

THANK-YOU LETTER

One Japanese prisoner was so grateful for the treatment he had received, he wrote a thank-you letter:

To All in the Australian Red Cross Hospital:
I am deeply grateful for the devotion with which you have nursed me. Thank you very much for everything that you have done. When you even took an X-ray of me, I broke down and cried in front of the soldiers. In doing this, even for an enemy soldier, made me think of Florence Nightingale. I think you know that every night, when I was in bed, in my heart the Gods reproached me. When I went to **** and the two gentlemen who spoke Japanese told me that I would be examined by the military police, I decided to tell them everything and take my punishment.

My wound has healed ... From the bottom of my heart I thank you. I think that the spirit of the Red Cross will continue forever, without differentiation of enemies. You will laugh at me, but I have wept at your devotion without distinction of friend or foe.

Others had a similar experience of being captured. Lieutenant Colonel Yasuse Shibazaki, an engineer in charge of a road surveying team, said:

> The only time I met any enemy soldier was after the end of the war, and they were Australians. I felt that the troops I was fighting against were sincere in everything they did. They were glad the fighting was over. They knew what our situation was. The Aussies showed much kindness towards us, much more than we ever expected. Our troops at the close of the war were weak and sick. The Australian government produced timber and other material for us to construct a field hospital. The Australian government was very kind to us; so was each individual soldier ... While we were dug in, in our positions in the mountains, several Australians came up to the mouth of our holes and tossed in a couple of hand-grenades. One needs lots of courage to do that. As for their weak point, that is whenever a patrol of five or six men went on patrol, they would always be close together. When one got hit, a second would try to help the wounded soldier by coming to the spot he was hit or try to pull the wounded buddy out of sight. We took advantage of this and killed the second enemy.

At home in Japan, morale collapsed, as Dr Kawai recalled:

> When the B-29 raids began the people really knew the war was lost. Before that they knew some islands had been lost, but islands mean nothing to the ordinary man. When the big raids came, the feeling of defeat began. But the B-29 raids went beyond the point of criticism. People felt that they were all in for it, and there was no purpose in criticism, at least not criticism of the government.
>
> 'There was increased criticism, however, of the ARP. They were criticized because they were always changing their directives and people came to think they didn't know what they were doing. But generally the raids were too big for mere criticism of the government. They were beyond that. People had completely lost confidence in the governing group.
>
> The fire raids were worse than the high explosives because they came at night. One night, one of the first raids, 100,000 people were killed when the bombers hit a slum area. This caused a hopeless

feeling, but there was no real panic yet because the affected people were not influential. If the raid had come in a 'better' area, the victims would have been able to spread more concern.

There were many strange things after that raid. For instance, the victims were evacuated to private homes in a nearby good residential section. They were so pitiful that their hosts were kind and gave them all kinds of attention. But the reaction was just the reverse of what was expected. Instead of being grateful, the slum people resented the fact that in war, while they were suffering, people should be having such luxuries, ones they couldn't dream of having even in peace. So they looted the houses wholesale, and the police could do nothing about it. They were tough people from one of the worst slum areas. After that people were evacuated not to private houses but to schools and public buildings.

But the B-29s soon bombed the good sections also and then all were in the same boat. The amount of feeling varied with the individual, but by the time the Marianas were captured, the intellectuals were certain that the war was lost. The real terror for the people came with those leaflets naming the places to be bombed. When you did that and then bombed the places named, then there was real terror.

The weekly newspaper *Mainichi* claimed that the US were going to run out of B-29 Superfortresses, fuel and crews to man them, but this was whistling in the wind. And the Japanese people were not fooled. Even before the B-29 Superfortresses began coming in from the Marianas, they were terrified of what was to come. According to a student writing in 1943:

Japanese correspondents in Germany have described the havoc wrought by Allied bombers in German cities, which are known to be much more solidly built than Japanese towns ... The people's reaction is: 'What can we do when the authorities do nothing? Our cities will be simply wiped out.' Similarly the government's attempts to harden people's nerves and prepare them against panic are having only negative results. I myself know families who would not allow their children to go far from home on sunny days last summer when everybody constantly expected air raids. The danger of air raids is freely and constantly discussed in the secrecy of family circles and fear is undisguised among friends in universities, factories, and practically all circles where one can talk frankly.

He also reported that 'The government's oft repeated guarantee that the Japanese homeland will never be directly attacked is spurious.' And the country was ill-prepared:

> It is now popularly known that Tokyo's shallow subways will not afford protection against heavy bombs. Other cities are without shelters and those built, in spite of a severe shortage of construction materials, including steel, cement and even timber, are most inadequate ... The greatest emphasis is laid on fire-fighting and all civilians, even women, are forced to train for two hours every morning from 5am to 7am, but the primitive methods used are characterized by the fact that the authorities are giving prizes to those who are able to throw water highest out of buckets.

It is little wonder that anyone who had relatives in the countryside and was not required to work in the factories fled.

THE FALL OF SAIPAN

The turning point came with the fall of Saipan in the Northern Marianas, which was taken by the US Marines on 7 July 1944 – more than a year before the end of the war – after a suicidal defence, during which some 8,000 civilians jumped off the cliffs. This allowed land-based B-29 Superfortresses to take off within range of Japan. The loss of Saipan was such a setback that Hideki Tojo and his entire cabinet resigned, to be succeeded by the government of General Kuniaki Koiso, which promised to carry on the fight with renewed vigour. Prince Higashi-Kuni, army general, member of the Supreme War Council and commander in chief of the Home Defence Headquarters, said:

> The war was lost when the Marianas were taken away from Japan and when we heard the B-29s were coming out. We were informed by foreign cable that the B-29s ... flew at the rate of 600km per hour at 13,000m high. We had nothing ... that we could use against such a weapon. From the point of view of the Home Defence Command, we felt that the war was lost and said so. If the B-29s could come over Japan, there was nothing that could be done.

But the people were not told. Mr Abe, minister for home affairs, explained the government's policy:

> The reason we had no definite policy of air-raid shelter protection for the citizens is that we did not unduly wish to alarm our citizens concerning the necessity for underground shelters as we feared it would interfere with normal routine life and have some effect on war production. We did encourage citizens who could afford it to build their own family air-raid shelters.

After the high-altitude fire-bombing of Tokyo on the night of 9–10 March 1945, Tokyo Radio could still bluster:

> If by any chance the enemy believed that he could demoralize the Japanese people, he has made a big mistake. The Emperor of Japan, on the morning of 18 March, deigned to pay an unexpected personal visit to the stricken districts of the Capital. He went on foot, exposing himself to the cold March wind. All the people, touched by his sympathy, renewed their determination to prosecute the war, saying: 'This is a sacred war against the diabolical Americans.'

However, in a later broadcast, Tokyo Radio itself drew a rather odd comparison:

> The sea of flames which enclosed the residential and commercial section of Tokyo was reminiscent of the holocaust of Rome, caused by the Emperor Nero.

Later, the Japanese simply gave up, as Mr Abe explained:

> I believe that after the 23–24 May 1945 raid on Tokyo, civilian defence measures in that city, as well as other parts of Japan, were considered a futile effort.

According to the Japanese government's official statistics, air attacks on Japan killed 260,000 people and destroyed 2,210,000 houses, leaving 9,200,000 homeless.

After the Allied landings on Okinawa, the Koiso cabinet fell and on 7 April 1945 the emperor appointed Baron Suzuki, a retired admiral and president of the privy council, as premier. Suzuki explained the difficulty of his situation:

> I was naturally in a very difficult position because, on one hand, I had to carry out, to the best of my ability, the mission given to me by the Emperor to arrange for the conclusion of the war, whereas if anyone heard of this I would naturally have been attacked and probably killed by people who were opposed to such a policy. So that on one hand, I had to advocate an increase in war effort and determination to fight on, whereas through diplomatic channels and any means available, I had to try to negotiate with other countries to stop the war.

On 1 May, the Imperial General Staff lamented the suicide of Hitler and the execution of Mussolini and announced a new policy of 'Nippon single-handed against the world'. On 5 June 1945, they decided to hold a 'Vassal's Conference' to decide on the future war guidance. As a result, Secretary of the Imperial General Staff Tanemura had to visit the 'high-spirited General Tojo in his half-burnt house' to go through the agenda, 'since I felt sorry for him'.

> In order to explain the agenda of the Vassal's Conference to General Koiso also, I arrived at the Zushi Station at 2000 hours wearing my national uniform, but due to the darkness I could not find his residence. Therefore, a Navy Petty Officer and I slept in a cheap lodging house near the station and were annoyed by the fleas and bedbugs.

He caught up with General Koiso the following day and 'left after eating white rice which I had not eaten for a long time'.

On 9 June, following the conference, a new 'Gist of the Future War Guidance', was issued, saying:

> Policy: Based upon the firm belief that loyalty to His Majesty should be fulfilled even though one should be born seven times, the war must be accomplished completely with the unified power of the land and the unified power of the people in order to protect the nationality of our nation, to defend the Imperial Domain, and to attain the object of the war of subjugation.

Meanwhile, however, overtures were being made to the Allies via Moscow, as the Soviet Union had not yet declared war on Japan. But the negotiations faltered when Stalin and Molotov headed for Berlin to attend the Potsdam Conference. One of the results of the conference was the Potsdam Declaration, demanding Japan's unconditional surrender. When some began to voice their fear that the Soviet Union would break its neutrality agreement and attack Japanese forces in Manchuria, Secretary Tanemura berated his colleagues for defeatism. They should be planning for victory on the mainland, he said. The following day he wrote in his diary:

> In the evening, I received an unofficial order from the Chief of the Military Affairs Bureau, Yoshizumi, transferring me as a staff officer to the Korean Army. Simultaneously with thanking my superior for the favour of giving me a place to die at this final phase of the war, I left the Imperial General Headquarters after five years and eight months with the feeling of utter shame in my inability to serve His Majesty, which led to the current situation. I will compensate for my past crime by burying my bones on the front line.

Tanemura was captured in Korea and spent four and a half years in a Soviet prisoner-of-war camp before being returned to Japan in January 1950.

THE DESTRUCTION OF HIROSHIMA
Meanwhile, on 6 August 1945, the atomic bomb was dropped on Hiroshima. One middle school student in Hiroshima described what happened:

> I'll never forget that day. After we finished our morning greetings in the schoolyard, we were waiting in the classroom for our building demolition work to begin. Suddenly a friend by the window shouted 'B-29!' At the same instant, a flash pierced my eyes. The entire building collapsed at once and we were trapped underneath. I don't know how long I remained unconscious. When I came to, I couldn't move my body. Cuts on my face and hands throbbed with pain. My front teeth were broken and my shirt soaked in blood. As I crawled along, encouraging myself, I somehow managed to poke my head out of the wreckage. The school that should have appeared before my eyes was nowhere to

be seen. It had vanished and only smoldering ruins remained. Beyond the school toward the center of town, all I could see was a sea of flames. I was so terrified I couldn't stop shaking. Moving my body a little at a time, I was finally able to work free of the collapsed structure. Making sure to head upwind to escape the fires, I made my way staggering haphazardly through the rubble of the city.

Fourteen-year-old Akihiro Takahashi was attending assembly at Hiroshima Municipal Junior High School, 1.5km (nearly a mile) from the centre of the blast.

We were about to form lines facing the front, when we saw a B-29 approaching and about to fly over us. All of us were looking up at the sky, pointing out the aircraft. Then the teachers came out from the school building and the class leaders gave the command to fall in. Our faces were all shifted from the direction of the sky to that of the platform. That was the moment when the blast came. And then the tremendous noise came and we were left in the dark. I couldn't see anything at the moment of explosion ... We had been blown by the blast. Of course, I couldn't realize this until the darkness disappeared. I was actually blown about 10m. My friends were all marked down on the ground by the blast just like this. Everything collapsed for as far as I could see. I felt the city of Hiroshima had disappeared all of a sudden. Then I looked at myself and found my clothes had turned into rags due to the heat. I was probably burned at the back of the head, on my back, on both arms and both legs. My skin was peeling and hanging like this. Automatically I began to walk heading west because that was the direction of my home. After a while, I noticed somebody calling my name. I looked around and found a friend of mine who lived in my town and was studying at the same school. His name was Yamamoto. He was badly burnt just like myself. We walked toward the river. And on the way we saw many victims. I saw a man whose skin was completely peeled off the upper half of his body and a woman whose eyeballs were sticking out. Her whole body was bleeding. A mother and her baby were lying with skin completely peeled off. We desperately made a way crawling. And finally we reached the river bank. At the same moment, a fire broke out. We made a narrow escape from the fire. If we had been slower by even one second, we would have been killed by the fire. Fire was blowing into the sky becoming four or even five metres high. There was a small wooden bridge left, which had not been destroyed by the blast. I went over to the other side of the river using that bridge. But Yamamoto was not with me any more. He was lost somewhere. I remember I crossed the river by myself and on the other side, I plunged myself into the water three times. The heat was tremendous. And I felt like my body was burning all over. For my burning body the cold water of the river was as precious as treasure. Then I left the river, and I walked along the railroad tracks in the direction of my home. On the way, I ran into an another friend of mine, Tokujiro Hatta. I wondered why the soles of his feet were badly burnt. It was unthinkable to get burned there. But it was undeniable fact the soles were peeling and red muscle was exposed. Even I myself was terribly burnt, I could not go home ignoring him. I made him crawl using his arms and knees. Next, I made him stand on his heels and I supported him. We walked heading toward my home repeating the two methods. When we were resting because we were so exhausted, I found my grandfather's brother and his wife, in other words, great uncle and great aunt, coming toward us. That was quite a coincidence. As you know, we have a proverb about meeting Buddha in Hell. My encounter with my relatives at that time was just like that. They seemed to be the Buddha to me wandering in the living Hell.

On 8 August, the Soviet Union broke off diplomatic relations and declared war. The following day a second atomic bomb was dropped on Nagasaki. The Potsdam Declaration was accepted by the Emperor on the 14th. However, there was little support for this decision among his advisors. According to Admiral Toyoda, chief of the naval general staff and a member of the six-man Supreme War Guidance Council:

> I might add, that even on 15 August, when the Imperial Rescript to terminate the war was actually issued, we found it difficult to hold

down the front-line forces who were all 'raring to go', and it was difficult to hold them back.

On 15 August 1945 – the 15th day of the eighth month of the 20th year of *Showa* – Emperor Hirohito broadcast for the first time to his people, telling them they must 'endure the unendurable'. But he did not have the support of his officers. Major-General Miwa told his captors:

As far as the army is concerned, the termination of the war was declared by the Emperor and not by the Army.

Lower down the ranks, the feeling was different. George Fukui fought on Cebi Island in the Philippines opposite the 21st Reconnaissance Troop of the Americal Division. After the war he said:

My parents expected me to become a Japanese citizen with the proper Japanese spirit ... in a militaristic and totalitarian country such as Japan was back in those days, you would naturally be forced to make a drastic change in thinking. That's what happened to me. I became almost more American than an American because I was able to compare values. To this day I root for America in the Olympic games, believe it or not. I prefer the sight of the Old Glory to the flag of Japan. The sound of your national anthem is real music to my ears. The anthem of Japan, which is not even officially recognized as such, lauds the emperor and every time it is played I plug my ears. I thought I was about the only guy to do so in our veterans' association but to my surprise I found that there are other guys like me. I am not a very loyal Japanese, I'm afraid. You might regard me as a misplaced American.

BIBLIOGRAPHY AND SOURCES

ATIS 506 Extracts from *Home News* published by the Voluntary Aid Organisation of Hatano village, Gona Village area, 6 December 1942 207

ATIS Spot Report 153, received 4 October 1943, collected by Martin Marix Evans 203–205

Barker, A.J. *Panzers at War*, Ian Allan, London, 1978 16–20

Bodenmüller, Eduard *Diary of a Tank Gunner*, Europa Books, New York, 2004, www.europabooks.com 123–24, 124

Brustat-Naval, Fritz *Ali Cremer: U 333*, Ullstein, Berlin, 1998 [1982] 40

Cawthorne, Nigel *Steel Fist: Tank Warfare 1939–45*, Capella, London, 2003 15, 43, 47

Fuchida, Mitsuo *From Pearl Harbor to Golgotha*, Sky Pilot Press, San Jose, California, 1953 55, 157, 147, 147

Giese, Otto and Wise, James E. Jr *Shooting the War: The Memoirs and Photographs of a U-Boat Officer in World War II*, Bluejacket Books, Naval Institute Press, Annapolis, MD, 2003 38

Giuglaris, Marcel *Le Japon perd la guerre Pacifique, de Pearl Harbor a l'Hiroshima* [published in English by A. Fayard, 1958] quoted in *The History of World War II* by Lt-Colonel E. Bauer, Orbis Publishing, London 1979 154, 157

Graf Spee 1939, The German Story, based on captured German records. Copy in the Harwood papers; also in the Parry papers in the Imperial War Museum 32

Guderian, Heinz *Panzer Leader*, Michael Joseph, London, 1970 12

Guillain, Robert *I Saw Tokyo Burning: An Eyewitness Narrative from Pearl Harbor to Hiroshima*, translated by William Byron, John Murray, London, 1981 155, 154

Hirschfeld, Wolfgang *Feindfahrten* [Enemy Hater], Kaiser, Munich, 1998 [1982] 39

Hohjo, Sei-ichi 'The Nine Heroes of Pearl Harbour Attack', *Contemporary Japan: A Review of Far Eastern Affairs*, Foreign Affairs Association of Japan, Tokyo, Vol XI, No 4, April 1942 153, 151, 153, 152

International Military Tribunal for the Far East, Exhibit No 1850. Material from page 2 of a captured diary, quoted in *Prisoners of War and their Captors in World War II* by Bob More and Kent Fedorowich, Berg, Oxford, 1996 202

Kuno, Captain Masanobu, final letter quoted on wgordon.web.wesleyan.edu/kamikaze/writings/kuno/index.htm 264

Liddell Hart, B. H., ed. *The Rommel Papers* William Collins, London, 1953 13, 14

Luettwitz, General der Panzertruppen Heinrich Frhr. von *ETHINT-41 XLVII Panzer Corps Investment of Bastogne*, 13 Oct 1945 93

Mölders, Fritz, an account [originally published in *Mölders und seine Männer*, 1941] quoted in Just, Günther *Die Ruhmreichen Vier* [The Famous Four, portraits of 4 ace German pilots], National-Verlag, Hanover, 1972 14

Mulligan, Timothy P. *Neither Sharks Nor Wolves* Naval Institute Press, Annapolis, MD, 1999 38

Neitzel, Sönke *Abgehört: deutsche Generalie in britischer Kriegsgefangenschaft 1942–1945* [Transcripts of Combined Services Detailed Interrogation Centre (CSDIC), Document 92, released in 1996], Ullstein/Propyläen, Berlin, 2005, translated by Angus McGeoch 142

Okumiya, Masate, and Horikoshi, Jiro, with Martin Caidin *Zero!* Cassell & Co, London, 1957 149, 151

Prange, Gordon W., with Donald M. Goldstein and Katherine V. Dillon *God's Samurai: Lead Pilot at Pearl Harbor*, Brassy's (US) Inc., Washington, 1990 151

Records of the Office of the Judge Advocate General (Army), War Crimes Section, RG 153 File 51-54, Atrocities by the Japanese Medical Department, NARA, Maryland. Quoted in *Prisoners of War and their Captors in World War II* by Bob More and Kent Fedorowich, Berg, Oxford, 1996 203

Rommel, Erwin Letter to his wife, 1 November 1942, quoted in *The Rommel Papers* by B.H.

Liddell Hart (ed), William Collins, London
  1953 42
Schmidt, Heinz Werner *With Rommel in the
  Desert* Harrap & Co, London, 1951 42
Takahashi, Akihiro, Testimony from *Hiroshima
  Eyewitness* produced by the Hiroshima Peace
  Cultural Centre and NHK, quoted on www.
  inicom.com/hibakusha/akihiro.html 278
The Outline of Atomic Bomb Damage in Hiro-
  shima. Booklet quoted on International
  Schools Cyber Fair 1998 Project website at
  www.hiroshima-is.ac.jp/Hiroshima/radia-
  tion.htm – site no longer exists 277
Tsuji, Colonel Masanobu *Singapore – The
  Japanese Version*, translated by G.W. Sargent,
  Ure Smith, Sydney, 1960 166
Uemura, Lieutenant Masahisa: final letter of,
  quoted on wgordon.web.wesleyan.edu/ka-
  mikaze/writings/uemura/index.htm 265
Westphal, Hans Jürgen. Interviewed by author
  August 2006 133–136
Williams, Andrew *The Battle of the Atlantic*,
  BBC Worldwide, London, 2002 37, 39, 41
www.kbismarck.com/archives/debriefing4.
  html 34
www.kbismarck.com/archives/debriefing5.
  html 36
www.kbismarck.com/archives/debriefing6.
  html 35
www.kbismarck.com/crew/interview-brzonca.
  html [interview carried out in English] 35
Yoshioka, Tadakazu, Commander of the
  26 Air Flotilla, Diary of 24 March–18
  June 1945. Taken from him at Botolan,
  Zambales province, Luzon 19 June 1945
  266–267

IMPERIAL WAR MUSEUM
Kubota, Sub-Lieutenant Kumataro, Diary,
  Jap. AL 5310 161–66, 167–176, 178–201
Kyoku, Nippon Joho, Historic Imperial
  Rescript issued at the outbreak of Dai Toa
  Senso, 8 December 1941 AL 5180 159

Duxford Collection
Hitler's Political Testament 137
Hitler's Private Testimony 136
Interrogation Reports 1939, Volume I 40

Shiojiri, Seitchi Manuscript of *Lost Troops*,
  published in Japanese in Bungei Shunji January 1946, English translation dated 1948,
  Kyoto 210–211, 212, 213–215, 216

**SECOND WORLD WAR EXPERIENCE
CENTRE**
Everyone's War, Issue No 7, Summer/Spring
  2003 37–41
Leibich, Gotthard. 8 Coy, 352 Div. Omaha
  Beach. Tape 1962, collected 1 June 2005 by
  Martin Marix Evans and Angus McGeoch
  64
Mertens, Alfred. 716 Reg Normandy LEE-
  WW/2004-2638 pp 11–14 relate to D Day,
  collected, 1 June 2005 by Martin Marix
  Evans and Angus McGeoch 64–65

US ARMY ARCHIVES
Seized Documents, microfiche 10-SR-67 148
Translation of captured enemy diary taken
  from the body of a dead Japanese officer
  after the battle on Attu Island in the Aleutians, 1 June 1943 228–231

US ARMY HERITAGE COLLECTION
10-SR-15 202; 10-SR-98 225
Fujino, Hideo, Notes to the 1964 English
  translation of *Raft of Death*, Tokyo, 1956
  232–233
Fukuzo Obara Papers 235–60
Winckelmann O'Neal, Ulrike Typescript of
  Jahresringe [Annual Rings] *An Autobiography
  of Herbert Otto Winckelmann* Louisiana, 1994
  12, 13, 15, 30–31, 47–53, 62–64, 74–75,
  122–123, 140, 143

Infantry Americal Division
Captured Japanese diaries; excerpts of
  translations made in Guadalcanal cam-
  paign, December 1942–January 1943 18,
  219–222
Fukui, George, IJA, Garrison Force, Cebi
  Island, Philippines, letter to William
  McLaughlin 279

US ARMY MILITARY HISTORY INSTITUTE
George R. Allen Papers 1943–45, *Memoirs –*

13 Company, 89 Regiment, 12th Volksgrenadier Division   119, 120–121

Memoirs of Horst Helmus, gunner number one in the 1st Company, 26 Battalion of 26th VGD, translated by Mrs Kovacs, Aachen, 1983   88

Memoirs of Gunther Holz, 12 Tank Destroyer Battalion, 12th Volksgrenadier Division, translated by Heinz Brandt, Stolberg 1982   82, 111, 119

Memoirs of Leonhardt Maniura, 9th Parachute regiment, translated by Mrs Kovacs, Aachen, 1983   88, 107

Memoirs of Klaus Ritter, 12 Tank Destroyer Battalion, 12th Volksgrenadier Division, translated by Heinz Brandt, Stolberg 1982   81, 85–87, 110, 115–116

Memoirs of Alfons Strüter, engineer in the engineering platoon of the Jünclear Regiment 39, 26th VGD, translated by Mrs Jehmaun, Aachen, 1983   80, 105

Memoirs of Willy Volberg, paratrooper   83, 84

US GOVERNMENT PRINTING OFFICE

Mission Accomplished: Interrogations of Japanese Industrial, Military, and Civil Leaders of World War II, prepared by the Assistant Chief of Air Staff, Intelligence Headquarters Army Air Forces, 1946   159, 209, 225, 226–27, 240, 262, 263, 264, 268, 269, 271–272, 273, 274, 275, 278, 279

Strategic Bombing Survey Europe, D785, U6.64b Effect of Bombing on Morale, 1946   56–57, 58, 59, 60, 61 141, 142

US NATIONAL ARCHIVES AND RECORDS ADMINISTRATION

Japanese material RG165 Stack 390 Row 33 Compartment 25 Entry 79 box 276   160, 177, 207, 209, 223, 233–235, 267–268, 270; box 277   206, 231

PICTURE CREDITS

1 Ardennes offensive © Corbis; 2 German advance © Corbis; 3 Berlin Armoury © akg-images; 4 Red Army in Berlin © popperfoto.com; 5 Afrika Korps © akg-images; 6 German troops in Africa © akg-images; 7 Heinz Guderian © akg-images/ullstein bild; 8 Eiffel Tower © akg-images; 9 Captain Langsdorff © Topham Picturepoint; 10 German army in Paris © PA Photos; 11 Ruins of Nuremberg © PA Photos; 12 German soldiers in Paris © akg-images/ullstein bild; 13 Paris under occupation © akg-images/ullstein bild; 14 Erwin Rommel © PA Photos; 15 Attack on Poland © akg-images; 16 Russian front © akg-images; 17 German soldier in Russia © akg-images; 18 U-boat crew © akg-images; 19 U-boat interior © akg-images; 20 V-1 rocket © akg-images; 21 V-1 rocket © akg-images; 22 Japanese troops © Corbis; 23 Japanese troops © Corbis; 24 Kamikaze pilots © PA Photos; 25 Kamikaze attack on ship © PA Photos; 26 Japanese POWs © popperfoto.com; 27 Hiroshima © akg-images; 28 Hiroshima survivors © akg-images; 29 Allied bombing in Japan © Corbis; 30 Execution of prisoner © Time & Life Pictures/Getty Images; 31 Japanese POWs © Corbis. UK COVER: Front: German soldiers © Nik Cornish at Stavka; Back: Kamikaze pilots © PA Photos.

INDEX